CUT FLOWERS and FOLIAGE PLANTS
for all seasons

Cut Flowers and Foliage Plants

for all seasons

H. G. Witham Fogg

John Bartholomew and Son Ltd.,
Edinburgh.

First published in Great Britain 1972
by John Bartholomew & Son Ltd.,
12, Duncan Street,
Edinburgh, EH9 ITA.

ISBN 0 85152 902 x

Printed in Great Britain by
Bristol Typesetting Co. Ltd.,
Barton Manor - St. Philips, Bristol.

Contents

PART I

CHAPTER 1

ADVANTAGES OF HOME GROWN FLOWERS

FLOWERS are now an essential part of the living-room, and modern flower arranging is a domestic art. The display of blooms in bowls and vases of all types provides an opportunity for the creation of colour harmonies and patterns which please the eye and bring life and beauty to the rooms in which they are placed. Flowers can often express sentiments which are difficult, if not impossible, to put into words.

Like almost all commodities, the cost of florists flowers is advancing. This being partly caused by the increased demand, especially in view of the splendid work and resultant publicity created by the activities of the National Floral Arrangement Societies. There are now branches in most parts of the country and arrangement classes are held in many centres.

At one time floral art was more or less limited to the use of exotic plants and flowers which needed a heated conservatory or greenhouse for their cultivation. The tendency now is towards greater simplicity which permits the use of a very wide range of flowers, many of which because of their pleasing appearance, have enabled much more satisfying results to be obtained. A wide range of flowers is always available from florists, but there is great satisfaction in actually raising and watching the development of plants from which the flowers are produced.

In addition, more kinds can be used for indoor decoration when little time is lost between cutting and being placed in water. Many species are never seen in florist shops because they do not travel well, and many wilt if not given water immediately they are gathered.

To overcome the objection that the cutting of blooms spoils the garden display, especially where the demand for flowers is heavy, it is usually possible to grow the plants in a separate plot. There are some plants too, which respond freely when their blooms are cut regularly, for they produce another display in a short time which is why they are sometimes referred to as ' cut and come again ' plants.

It is essential to grow the right type of flowers and foliage for cutting. The aim should be to concentrate on those subjects which are long lasting with good strong stems and which take water readily.

While the aim of most cut flower growers may not be to produce prize winning blooms, it is important to provide the best possible growing conditions which will enable the plants to give of their best. Well grown under healthy conditions they will produce more and better blooms which are much less likely to succumb to disease or pest attacks.

Another aspect of flower growing worth remembering is that it provides exercise and relaxation which are most important to all of us in these days of stress and strain of modern living. There is something satisfying in planning and planting flower beds and borders and a sense of achievement as the development of the plants is watched from their earliest stages until they produce their attractive blooms.

While we are concerned with growing the actual flowers we must not forget that for good balanced development the health of the foliage is vital. Plant life begins and ends in the green leaves. It is this green colour that shows the presence of chlorophyll the pigment which acts as a bridge between the plant and its energy supply. This green colouring develops in light without which the foliage turns pale and the plant becomes weak.

On the surface of the leaves, generally on the undersides, there are tiny valves known as stomata. These are the lungs or breathing pores which must be kept working if the plants are to grow healthily.

Sufficient moisture is another essential for regular development, for during daylight there is an escape of water vapour from the leaves into the atmosphere. This is known as transpiration and moisture needs to be replaced through the roots so that all the plant cells remain inflated and there is then no wilting.

So long as the plants themselves are functioning properly flowers will develop normally. Proper cultivation means that the plants will remain in good condition longer, and the flowers for cutting will be stronger with firmer stems carrying blooms of good colour and long lasting ability.

What are the qualities we can expect from cut flowers we can grow in the garden? Among those most desirable are the following:

easy culture, long lasting ability, little or no staking, strong stems, a wide colour range, and different formations such as daisy-like flowers, spikiness, or branching habit. In addition, there are many plants which have attractive foliage both as regards shape and colour.

With thought and planning it is not beyond the ability of the average grower to be able to provide cut blooms from the garden all the year round. This of course implies the use of annual, biennial and perennial subjects and our purpose now is to show how this can be achieved.

Where the aim has been to grow flowers specially for cutting, the next step; having gathered the blooms is to treat them in such a way that they retain their beauty for the longest possible time.

The art of flower arranging as an expression of individual personality is easy and relaxing in these tension-ridden times, because you are fundamentally pleasing yourself and enjoying working with the most beautiful materials nature provides. Flower arranging brings a fresh interest in colours, textures and forms and stimulates a new appreciation of light, shade, depth and quality.

Successful flower arranging in the home does not require mastering the rigid rules and regulations of flower shows and competitions. Common sense will tell you not to site your arrangements in direct sunlight or near heating appliances; in draughts or in danger spots where the containers can easily be knocked over. Trial and error will quickly demonstrate that plain backgrounds are more suitable than fussy patterned ones. Flowers can be used to pick up colours and textures of backgrounds. Light colours will show up best against dark panelled walls and vice versa.

Too many flowers jammed into a container will look wrong, and tall stemmed flowers in a miniature container will look out of place. Use spring flowers in bud, just when they are showing colour, to ensure the longest possible vase life. After cutting place the stems in 2 in. of water with the chill off, for one hour before arranging. This ensures that the flowers are turgid and will remain in good condition.

Daffodils, iris and hyacinths have stiff stems. If tulip stems become limp after cutting, wrap the tulips firmly in newspaper before standing them in the bucket of water. This will stiffen and straighten them. Daffodils exude a milky fluid which can affect the vase life of other spring flowers. The remedy is to place daffodils in a separate container of water before arranging them with other flowers.

Create your arrangement in your mind's eye first, taking into consideration the background, the flowers, foliage and containers you have available. Choose a container of the right size, shape and colour to give a balanced appearance and to tone or contrast with your flowers. Ensure that your pinholder, wire mesh, foam base or other fixing material is firmly placed in the container. Arranging flowers with water already in the containers is easier, because the water provides better balance, but don't forget to top up when the arrangement is completed. Stems placed so that they radiate from a central point make more effective arrangements than stems that cross one another above the mouth of the container.

Floral colours rarely clash which means you can mix colours almost as much as you like, especially when foliage is plentifully used. Flowers massed in blocks of colour are more effective than flowers of different colours scattered through an arrangement. Colour can be used for harmony or contrast with heavier colours reserved for the base and centre of any design.

Spring flowers in particular are very cheerful and make a great deal of difference to any room. Although they can be placed straight into a vase or bowl, with a little care, a satisfactory arrangement can be made which will make the flowers look even better.

Arranging flowers for the house need not cause worry for it is not like entering a competition. One can forget rules and regulations, classes and themes. There is something satisfying in placing the flowers as one likes for this affords freedom of expression. Simplicity is really the key to easy flower arrangement.

Every flower should be given a chance to look its best. This means that you will need to use stems of differing lengths. All flowers should have sufficient room to be seen. Not only so, they should be allowed enough room for their expansion into full bloom. It is sometimes helpful in starting an arrangement to use the basic shape of a triangle. For this, place 3 flowers in key positions and work from there.

It is not necessary to have a lot of expensive equipment and most materials are readily available in the home. These include ordinary vases and bowls, as well as copper vessels, entrée dishes and various baskets into which water containers can be placed. In many cases a little 2 in. mesh wire netting is invaluable for crumpling up to hold stems in deep containers, while pin holders of various sizes allow individual flowers to be inserted exactly where required. This also applies to oasis and florapak.

Candle-cup holders are a sound investment for the more

adventurous flower arranger and florists also stock cone-like tin holders which can be affixed to a cane or stick to give added height to an arrangement.

To keep flowers in perfect condition, they should be placed up to their necks in water a few hours before arranging. Green foliage too, should be treated similarly. In the case of coloured foliage only the ends of the stems should be placed in water.

Special care is needed in respect of some types of material. Woody stemmed shrubs and flowers should have their ends split or crushed to facilitate the intake of water.

Hollow stemmed flowers such as delphiniums should have their stems filled with water, the ends being plugged with cotton wool before they are placed in deep water. In the case of roses as well as having their woody stems crushed, the thorns should be removed which makes it easier for carrying and subsequently arranging.

Poppies and other subjects which emit sticky sap should have the ends of the stems held over a flame as soon as possible after cutting. This will seal the cut surface and prevent loss of sap.

Short stemmed flowers being used in a shallow container are best fixed into a pin holder or into small mesh wire. Simple or plain vases and containers are best, so that they do not overshadow the actual flowers.

Whenever possible, the aim should be to cut flowers in the morning or failing this in the evening rather than in the heat of the day. Plunging the stems in water immediately, means that there will be much less possibility of wilting.

Various ingredients have been used in endeavours to make flowers last a long time. Many of them seem quite useless. These include copper coins, aspirins and bicarbonate of soda. There is some evidence that the latter is of help, but sugar has shown the best results. A small piece of charcoal put into the vase helps and keeps the water sweet with less possibility of the lower leaves becoming slimy, although it is a good plan to take off most of the lower leaves before the stems are placed in water.

There is on the market, a preparation known as Chrysal, which is probably the best for helping flowers to remain in good condition for a long time. Much can be done by keeping the flowers out of direct sun and draughts and away from fires. When used in the living-room, it is beneficial to take them into a cooler place at night. Lastly, the vases should always be kept topped up with water.

CHAPTER 2

PLANNING AND PLANTING A CUT FLOWER BORDER

WHATEVER else may be required in the garden there are few if any gardeners who would willingly be without a good border of hardy plants. Such a border has a number of advantages. It always proves an attraction if properly made and stocked, and when planted, it is not difficult to keep in good order. There is another very important aspect to consider, for by making a proper selection of plants it is possible not only to have some colour in the garden throughout the year but at the same time to be able to provide a succession of cut flowers.

In a garden of average or even small size it is a good thing to design the border so that it avoids a more or less oblong shape. More often than not, the background will be a hedge or fence, although sometimes it will be an island bed approachable from both sides. In the latter case, the taller plants must be placed towards the middle of the bed otherwise the higher growing subjects will be put at the back. Whatever design is decided upon, it is best to sketch out a plan before commencing the work. One can then get an idea of what the finished border will look like when seen from the window or door, as well as from other parts of the garden.

A flower border can be and usually is, left undisturbed for 4 years or more. It will therefore be seen that good preparation is important. The first essential is that the site should be well drained and if it is not naturally so, steps to ensure the easy getaway of excessive moisture must be taken. Then dig the ground two spits deep, incorporating plenty of manure or other organic material while bone meal 2-4 oz. to the square yard should be added to the top spit. In the case of light dry or chalky soils the more humus forming material which can be added the better the plants will grow. As far as possible digging and manuring should be done several weeks in advance of planting. If the frost gets to the surface soil so much the better for it will then crumble well and help to make planting easy.

Before dealing with the selection of varieties it would be wise to consider the planting. Here again a plan should be made out to avoid wrong planting.

While perhaps the ideal border may be one where all the taller plants are at the back, and the remaining subjects gradually lessen in height until the front of the border is reached, I am in favour of some plants of medium height being placed a little way back so as to create little dells and undulations. Planted thus it is possible to look at the border from all angles, and to see, if care has been taken in selecting the subjects used, a delightful kaleidoscope of colours which both blend and contrast. From this it will be obvious that width is quite as important as length, for a very narrow border will never look effective.

Coming to the actual planting always make the holes large enough to allow the roots to be spread out fully. Plant with a trowel or spade. Make the soil firm around the roots and re-tread it after the plants have been in 10 days or so. Groups of 3 or more of one variety are better than straight lines, and in addition this ensures that there are sufficient flowers of one subject to cut at one time. When established, all the plants will need annually is the cutting off of flower heads before they sent seed, and wherever possible, a yearly spring mulching of compost, peat, strawy manure or anything similar, while after the third year, bone meal worked into the surface in the autumn will prove very beneficial.

It is not possible here to give particulars as to the exact placing of the plants in the border but it will not be difficult to find in any good nurseryman's catalogue plants of varying heights. For convenience it is simpler to place them in 3 groups, tall from 4-6 ft.; medium 2-4 ft.; and short under 2 ft.

In many perhaps most gardens it is not possible for reasons of space to make separate beds or borders of perennials, annuals, bulbs or shrubs. This means that many of us have to use all of these subjects in one cut flower bed. Obviously it is better where each of these groups can be planted separately, but the mixed border can be a really good feature as well as supplying cut flowers. It does mean, however, that special care is needed in the choice of what is planted so that colour is actually available from January to December and not simply during spring and summer when there is usually an abundance of cut flower subjects available, in most gardens. Properly chosen according to the site available many perennials associate well with shrubs in a permanent garden feature.

Then there is the foliage bed or border. Here the range of colour is much wider than often supposed. The shades of green alone will surprise those who have not tried this type of border. The silver, grey, gold, orange, red and beautiful autumn tints of many subjects can provide real pleasure to gardeners who have not previously grown foliage plants.

There are excellent possibilities for those who wish to plant a scented border of plants and shrubs. These include both flowers and foliage and of course takes in annuals such as mignonette and sweet peas.

What about a bee border? Gardeners partial to honey and who keep bees can plant a selection of perennials attractive to these insects, and for this purpose no different culture is needed. Here are some excellent easy to grow ' bee plants '. Anchusa, aquilegia, aster, campanula, centaurea, eryngium, echinops, gaillardia, helenium, lavender, monarda, nepeta, penstemon, papaver, physostegia, rudbeckia, scabious, sedum, solidago and statice. Annual plants which attract bees include: bartonia, centaurea, linaria, nigella, phacelia and echium.

At some time or other, most of us feel the need of satisfying some form of creative expression and the growing of cut flowers and foliage provides great scope for this objective. The great variation which can be produced each season and the changes which can be made in successive years ensure that one does not slip into a rut.

CHAPTER 3

PROPAGATION. SEED, CUTTINGS, DIVISION

AMATEUR and professional gardeners alike, find pleasure and reward in propagating plants and there are many methods of increasing a stock which can be carried out without technical knowledge. Sometimes remarkable results have been obtained by simply sowing seeds and awaiting the results. On other occasions success has been achieved after long and patient experiment. The raising of apple, Cox's Orange Pippin, probably the best known of its kind, is an example of success without labour.

Records show that Richard Cox, a brewer, born in 1776, sowed seeds from apple Ribston Pippin and from one of these pips he obtained the now famous Cox's Orange, while from another has come Cox's Pomona, an excellent dessert variety.

Then we have the work of Henry Eckford with sweet peas. He worked long and meticulously to achieve a flower with a wavy back petal and which has now been developed into the modern large flowering varieties we know as Spencer sweet peas.

Another name well known in gardening circles is that of George Russell, a gardener in the Midlands, who experimented for many years before he secured the breakthrough we now know as Russell lupins. Similarly, there have been other plants which have been increased in size, with colour range widened and the constitution of the plants improved. Whether we propagate by seed, cuttings, bulb offsets, or divisions, we should aim only for the best quality, for it is useless retaining plants which are not an improvement on varieties already in cultivation.

Although knowledge and perseverance are essential we must work in accordance with the laws of nature. To do otherwise will result in failure.

SEED SOWING

To many gardeners, the problem of exactly when to sow seed is

B

not always easy to solve. For so often when ' the book ' says sow at a certain date, either or both soil and weather conditions may be quite unsuitable. The fact is, that it is more important for the soil to be in the right condition than it is to sow on a particular date.

In the past there has been a too rigid adherence to the belief that unless seed is sown at a specific time, the resultant crop would not be satisfactory.

Outdoors the soil is right for sowing purposes when it can be easily worked with a rake, and when it crumbles easily and does not pull when the rake is moved over the surface. The three essential needs for free germination and good growth are: moisture, warmth and air. Moisture will come from the soil, but if the ground is too wet there will be no room for air. This is why the seed bed should be made where there is no possibility of water draining on to or remaining on the seed. For warmth, we usually rely on the sun, although this is where cloches and other glass structures can be useful, since if placed over the soil a week or two before the seed is sown, the soil temperature is raised considerably. Ideally the right soil temperature for easy good germination is at least 50 deg. F. In practice it is very often considerably lower.

Most seeds are sown in rows, although hardy annuals look more pleasing if clumps or groups are planned, a more natural effect is then obtained, since all the flowers may not be cut but some left to beautify the garden. Outdoor sowing should always be done on a calm day, otherwise the seed will blow about and fall irregularly, some being entirely lost. Drills or rows will vary considerably, both in depth and distance apart. The space allowed between the rows is largely decided by the subject being sown.

With hardy annuals, which are being grown solely for cutting, much will depend among other things, how tall the plants will grow, and if they are subjects which will make bushy specimens or those which grow tall and slender. There must always be room for natural development to enable the full quantity of flowers to be produced. Sow evenly, for seed obtained from reputable firms will under ordinary conditions, germinate well, and it is a waste of seed crowding them in narrow drills, besides leading to plants which cannot develop properly.

With most subjects some thinning out can be done. Some popular annuals such as cornflowers, nigellas, larkspur and eschscholtzias resent root disturbance and generally speaking do not transplant satisfactorily except perhaps, in showery weather. If left bunched together in rows, they will never make satisfactory plants.

Many half hardy plants can be started in warmth and a temp-
ature of 60 deg. F. is ample for a wide range of subjects. Seed can
be sown in pots or boxes of a simple compost of the John Innes
type. If seed is well spaced it will encourage early development and
this, with the pots and boxes kept fairly near the glass, should
result in shapely plants which will flower well.

Some kind of support will be helpful in preventing the young
plants from being flattened by wind and heavy rain. Bushy sticks
inserted at intervals or strands of string run each side of the rows
supported by bamboo canes every yard or so, will prove quite
sufficient. Should the weather become hot and dry in the spring,
a mulching of compost around the plants will keep the roots cool
and prevent the soil drying out rapidly.

CUTTINGS

While the majority of ornamental plants can be raised from
seed, the perennials, including shrubs are very often increased
vegetatively. There is a variety of ways of doing this and according
to the subjects being propagated, it can be by division, layering or
by taking stem cuttings or slips. The main advantage of these
methods is that the resultant plants are exact replicas of the parent
plants, whereas plants raised from seed often vary considerably in
many ways.

There are two main types of cuttings used in this method of
propagation. Soft wood and hardwood. The first is a shoot or section
of stem taken from a plant when it is growing. Examples are:
chrysanthemums, dahlias, and many herbaceous plants.

Hardwood cuttings are ripened shoots, particularly from shrubs,
and these will often root without warmth, while the majority of
soft wood cuttings need a little heat, or at least some kind of
protection to encourage rooting.

The finest, healthy plants should be selected for propagation and
those free from disorders. Having selected the right parent plant
next comes the selection of good short jointed growth. Choose
those which are firm rather than those having coarse bushy growth.

Make a clean cut at the base of a leaf joint or node. Then insert
the cutting in prepared compost giving a light watering to settle the
soil around the base.

While sufficient moisture must be available while the cutting is
making roots too much may cause damping off. Once the cuttings
are well rooted, and this can be determined by their perky appear-

ance they can be given more room, in some cases, potted up separately.

DIVISION

Hardy perennial plants can be divided in autumn or early spring. Any large healthy clumps should be lifted and separated either by really pulling the clump apart until strong healthy pieces have been secured, or by the old fashioned method of placing two forks back to back and moving these until the clumps are divided.

They should not be cut up by using a spade, since this makes it easy for disease spores to gain a hold. Plant up only strong, healthy outer portions and not the central parts which so often have grown weak and may be affected by disease.

In some instances propagation can be done by root cuttings and in the case of fleshy rooted subjects such as lupins, anchusas and Oriental poppies, this is probably the best method, since it is not easy to divide the clumps. For root cuttings the plants should be dug up after the flowering period is over, and the roots cut into small portions up to 3 in. long, cutting the top flat and the bottom slanting. These are placed 4-6 in. apart in sandy soil in the cold frame and left there until the following summer, when good young plants should have developed and will be ready for moving to their flowering quarters in the autumn.

Autumn is also the time to move seed-raised perennials to their final quarters. Although specimens raised early in the year can be moved to their final positions in the same season, wherever possible, if the seedling plants have been allowed plenty of room, they will benefit from being left undisturbed for another year. This should not be done with box or pot raised plants.

CHAPTER 4

HARDY ANNUALS FOR COLOUR

HARDY annuals have a life compass of 12 months or less. They die after flowering and consequently must be sown every year. They can be sown from March until May in positions where they are intended to flower in the summer and autumn, due regard being paid to their respective heights in relation to the surroundings of the positions in which they are to grow.

Among the wide range of plants grouped together as hardy annuals and which are so useful and dependable for many purposes in the garden a large number are ideal for cutting. The main reason for growing annuals is to provide flowers for cutting in the shortest possible time.

They are of most easy culture and many will grow and flower well, with even the most casual treatment. The most inexperienced gardener will have no difficulty in securing a wealth of bloom at very little cost. While a separate border of hardy annuals looks impressive, they may be used most effectively in all parts of the garden. However limited may be the space available there are annuals which will fit in and yield a plentiful supply of cut blooms. The fact that the seeds are cheap to buy, does not imply that the flowers they produce are inferior. This is not so and in addition, entirely different varieties may be grown in successive years.

We have seen from Chapter 3 how to sow the seed and raise the plants of annuals, so that now we will endeavour to list some of the best of the worthwhile hardy annuals which will look good and last well when cut. There are many interesting colourful species and varieties are rarely obtainable from the florist but which are ideal for all kinds of floral arrangements either when used alone or when mixed with other subjects.

Our aim now is to consider well tried favourites and to bring to notice other equally good and often more exotic looking flowers which will prove decorative for both formal and informal occasions.

Agrostemma githago. Often known as the Corn Cockle this is an old fashioned cut flower of easy culture, although the magenta coloured flowers on 1½-2 ft. stems are not to everyone's liking. It is the variety Milas which is the favourite the colour being rosy lilac paling towards the centre, the petals being lined and dotted black. This variety has stiff wiry stems 2½-3 ft. high the flowers which remain fully open in dull weather, being up to 3 in. in diameter. The linear foliage adds to the graceful effect.

Arctotis grandis, the African Daisy likes sun and a well drained situation. The flowers on long stems often up to 2 ft. are silvery white, having mauve centres surrounded by a narrow golden band, which appear from June to September. The foliage is covered with a fine white down.

Calendula. This is the Garden or Pot Marigold which has been grown in this country for centuries and was once valued for its medicinal qualities and is still used by herbalists. The plants flower continuously this characteristic giving rise to the name calendae in reference to the fact that the plants will often bloom at all seasons. Cut the flowers freely since this will cause more to develop quickly.

Seed can be sown in autumn for spring flowering, or in early spring for summer and autumn blooms. The plants prefer sun and good drainage but they will actually grow quite well under almost all conditions. They grow from 1-1½ ft. according to variety and the seedlings transplant without difficulty.

Varieties include: Orange King, Radio, with quilled petals; Indian Maid, orange with dark centre; Campfire, deep orange; Chrysantha, canary yellow and Golden King.

Ageratum. We usually think of ageratum as being bedding subjects but *A. mexicana* is a splendid half hardy annual with soft lavender blue flowers on 15-18 in. stems. This makes them excellent for cutting.

Alonsoa is another fine plant for pots or for planting outdoors in early June. These plants like sun and make bushy specimens of pyramidal growth.

A. acutifolia has vermilion red flowers on 2 ft. stems while the shorter growing *A. linearis* is scarlet, the foliage being finely toothed. Both bloom from July to September.

Amaranthus. The tall erect plants are showy in the border, their dense vivid spikes of colour providing a splendid contrast for other after pricking out the plants can be spaced in the garden 18 in. less prominent annuals. Germination usually takes 12-14 days and apart. One can reckon the long trails will develop in about 14 weeks from time of sowing and they go on appearing until cut down by frost.

A. caudatus, better known as Love-lies-Bleeding, has 2½ ft. long amaranth red tassels and it has a form viridis, which is green.

Butterfly Flower see schizanthus.

Felicia. Sometimes known as the Kingfisher Daisy this is a dainty annual which can be sown directly outdoors in May or raised under glass in April. It makes compact rounded plants usually no more than 4 or 5 in. high, the dainty royal blue flowers having a yellow disc of stamens. This makes them ideal for including in miniature arrangements and posies, while outdoors, their presence invites attention.

Aster. There are few more popular half hardy bedding plants than the annual China Asters, *callistephus* to give them their correct name. While most varieties do not flower before July they come in at a time when some of the other annuals are not quite so spritely and go on blooming until October.

The Single and Ostrich Plume types have been grown and appreciated for many years, but during the last 20 years new types have been perfected and distributed. Chiefly of American origin, they have been grown in this country long enough to enable their worth to be assessed under ordinary weather conditions.

Asters prefer a neutral or alkaline soil and acid soils should be given a dressing of lime in spring. A deep moist, but not wet soil will give best results. Light sandy ground can be improved by working in dressings of decayed manure or other humus forming material well before planting.

These showy flowers are splendid for cutting, although for this purpose, those with long stiff stems should be selected. Seed is sown in succession under glass from March onwards and in a temperature of 60 to 65 deg. F. Germination occurs in about 9 days and the seedlings are pricked out in the usual way and kept in a temperature of around 50 deg. F. until April. Then move them to the cold frame for hardening off. According to weather conditions and space, plants should be moved to their flowering positions in May placing them about 12 in. apart. China asters can also be sown where they are to flower in April, thinning the seedings to the required distance.

The following are among the best of the cut flower asters available today.

Tall Varieties – 2 ft. high

Californian Super Giant. Sometimes known as Perfection asters, this strain produces really huge blooms with long, loosely arranged shaggy petals not unlike Japanese chrysanthemums. Usually available in mixture.

Duchess. A vigorous growing erect and base branching strain with strong, rigid stems. The large flowers are fully double and incurved. Usually in mixture, although yellow and crimson are sometimes available separately.

Powderpuff mixed. Produces huge tightly double blooms 3 in. or more in diameter. A dozen or more blooms are sometimes open at the same time on each plant. The colour range is wide.

Super Princess. Very large double flowers with quilled petals toward the centre. Of branching habit with long, straight stems.

Medium varieties up to 18 in. high

Ostrich Plume or Ostrich Feather. Very large double flowers with feathery, recurving petals. Base branching and ideal for both garden and cutting. Wilt resistant.

Pompone mixed. An attractive strain which includes many bicolour double flowers.

Giant Comet. Large, fully double blooms with long curling petals in a wide colour range.

Single Marguerite mixed. This gives a gay and attractive display with prominent central stamens producing the effect of a cushion.

Super Chinensis is a strain having two rows of petals making it a more substantial flower with very long lasting qualities.

Victoria. This strain of compact habit has large blooms 5 in. or more in diameter carried on 15 in. stems.

Dwarf varieties up to 10 in. high

Daisy Mae. Brilliant yellow.

Dwarf Queen. Ball shaped flowers in mixture.

Thousand Wonders. Double flowers in a good colour range.

Remo. Forming bushy rounded plants with rosette-like flowers. All of these are suitable for short arrangements.

Cosmea bipinnatus. Natives of Mexico these plants often known as cosmos, are of value both for the flowers and feathery foliage. The flowers are carried on long stems the colours usually being white, pink or crimson all with a yellow central disc. Recently several new colours have been introduced including Goldcrest, semi-double glowing orange-yellow; Sunset, vermilion-red and Bright Lights, in tones of yellow, golden orange and red.

They make branching plants of anything between 2½ and 5 ft. the main flowering period being August and September. Normal half hardy treatment is required. Sow the seed under glass in March and move the plants to their flowering positions towards the end of May.

Although the flowers do not travel well, if the stems are plunged in water as soon as cut they remain decorative for a week or more.

Euphorbia heterophylla is a hardly annual which has fairly recently come into prominence as a subject for cutting. Sometimes known as the Mexican Fire plant or Hypocrite plant, it is easily raised from seed and has attractive leaves of mid green and, at the top of the stems, whorls of fiery scarlet bracts.

Soil is not important provided it is well cultivated and the site sheltered from prevailing winds. It can be grown in the cold frame and is a practical proposition for cutting from pots. Seed can be sown under cloches in April, or without protection in May.

To preserve their long lasting qualities the stems should be cut just as the small flowers, which appear at the centre of each stem, are fully developed and are the same scarlet colour as the topmost bracts. Place them in water immediately, leaving them in the cool for an hour so they take up water and remain turgid.

Euphorbia marginata or variegata is known as Snow on the Mountains, a striking plant with light green leaves variegated with white. One or two stems included in a floral arrangement can prove very telling.

Kochia scoparia is well known as the Burning Bush being useful for beds and borders. Their habit of growth gives them the appearance of a bearskin busby. The plants vary from 2-3 ft. in height and it is possible to introduce smaller specimens into a floral decoration. A form known as *K. childsii* retains its finely cut fresh green foliage throughout the season while *K. tricophylla* turns a rich russet red from late summer onwards.

Centaurea. This is the correct name for both Cornflowers and Sweet Sultan. Cornflowers are great favourites for growing in the garden and when cut. Of simple culture the finest plants and earliest flowers are obtained from an autumn sowing, mid-September being the best time. These plants will flower from May onwards at a time when cutting material is not too plentiful. Spring sowings can be made from late March onwards for producing summer and autumn blooms.

It is best to sow where the plants are to flower, although thinnings can be used too, if soil is kept on the roots, but usually they do not make such good plants.

Centaurea cyanus the original Cornflower, has several common names including Blue Bottle and Batchelor's Button. Among the best of these are: Blue Diadem, large rich blue flowers on sturdy 2-2½ ft. stems and Snowball, double white 12-15 in. high. Double Rose and Double Blue are both old favourites growing 2½-3 ft. Jubilee Gem rarely grows more than a foot high but produces vivid blue double flowers in abundance.

Carnival mixed, 3 ft. is notable for its veined and marked petals tipped with a different colour, while Polka Dot mixed, 15-18 in. has a gay colour range and is most suitable for cutting.

Centaurea moschata is the Sweet Sultan which produces sweetly scented fluffy, thistle-like heads in shades of purple, white and yellow. *C. imperialis* is the Giant Sweet Sultan and is now the most widely grown. The fragrant heads are twice the size of the ordinary Sweet Sultans the colour range being wider. Sown in spring they flower from July to September and if cut when young, will last in water 7 to 10 days in good condition.

Charieis heterophylla is often listed as Kaulfussia. These little plants are sometimes used for border edgings and on the rockery. They flourish in ordinary good soil and a sunny situation. The elegant plants produce deep blue daisy-like flowers on 5 to 6 in. stems from June to September. These are ideal for including in posies or miniature arrangements.

Clarkia. One of the easiest to grow and popular of all annuals flowers, they are excellent when a 'simple' cutting flower is required. Any open, sunny position suits this subject, seeds being sown in spring where the plants are to flower.

In windy exposed positions, it is helpful to provide some twiggy supports for the young plants which otherwise, might snap off at ground level. Clarkia also makes useful spring flowering pot plants if sown in August and September and kept under cool conditions.

Clarkia elegans is the species from which most of the double garden varieties have been developed. These grow 1½ to 2 ft. high and bloom from July to September. Among good named varieties are the following: Albatross, white; Enchantress, salmon pink; Glorious, crimson scarlet; Purple Prince; and Vesuvius, orange-scarlet. A reliable mixture will provide a wealth of bloom in a wide colour range.

C. pulchella is not quite so tall growing and has narrower leaves and divided petals. The colour selection is not so wide, although there are good mixtures available.

Coreopsis. The annual forms of this subject are often but incorrectly listed in catalogues as calleopsis. These annuals are splendid garden plants which easily grow in even poor soil. The colouring is chiefly confined to yellow with pleasing markings or zonings of brown or crimson. The plants vary in height and habit but all are of graceful growth and useful for cutting.

Sowings can be made outdoors from late April or for earlier flowering can be sown under glass in March. *C. drummondii* 1½-2 ft. high has yellow flowers the base of the petals being marked maroon. *C. tinctoria* grows up to 2½ ft. its rich yellow flowers being zoned maroon. It has many forms varying in height from 9 to 24 in. including The Sultan, maroon-crimson and The Garnet, crimson-scarlet.

Corn Cockle see Agrostemma.

Cornflower see Centaurea.

Cosmos. The bright green filigree foliage, long branching stems and the pleasing daisy-like flowers give this subject a special charm. In the garden they will bloom from July to October but used as cut flowers the petals fall after 3 or 4 days. Even so, they remain popular with arrangement enthusiasts.

Seed can be sown in late May where the plants are to flower or some growers treat them as half hardy annuals raising them under glass for putting outdoors at the end of May. Good garden soil and sunshine suits them.

C. bipinnatus growing 3-4 ft. high is available in several varieties including Sensation Mixed and the Crested Mixed, having double flowers. The *C. sulphurea* varieties include Klondyke, Orange, Flare and Orange Ruffles, while the new Bright Lights produces semi-double flowers in shades of yellow, golden orange and almost red tones.

Chrysanthemums. There are 3 main species of Annual Chrysanthemums *C. carinatum*, *C. coronarium* and *C. segetum*. The first is usually referred to as tricolor of which there are many handsome forms. The species itself has white petals which are bright yellow at the base, the dark purple centre making up the 3 colours, hence the term tricolor. Among the best named varieties of *C. tricolor*, growing about 18 in. high are *C. burridgeanus* with yellowish foliage; Northern Star, white with yellow ring at the base and a blackish-maroon central disc; and The Sultan, bronzy-red and yellow with a brown disc.

It is, however, the mixtures of *C. carinatum* or tricolor which are particularly effective either when growing alone or placed among other annuals. Apart from a wide range of 3 coloured single flowers, there are semi-double, double and beautifully fringed strains.

Chrysanthemum coronarium varieties have finely cut foliage. The species itself has pale yellow semi-double flowers. There are numerous garden varieties which have been derived from it. These include Golden Glory, 3 ft. high with large single, rich yellow flowers; Golden Crown, 3 ft. or more high, with double yellow flowers; Golden Queen and Primrose Queen form compact bushes not more than 18 in. high; while Tom Thumb Golden Gem is 12-15 in. high, making a useful pot plant.

Chrysanthemum segetum has 2 forms, grandiflorum with larger flowers and pumilum, of more compact habit. This species which has small single yellow flowers has given rise to many beautiful forms, all growing about 18 in. high. These include Eldorado, large yellow, black centre; Evening Star, golden yellow with dark disc; Morning Star, soft primrose with decorative glaucous-green foliage.

Dahlia. A fascinating and economical way of obtaining a stock of dahlias for cutting, is to treat this subject as an annual and sow seeds in warmth by the ordinary half hardy method. Any one who can grow asters and stocks should be able to raise dahlias from seed.

The seedlings are pricked out as usual, the plants being gradually hardened off for putting outdoors from the end of May onwards. They flower on 15-18 in. stems from mid July, according to weather and situation.

It is chiefly the singles and semi-double sorts that succeed in this way and a good planting of dwarf bedding dahlias will create a show in the garden and produce an abundance of cut blooms. If you need separate colours try Coltness Gem, scarlet, and its yellow form.

Delphinium Blue Mirror. Growing about a foot high this is one of the finest of all annual delphiniums. The large flowers on sturdy spikes are a vivid gentian-blue and last quite well when cut.

Dimorphotheca. The common names of this subject are Star of Veldt, and African Daisy. The latter name giving an idea of what the flowers look like. This subject prefers a sunny situation and soil on the light side. In dull weather the flowers remain closed as they do at night. Seed can be sown under glass early in April, but best results come from sowing into flowering positions from mid-

May onwards. Usually plants flower within 8 or 9 weeks from time of sowing. Growing 12-18 in. high the colours of D. aurantiaca hybrids take in apricot, buff, biscuit, yellow, lemon, orange and white, some having a dark centre.

Emilia. Better known as cacalia with the common name of Tassel Flower. This charming subject is not usually recognised among cut flowers, but for the miniature arrangements and posies, it is ideal. Its clustered flower heads of bright orange-scarlet which are freely produced from June to October, are carried on stems of a foot or more. Of most easy culture seed is sprinkled where the plants are to flower and lightly covered with fine soil. This plant looks better grown in irregular patches rather than in straight lines.

Eschscholtzia. Sometimes used in bunches of mixed flowers this subject loses its petals too quickly to be of much value for cutting. Even so, if cut when the buds are swelling they will often remain decorative for 2 or 3 days. The finely divided grey green foliage is specially attractive and useful for using with colourful flowers of all kinds. The common name for eschscholtzia is Californian Poppy although this refers generally to the orange-yellow variety. The Monarch Art Shades take in a glorious colour range of delightfully frilled flowers. Of easy culture eschscholtzias grow almost anywhere so long as the light is good.

Gaillardia. The annual varieties can be sown under glass or in the open where they are to flower. They bloom from July onwards on stems 15-18 in. high. Among named varieties are *G. pulchella*, crimson; *G. picta*, crimson tipped yellow; and *G. lorenziana*, double mixed with globular flower heads. G. Indian Chief is bronze-red. All of these are double and in addition there are single flowering sorts.

Gaura lindheimeri. While not striking this is useful for cutting. Its long graceful sprays of white and pink flowers show from July to October on 2-3 ft. high stems. It will grow well in good soil, the blooms being of value when used among colourful subjects.

Godetia. This is a popular annual of easy culture though the flowers are inclined to drop their petals quickly. Handsome when growing and when seen in vases, there are 2 groups of varieties. The first grows 12-15 in. high, the second between 2 and 3 ft. or when grown in pots, is even taller.

Seed should be sown from March to early May where the plants are to bloom, or for early flowers, a sowing can be made in well drained soil in autumn. Thin out the seedlings early to increase bushy, free flowering growth. While it is possible to use the thinnings these plants do not develop so well as unmoved specimens. Named sorts in separate colours as well as mixed are offered by the leading seedsmen.

Gypsophila elegans is a much used and valued annual. The plants have small leaves and much branched stems, producing numerous white flowers so useful for mixing with other colourful subjects to which they bring a sense of airiness.

By sowing in September early flowers are secured and further sowings can be made in spring and early summer to produce a succession of blooms.

Thin sowing lessens the need for thinning out. G. elegans Covent Garden is the best variety and there are also pink and crimson forms, all growing about 18 in. high. Soil containing lime will encourage finest results.

Helianthus. A number of the annual Sunflowers are excellent for indoor use. All grow in ordinary good soil and seed should be sown in flowering positions in spring. They bloom from early July onwards and apart from the mixtures, a number of separate named sorts are available, including Autumn Beauty, yellow with bronze zone; and Sutton's Red, yellow with chestnut-red band, all growing 3-5 ft. high.

Larkspur. The name delphinium comes from a Greek word, meaning a dolphin. It was once thought that the buds of certain species bore some resemblance to that sea animal.

Apart from the perennial forms so valued for the border, there are a number of annual types. Now usually known as larkspurs, they were once referred to as King's Spur and Lark's toes.

While seed can be sown in the spring, undoubtedly the best results follow an autumn sowing where soil conditions are suitable. Autumn sown plants are altogether more robust and bushy than spring sown specimens. They flower earlier and longer, since with their better root system they do not feel the effects of spring drought.

It is best to make two sowings, one say, during the first 10 days of September and another towards the end of the month. Choose soil in good conditions and well supplied with phosphates and potash which encourages a good root system and freedom from disease. Too much nitrogen leads to unwanted abundant, sappy growth likely to be cut by severe weather. Avoid freshly manured soil and sow where the ground is well drained without being dry.

Make the drills at least $\frac{1}{4}$ in. deep and in double rows about 18 in.

apart. Fortunately larkspurs will grow on various types of soil but for preference they should be given a good deep, rich well manured site. In southern and midland districts the plants come through a normal winter unharmed but in cold wet areas the seedlings benefit from protection especially during prolonged severe weather. Cloches or Dutch lights are useful for this purpose.

By the early spring the larkspurs will be growing nicely. Watch must be kept so that damage by pests such as cutworms and wireworms can be prevented before it becomes serious.

Once the flower stems begin to run up, and certainly as the buds begin to show, some support may be necessary for the tall growing sorts. This will prevent the plants from being flattened by strong winds or heavy rains. The spikes are cut with as long a stem as possible when 3 or 4 lower florets are opening.

The two best types of larkspur for both autumn and spring sowing are the Stock Flowered and Giant Imperial which grow 3-4½ ft. Apart from mixtures they are available in separate colours including Imperial: Blue Spire, Dazzler, scarlet; and Miss California, pink shaded rose. Of the tall Double Stock flowered, Rosamond is bright rose. The Hyacinth flowered double larkspurs growing only 1 ft. high are available in a mixture of neat habit with charming feathery foliage.

Lavatera. This is a very showy annual both in the garden and when cut. The seed should be sown in the early spring where the plants are to bloom. The plants should be spaced out well since they will develop into really bushy specimens. The stems, 2½-3 ft. high, carrying large numbers of semi-trumpet shaped flowers.

L. splendens is pink and there are both rose and white forms. The variety Loveliness is particularly showy with its rose pink blooms.

Leptosyne stillmannii is another hardy annual which can be sown in April and May where it is to bloom. The lemon yellow daisy-like flowers are particularly attractive, as is the double form Golden Rosette.

Leptosiphon is one of the most charming of all dwarf growing hardy annuals. Early flowering each plant produces large numbers of flowers which come into colour very quickly. The French hybrids, on 6 in. stems, produce tiny single flowers which spring in pincushion-like fashion from tufted foliage. They are ideal for miniature arrangements and posies.

Linaria. These are rather like miniature antirrhinums. They have the common name of Toad Flax, the flowers being continuously produced. The plants like sunny positions where the soil is well drained and on the light side. Sown in April the flowers appear in quick succession from June to October. These blooms too, are ideal for the smaller arrangements.

Linaria cymbalaria is sometimes known as the Kenilworth Ivy and although a perennial can be treated as an annual, particularly for its attractive trailing growths which can be used in many types of floral creations. Linaria maroccana hybrids take in a beautiful colour range including violet-purple marked with yellow.

Linum rubrum is the bright crimson annual Flax which is so easy to grow and so useful for cutting. The erect stems grow 12-18 in. high and bear large numbers of blooms throughout the summer and autumn.

Lupin. Apart from the well known perennial lupins there are a number of recently introduced varieties which can be treated as annuals, and of which the flower spikes make a useful contribution to arrangements. The mixture of annuals known as Dwarf Pixie Delight grow only 6 in. high producing flowers in a glorious mixture of colours.

Malope. Similar in habit to the Lavateras this is another subject which flowers continuously from July to October. They like the sun and look well both when growing and when cut mixed with other brightly coloured subjects. *L. grandiflora* has rose-red flowers and there are pink and white forms growing up to 3 ft. high. Particularly good is the variety Aphrodite which have trumpet shaped carmine-red flowers most freely produced and very effective against their own or other dark foliage.

Mignonette. This is much valued because of its fragrance although there are possibilities in the use of the foliage. An easy plant to grow it prefers a soil in which there is lime and which has been well prepared. If a sowing is made in September blooms will appear in the early spring, alternatively spring sowings will yield flowers from late June onwards. There are a number of species and varieties. Reseda odorata is the most sweetly scented, having greenish flowers, but a number of its varieties have reddish tinged flowers including Bismarck and Red Monarch, while Golden Goliath is tinged yellow.

Nasturtium. Although not always held in high esteem the nasturtium is most useful for indoor decoration. The foliage does emit a scent but this is not unpleasant and is unnoticed if the leaves are not bruised or rubbed. The colour range is exceedingly wide and both the shape and size of the leaves makes them suitable for

mones and freesias make a simple yet attractive display.

Cineraria maritima Of great value for greenhouse and conservatory decoration during the winter months. It can make an eye catching bedding plant display also. Although Perennial these subjects are usually treated as annuals.

using in all sorts of designs. The long trails of the climbing form are ideal for using alone or with other subjects.

Nasturtiums are easy to cultivate. Cover the seed with ½ in. of soil and germination soon occurs. They do well in quite poor soil and often go ona blooming until early winter. If grown in shade the foliage will be abundant but flowers will be fewer.

The new dwarf Compact Jewel mixed strain has a remarkable colour range. The variety Empress of India has dark foliage and crimson flowers while Ryberg Perfection has variegated leaves.

Nemesia. Chiefly used as a bedding or edging plant, this subject is also excellent for pots. It makes a good cut flower. Although frequently grown as a mixture there are many separate colours including blue, red, pink and orange. Sow seed under glass in early spring and move plants to outdoor positions at the end of May.

Nemophila insignis grows only 6-8 in. high and is charming in miniature decorations and posies. The clear sky blue flowers have white centres. Sow seed where the plants are to bloom, either in spring or September. According to when the seed is sown flowers will be available from May onwards.

Nigella. Better known as Love in the Mist and sometimes as Devil in the Bush, this is another plant of the easiest culture. The flowers on 12-18 in. stems are surrounded by light green feathery foliage. The best known variety is Miss Jekyll – cornflower blue, and there are dark blue and white forms. The mixture known as Persian Jewels contains a wide colour range including shades of pink. The seed pods dry well and can be used for winter decoration. Sow in autumn or spring.

Saponaria is another easily grown hardy annual of which the flowers are often cultivated for cutting by both gardeners and market growers. Like gypsophila the flowers are frequently used for mixing with sweet peas and other cut flowers.

For early flowering sow seed in the open ground in September and successive sowings can be made from March to May. *Saponaria vaccaria* produces sprays of rose pink, while its variety rosea has rather larger flowers. There is also a white form. Better still is Pink Beauty which is now the most widely depended on variety.

Senecio. In this large family there are many sections among which is Jacobea elegans of which seed can be sown in flowering positions in early May. The plants like the sun and ordinary good soil and bloom from early July onwards. Usually offered as mixed the colours include: crimson, mauve, purple, rose and white. The

C

double flowers look like little pompons on 15-18 in. stems and are quite long lasting.

Scabious. Often known as the Pincushion Flower the Sweet Scabious is one of the most valuable of all cut flowers the long lasting blooms being carried on wiry stems. They can be grown as hardy annuals, but if treated as half hardy subjects they will come into flower earlier.

The older type has flowers with an outer row of broad petals and a flat pincushion-like centre making them quite attractive. The newer strains are made up of broad petals which are so placed as to produce a cone-like shape.

Any good soil and a sunny situation suits them. In open windy positions it may be necessary to support the flower stems which grow between $2\frac{1}{2}$ and 3 ft. high.

Senecio laxifolius

Scabious are available in many separate colours such as white, rose, violet, pink, crimson, yellow and maroon.

Sweet Peas. This is a true hardy annual with normal life span of about 12 months. The sweet pea has a long flowering period, growth is free and luxuriant above and below ground level. Following nature we find that seeds ripen and are shed in the later summer, and autumn. Therefore this is the natural time to sow, a supposition borne out by experience, for better results follow an autumn sowing.

This subject is much hardier than is often supposed and will withstand the frosts we get in this country nine seasons out of ten, without any protection. It is 100% hardy if given the protection of a cold frame or cloches, provided always the glass is not placed over the plants except during very frosty or very wet weather in winter. Any attempt at coddling or forcing is resented at all stages of growth. Left to its own devices, without crowding or hampering the plants grow luxuriously therefore overcrowding at all stages is wrong. The plant likes sunlight, therefore, choose a position in the garden that is open and sunny all day long.

Apart from the fact that sweet peas do not like too much chalk, they will grow well in almost any kind of soil to be found in this country. The root system is naturally deep and wide searching so for best results we must provide conditions whereby the roots can develop in a normal manner by digging deeply or trenching, although many growers do not move the soil beyond one spit deep.

To sustain a free, luxuriant haulm growth and freedom of flowering over a long period, feeding agents should be given liberally and of such a nature that they release their nutriment gradually over a lengthy period. Animal manure or other organic agents should be used in preference to chemical fertilisers. Bone meal is excellent, but should be used in conjunction with animal manure. Where the latter is unobtainable, use good compost and bone meal with a top dressing of wood ash in spring. Most soils benefit from a dressing of lime scattered on the surface in winter. From mid March to late April the seedlings are transplanted, using a trowel or dibber, not less than 6 in. apart in single or double rows. Some growers plant out without disturbing the ball of soil round the roots, others prefer to gently shake off the old potting soil. Support the plants immediately with small twigs, to prevent slug or wind damage. Later give them permanent supports. Exhibition growers prefer 8 or 9 ft. bamboo canes fastened to a light framework.

When plants are about a foot high pruning or restriction of

growth commences. Each plant has all growths nipped or cut away except the strongest basal side growth and this is trained up the cane by means of wire split rings or raffia ties. Thus we see that a plant which has been encouraged to develop its root system to the utmost underground has its growth above the ground pruned and restricted very considerably.

Naturally, what growth is produced, leaves, haulm, stems and flowers are much larger than had the plant been allowed to develop naturally. That in brief, described exhibition culture sometimes called the cordon system. There are many details one could mention, such as the need for removing side or axil growths at an early stage, removing tendrils before they develop, precautions against greenfly, that worst of all enemies of the sweet pea.

For general garden culture and cutting for indoor decoration the plants can be allowed to grow naturally on bushy sticks and are just as easy to cultivate as culinary peas.

There are various types of sweet peas, but undoubtedly the large flowered Spencer sorts are the most satisfactory for cutting purposes. These are available in a wide colour range and the following are among the best sorts: Magestic and White Ensign, white; Geranium Pink, rose pink; Carlotta, carmine; Sun Dance, orange-salmon; Scarlet Ripple, scarlet; Hunters Moon, cream; Noel Sutton, mid blue; Signal, crimson Leamington, lavender; Pangbourne, mauve; Ballerina, cream with rose picotee edge and Sally Patricia, salmon pink.

The super scented Old Fashioned sweet peas are particularly useful for cutting, not only because of the strong perfume, but for their daity appearance. There are fewer flowers per stem and there is no waviness but the spikes are both dainty and graceful.

Apart from these a number of other strains are in cultivation including the Galaxy multifloras which are sweetly scented and produce long stems bearing 5-7 florets making them very useful for cutting. In addition numerous dwarf strains are in cultivation.

Apart from sowing seed in the autumn in pots and keeping them in the frame it can be sown in warmth in January and February or directly into the open ground from the end of March onwards. Cover the seed with ½ in. of fine compost. Only the hard black seeded sorts need chipping.

Zinnias. During recent years the zinnia has become a valuable cut flower. Although of Mexican origin, it is a plant which will grow well in this country so long as it is given an unexposed position. It does best in loamy soil and in dry and sunny aspects.

Zinnias have the reputation of being a little difficult to raise and there is no doubt that, in their early stages, the plants do need care and attention. Most losses occur through dampness, draughts, cold and poor light. Irregular temperatures are also disliked.

For maturing outdoors, sow in April in a temperature of not less than 65-70 deg. F. Seed can also be sown in May but this means later flowering. Sow thinly in trays or pans of fine compost. Since the seedlings are subject to damping off disease, sterilised soil is used by many growers. Alternatively, the trays or pans can be watered with a solution of Cheshunt Compound.

Germination is usually quick and once the seedlings are clearly seen, the temperature can be reduced to around 60 deg. F. Thin sowing will do away with pricking off, since this operation often leads to a check in growth.

Carefully harden off the seedlings so that by the end of May they are ready for planting outdoors, spacing the plants 8 or 9 in. apart. The main outdoor flowering period is during August and September. Zinnias are divided into three main groups: 1, the tall large flowered types which are usually disbudded, 2, the intermediate varieties, and 3, the dwarf growing and small flowered sorts, including the Lilliputs and Tom Thumb types.

The dahlia flowered, Californian Giants and Burpee Giants are the most popular of the large zinnias all being available in separate colours and mixtures. The Fantasy and Scabious flowered types are the best of the intermediates. The dwarfer growing small flowered sorts, are more suitable for bedding than for cutting.

The blooms should be cut when the flowers are just opening. Cut too soon, the stem is soft and the head liable to bend and become useless for indoor decoration. The lower leaves should be removed for if too much foliage is retained the flowers seem to flag quickly.

CHAPTER 5

BIENNIALS

COUPLED with bulbs, biennials make up a large part of the cutting flowers for spring display. Biennials are sown one year for flowering the next season. Timing is important for the main reasons for the plants sometimes proving disappointing, is either late sowing or transplanting too late. If your plants are in their growing positions by October they will become established before severe weather. May is a good month for sowing, but if it is left until after June, weather and soil become dry and growth is arrested.

Seed is often sown in trays or pans when of course, better control can be had over sowing and initial cultivation. Open ground sowing is really best since it enables the little plants to begin to make a fibrous root system from the earliest stages of growth.

Select a site where the soil is in good heart and work it down to a fine tilth. Sow the seed in drills 12 to 15 in. apart, covering the seed lightly. If slugs are troublesome in other parts of the garden a few applications of slug bait should prevent any serious damage.

Plants are best removed after their flowering period is over, otherwise they clutter up the soil unnecessarily.

Brompton Stocks. This is one of the most popular of spring flowering subjects. It is really best treated as an half hardy biennial, for in exposed gardens the plants are better wintered in the cold frame and planted out in spring. In warm southern and south western districts they can actually be bedded out in autumn.

Sow the seed in June and July in prepared beds in a warm situation, if possible in a frame or where cover can be given with cloches. Such cover will give protection from excessive winter dampness. This is a great help since stocks are liable to damp off if subjected to excessive moisture in the seedling stage.

Thin out early and a second transplanting later will encourage the formation of a good fibrous root system and make it possible to remove any tap roots which may show signs of developing. The plants prefer a good deep soil and never give of their best in thin shallow ground. The flowers, which appear on 18 in. stems, are of compact habit and available separately in crimson, rose, mauve and white, although a good mixture is usually grown.

Canterbury Bells. Botanically identified as Campanula media, these are old world favourites and delightful for an early summer display both in the garden and for cutting purposes. They are particularly valuable in that they grow up to 3 ft. high and are, therefore, most useful where larger decorations are being planned. They should be sown in June or July, since they like a long growing season and the aim should be to have the young plants in their final positions by mid October.

The seed is small and to ensure thin sowing it should first be mixed with sand. Very shallow covering of soil is needed. There are single and double forms, in shades of blue, pink and white, while the Cup and Saucer varieties are particularly attractive. A newer strain of Canterbury Bells known as Bells of Holland, growing only 1½ ft. high, is particularly useful, being extremely free flowering in a delightful mixture of pink, blue, white and mauve.

Digitalis. This is one of our British flowers and familiarly known as Foxglove. The original D. purpurea, with purple flowers is the type plant, but a number of varieties have been introduced, including those having white, pink and spotted flowers, as well as one strain which produces its flowers all round the stem.

There are a few Foxgloves of perennial duration, but the usual practice is to treat them as biennials. Fortunately digitalis produces plenty of seeds, and there are always lots of self sown seedlings appearing round the plants.

D. ambigua while not brilliant, is different, since it freely produces attractive yellow flowers of which the insides are lightly veined brown.

D. ferrugineum has yellow flowers on 3½-4 ft. spikes and foliage tinted an unusual rusty-brown.

D. lanata has 2-3 ft. spikes of greyish-white flowers which are quaint rather than pretty, but most useful for bringing a touch of the unusual into flower arrangements.

Hesperis matronalis is best known as Sweet Rocket, while another common name is Dame's Violet. It is somewhat like a Stock in appearance, the toothed leaves being hairy. On 2½-3 ft. stems, the plants produce violet-lilac or white flowers. The name hesperis comes from the Greek ' hespera ' meaning evening, at which time during June and July, the flowers are most fragrant.

Sow the seed in May or June in pepared beds in a good soil which remains moist. A dusting of lime will be helpful before the plants are moved to their final positions in early autumn, selecting a light soil which does not dry out. The flowers need treating carefully when cut, for if the stems are not placed in water immediately, they are likely to wilt quickly and prove disappointing.

Lunaria biennis. This plant is widely known as Honesty and in some parts of the country it is referred to as Moonwort because of the shape of the seed vessels. An erect growing plant, it produces broad, pointed leaves and 3 ft. branching spikes of mauve flowers which open in May and June.

Seeds are sown in prepared beds of good, but not over rich soil, in May, the plants being moved to their flowering quarters in August or early September. Allow at least a foot between the plants. Cut the spikes in autumn, when the seed pods have formed. If the outer skins are removed, the glistening transparent white ' moons ' will be revealed. They look admirable used in an arrangement of leaves and autumn flowers.

There are several varieties, the most popular being Munstead Purple. Other colours include: white, mauve and crimson. The white variety is sometimes used as fresh flowers in summer but this subject is usually grown for the dried ' moons ' which are sometimes dyed various colours.

Myosotis. This is the well known Forget-me-not for so long grown in British gardens. There are a number of species and although some are perennials they are not reliably hardy and even when they come through the winter they are usually very untidy looking. It is, therefore, best to sow annually.

The main trouble with many of them is that they seed so freely dropping their seed all round the plants so that self-sown seedlings quickly lose their distinctive character.

Seed should be sown during May and June. Thin out the seedlings before they become crowded and weak and move the plants to their flowering places in October or early November.

Myosotis like a position where they never lack moisture and will succeed in partial shade although they flower more abundantly in sunny situations.

The naming of Forget-me-nots is somewhat confused. In seed catalogues they are usually offered as *Myosotis alpestris* or *M. sylvatica cultivars* such as Victoria, bright blue; Marine, mid blue; both 6-7 in. Royal Blue, indigo blue and Carmine King, rosy-carmine, grow 10 to 12 in.

M. palustris, the water Forget-me-not is useful for growing in wet ground or at the edges of ponds or streams.

Sweet Williams. These members of the dianthus family are really perennials, but are usually best treated as biennials, since they are so liable to become straggly and in poor condition after cold weather. In warm, sheltered positions there is no doubt that the plants would come through the winter without difficulty.

Seed is sown in the open ground from late April onwards, and being small, is best mixed with coarse sand. Sow thinly and prick out early. The seedlings should be transplanted to beds, allowing 8 or 9 in. between the plants so that they do not become drawn and weak. Subsequently they can be moved to their flowering positions, where they should be placed not later than the end of October. Ordinary good soil is quite suitable, although lime is liked.

There are a number of good named varieties available, including Scarlet Beauty, Pink Beauty and Dunnett's Deep Crimson, the latter having dark foliage as well as flowers. The auricula-eyed mixture is old fashioned but still very attractive. A much newer strain known as Messenger mixed, flowers 14 days earlier than the older types and has a rich, bright colour range. All of these grow 1½-2 ft. high, although often they remain about 18 ins.

The dwarf double mixed are quite distinct, rarely growing more than 10 in. high. They form compact, uniform plants and during June and July produce 60 to 70% double flowers in a bright and effective colour range.

Wallflowers are perennial plants sometimes making quite shrubby growth but they are usually treated as biennials being sown in the early summer to secure flowering plants the following year. Of simple cultivation they like well drained soil. They are susceptible to club root, so that a well limed soil should be selected for growing the plants.

The seed is usually sown in a prepared bed, and covered by about ¼ in. of soil. Thin out the seedlings early, before they become crowded and move to their flowering quarters in October, although planting can also be done in the early part of the year when weather and soil conditions are favourable. Firm planting is essential and this combined with the pinching out of the growing points, will encourage side shoots to develop.

The range of varieties is wide, as will be seen on reference to seedsmen's catalogues. The following are among the most reliable cultivars; making excellent cut blooms with pleasing fragrance.

Blood Red, deep crimson; Cloth of Gold, bright yellow; Eastern Queen, apricot changing to bright red; Fire King, brilliant orange; Ivory White, creamy-white; Orange Bedder, orange-apricot; Ruby Gem, ruby-violet; Vulcan, velvety-crimson; and Scarlet Emperor, pure scarlet.

In addition there are first class mixtures including: Monarch, Fair Lady, 1 ft.; and Tom Thumb mixed, 9 ins. Less common is the double mixed, growing $1\frac{1}{2}$ ft. high.

Cut the spikes when several of the lower flowers are open and with the stems as long as possible. The lower leaves should be stripped off the base of the stems, since this will prevent fouling of the water.

CHAPTER 6

RELIABLE PERENNIAL PLANTS

HARDY perennial flowering plants have an advantage over other groups of plants in that they can be left in position for 3 or 4 years or even longer and still produce first class flowers for cutting.

The range of easy to grow species and varieties is very wide indeed and includes not only the more familiar subjects but many elegant and exotic-looking flowering plants.

Hardy perennials have often been referred to as the mainstay of the flower garden and they well deserve this title, for unless you are a purist, and keep all perennials strictly separated from other plants, it is possible to grow bulbs and annuals in the same beds and borders and in so doing ensure that there is cutting material available throughout the year.

Some plants form tufted fibrous roots which are liable to exceed their allotted space and action is necessary to prevent their smothering nearby less rampant subjects, although much can be done by careful selection and placing of the various species.

Many perennial plants have attractive foliage which can also be used for cutting. Sometimes, the addition of just a couple of leaves will greatly improve a floral display.

Hardy perennials of today are undoubtedly superior to those available in the past and those listed can be relied upon to produce a plentiful supply of blooms under ordinary good cultivation.

Acanthus. This plant is grown almost entirely for the beauty of its foliage, which is handsome and shiny green with beautiful scalloped edges. It does best in partial shade and likes moisture, although drainage should be good. Left in position for a few years it forms a stately tall plant.

A. mollis is the most commonly cultivated species often referred to as ' Bear's Breeches ' with leaves up to 2 ft. long. It has a larger leaved form known as *A.m. latifolius*, with purple and white flowers shaped like dragon's heads. *A. spinosus* grows 3 ft. high having long strap-like leaves deeply cut and armed with white spines, making the foliage even more handsome. A form known as A. spinosissomus is dwarf growing and more spiny and both have flowers of a purplish colour.

Propagation is by division in the spring or autumn, by root cuttings in spring, or from seed.

Alchemilla. Often known as 'Lady's Mantle' these are small growing plants of interest for their evergreen foliage, the flowers being insignificant. In the garden they are of value because of their ability to thrive under trees or in other shady places. It is where individual leaves are required to complete a floral design that these plants are of value to the flower arranger.

A. Alpina has foliage shaped like a miniature lupin but the leaves are soft and silvery looking. *A. vulgaris* grows a foot high, the foliage in this case being green.

Propagation is easy by division in the spring.

Achillea. Several species and varieties are most useful for cutting. *A. eupatorium* or *filipendulina* is a favourite, producing from July until September, flat, golden heads on strong 4 ft. stems. It has a value for mixing with other colourful flowers, while its silvery grey-green foliage is an extra asset. It lasts well and in fact, is sometimes used with 'everlasting' flowers.

From *A. eupatorium* have come several varieties including the 5 ft. tall Gold Plate, which is well named, while 'Parker's Variety' is especially good for drying for winter decoration. As a smaller, daintier grower, the newer variety Coronation Gold, should be grown. Its flat heads on upright 2½ ft. stems clothed with grey leaves, are very long lasting.

Achillea ptarmica and its varieties are quite different and provided they have a soil containing plenty of organic matter and never lack moisture, they will produce an abundance of flowers. From the free growing creeping root-stocks, there arises a plentiful supply of flower stems. The varieties Perry's White and The Pearl have double white, button-like flowers over a long period during the summer. While they are much used by florists for wreaths and other purposes, there is however, nothing depressing or funereal-like about these flowers.

A. millefolium, Rose Queen and Cerise Queen although not quite so choice, are nevertheless good cut flower varieties. Plants of these are best divided every two years.

Aconitum. These have nothing to do with the little tuberous Winter Aconite, but are tall growing perennials flowering from the end of June until late August. Not unlike delphiniums, they are useful where 'spiky' blooms are needed. *A. wilsonii* is a lovely pale blue; *A. napellus* bicolor; Newry Blue and Sparks Variety, are less tall than some of the others. The thickish tuberous-like roots are said to be poisonous but if they are handled with care there is no risk or harm.

Agapanthus. These are useful as cut flowers. Although usually grown in tubs or large pots these plants are hardier than generally supposed. They like well drained soil and plenty of moisture in summer. After a severe winter they are sometimes slow to start into growth but soon make headway. *Agapanthus africanus* often known as umbellatus, has rather drooping rush-like leaves and in August it produces on 18 in. stems, fine heads of violet blue flowers.

A. campanulatus or *moreanus* has narrower leaves and rather shorter stems with pale blue flowers. When necessary divide in spring.

Anemone japonica. Most effective when used alone or with other flowers. A cool well drained, rich in humus soil is needed. So long as the stems are plunged in water as soon as they are cut, they will remain fresh for a week or so. Since they flower from the end of August onwards their value will be obvious. Among the good varieties there are, A. japonica alba, white; Louise Uhink, also white but dwarfer and cleaner looking; Queen Charlotte, rose-pink; Marguerite, large semi-double pink and Prince Henry, rosy-red.

Anthemis. This is a sun loving family of plants. While some species have little merit as cut flowers, there are other chamomiles, to give them their common name, which are of great value. These are chiefly varieties of the yellow *A. tinctoria* of which Perry's Variety, Mrs. Buxton and Loddon Gold are good.

These however, are surpassed by Grallagh Gold and Beauty of Grallagh both of which make very bushy plants 2 ft. high and sometimes nearly as much wide. From June to August the plants are literally smothered with rich golden daisy-like flowers of fine lasting quality. Grallagh Gold is stiffer growing rarely needing support which is a great asset. Spring planting is best, a good, but not rich soil being selected. If the plants are cut back in August some of the fresh growths produced will give late flowers and the new leaves will in any case give winter protection to the roots. Propagate by cutting or divisions.

Aquilegia. Summer flowering perennials which have been grown in this country for centuries, the Columbines have an attraction of their own. The old name of Granny's Bonnet was applied to the earliest known species most of which had short spurs. The modern trend, however, is for long spurred flowers although both types look well in any floral decoration.

The colour range is fairly wide, and although the mixed strains such as Mrs. Scott Elliott's, and the newer McKana hybrids, are very good, the separately named sorts are preferred by some gardeners. Of these A. Crimson Star; Mrs. Nicholls, blue and white; and the yellow A. longissima last well.

Seed is sown during July or August either in pots or boxes under a cold frame and transplanted to flowering quarters in October, or if insufficient growth has been made keep them in boxes after pricking out, until the early spring. Aquilegias like an open, sunny situation and a fairly rich soil, which does not dry out during the summer. They flourish in chalky ground but will often die out in very heavy soil.

Since the hard seed is often slow in germinating, it is a good plan to rub it smartly with sand paper before sowing. The slight scratching thus caused will lead to earlier growth. These flowers do not travel well, but gathered from the garden and placed in water at once, they remain in good condition a long time.

Alyssum saxatile. This plant is largely used in the rock garden or front of the border. It has more or less evergreen foliage and heads of charming yellow flowers, giving rise to the common name of Gold Dust. Light soil and plenty of sun are required for finest results. The flowers on 6-8 in. stems appear with great freedom from April to June. Established plants can be kept shapely by shortening the longest growths after flowering.

Propagation is easy by seed, excepting in the case of the double forms which must be raised from cuttings or division. Alyssum saxatile citrinum is lemon yellow, and the form compactum rich yellow. A.s. plenuum and A.s. Dudley Neville are both deep golden yellow.

Anaphalis is known as the Pearly Immortelle because the bunches of white fluffy calyces can be dried and used as everlastings. It is these which florists sometimes dye so that they become red, blue or white, allowing them to be used in all manner of floral resigns.

A. margaritacea has upright 1½ ft. stems clothed in dense greyish foliage. *A. triplinervis* has woolly silvery-grey leaves the flower stems being about 10 in. high.

Bergenia. This old fashioned plant classed in the past as megasea and saxifrage makes an excellent ground cover. The stocky creeping root-stock sends up large shining, leathery leaves of rich green invaluable for using in indoor decorations, particularly when in autumn, the leaves begin to turn yellow or scarlet. It has the common name of Pig's Squeak, because if the leaves are placed between the finger and thumb and pulled sharply towards the tip, a squeaking sound is emitted.

These leaves when used indoors, will last 3 or 4 weeks in good condition. The foliage left on the plants in the winter usually turns a beautiful brownish tinge, which is another reason why the leaves are of such value to flower arrangers both in winter and summer.

Bergenia cordifolia is the best known species its thick reddish stems producing from February onwards, dense heads of magenta-pink the leaves being slightly heart-shaped. *B. crassifolia* has large spoon shaped leaves which become mahogany tinted in winter. B. ligulata has narrower leaves with apple blossom pink flowers on 12 in. stems. All like partial shade and cool growing positions.

Propagation is by division after flowering, when soil and weather conditions are suitable.

Armeria. Often known as Thrift or the Sea Pink, these hardy plants form little evergreen hummocks thriving in poor soil and withstanding drought well. From May onwards rounded heads of pink flowers are produced on strong slender stems of about 6 ins. This subject is useful where short stemmed blooms are needed. The more they are cut, the more freely they appear and they last well in water. They like the sun and chalky, porous soil. Among the best are, *A. maritima laucheana*, and Bee's Ruby. Propagation is effected by dividing the plants after the flowering period is over.

Asclepias tuberosa, is a striking plant, worthy of greater use. During August and September it has quite large flattish heads of intense orange, often 6 ins. in diameter, produced on 18-24 in. stems. Each individual floret is of a shiny waxy appearance. Sometimes a temperamental plant it dislikes lime as well as a heavy, badly drained site. It has a tap root and dies right down in the autumn, sometimes not reappearing until quite late in the spring.

Asters of a perennial habit are a ' must ' for the cut flower grower. Very many of them are best known as Michaelmas Daisies, and the majority will stand quite casual, almost rough treatment. Even so, few plants respond so readily to a little extra attention. To obtain a really fine display of good sized flowers, a fairly rich soil, containing organic matter, should be provided and the plants can be further helped by giving a few applications of liquid manure when they are in full growth. Avoid hot, dry soils, and draughty positions, both of which encourage mildew which sometimes so disfigures the entire plants.

Since the roots spread quickly the plants should be divided every 3 years. Propagation is easy, either by detaching strong outer portions of the roots in the spring, although the best method is to secure cuttings in the early spring and pot them up, planting them in their flowering positions during April and May.

As to the species and types, the little alpines varieties are good for cutting, although the flowers are short. The Aster amellus varieties from 2-2½ ft. high, have from August until October large single flowers, many of which are up to 2 ins. across. All are excellent for cutting since the stems remain upright without supports, unless grown in exposed windy places. There are many varied varieties in shades of blue and pink.

Aster acris grows 2-3 ft. high, each stem having very many small, star-shaped flowers with conspicuous yellow centres. *A. ericoides* is the name of another small flowered group, the wiry branching stems 2½ ft. high carry large numbers of starry white flowers with golden centres. The leaves are small and pointed and it is an excellent cut flower plant.

A. cordifolius is a charming species with graceful arching stems so useful for indoor decoration. The cultivar Silver Spray has really long sprays of silvery-lilac flowers. The majority of the Aster novae angliae varieties are of little use for cutting. The variety Harrington's Pink is an exception. They like a good soil, containing plenty of organic matter.

It is the *Aster novae belgii* varieties which are so widely grown. The following are among the best, although some have been in cultivation for a good many years. Apple Blossom, a delightful shell pink; Beechwood Triumph, rosy-red; Ada Ballard, mauve-blue; Blandie and Choristers, fine whites; Crimson Brocade; Eventide, violet-blue; Festival, orchid purple; Gayborder Royal, bright purple; Marie Ballard, pale mauve-blue; Plenty, pale blue; Royal Velvet, violet; The Cardinal, rosy-red; and Winston Churchill, rich deep red.

Aster hybridus luteus, a hybrid between Aster aeris and a Solidago (Golden Rod), produces from August onwards long sprays of small yellow flowers. Gathered when they are just opening the blooms last a really long time in water.

A. linosyris is easy to grow, its 2½ ft. stems being laden with deep sulphur yellow flowers in September, excellent as a cut flower, the plants do not need staking.

Aster yunnanensis Napsbury is not unlike an amellus variety. The blooms appear from late July on strong 18 in. stems and are

planted herbaceous border with tall plants at the back and shorter at
ont.

A heavily planted bed just beyond a patio provides a vista from the window and also wafts a lovely fragrance into the house.

of a rich cornflower-blue colour, with a conspicuous yellow centre. It does well in ordinary soil and full sun, but good treatment is well repaid.

Mention must be made of the dwarf perennial asters which are so effective in the front of the border, and make excellent pot plants. They are excellent when short stemmed cut flowers are needed. Planted in April they will give a really gorgeous display from early September onwards. Good varieties readily available and of which the flowers last well when cut are the following: Nancy, pink 9 ins.; Victor, lavender-blue 6 ins.; Diana, pale pink 9 ins.; Remembrance, lilac 12 ins.; Hebe, strawberry-pink 10 ins.; Margaret Rose, rose-pink 9 ins.; and Vesla, shell-pink 9 ins.

Astilbe. Although not much used for cut blooms the elegant feathery spikes of the japonica varieties will last some days in water. There are forms producing pink, red and white flowers. Strong young plants put into 6 in. pots during the winter and kept in gentle heat, will give a really lovely display in the house during the spring and summer.

Campanula. The peach leaved bell-flower as Campanula persicifolia is frequently called, is among the very best plants for grouping or using as individual specimens. Flowering as they do in June, the plants make admirable companions for other perennials such as lupins, pyrethrums, oriental poppies and irises, which flower at the same time. Together, these form a real colour display without appearing gaudy. It is a fact that inferior forms of C. persicifolia have in the past been grown and distributed. This is a pity, since there are really good named varieties to suit all tastes.

Perhaps the trouble is that these plants seed freely and it is easy to grow on inferior self-sown seedlings, which, as with other plants, grow fast, often making the biggest specimens.

Of the varieties of persicifolia, Telham Beauty, has large expanded bells of light lavender-blue. It has been given an Award of Merit as has the double white, Fleur de Neige. These were followed by such sorts as: Beechwood, mid-blue; Pride of Exmouth, double blue; Moerheim, semi-double white; Wirral Belle, violet blue; and the single white, Snowdrift. Campanulas do not travel well, for the flowers will soon bruise.

To maintain the vitality of the stock, it is essential to lift and divide the plants every 2 or 3 years.

Campanula lactiflora is another fine, tall, border perennial, growing 5 ft. or more high. Each plant produces many large spikes, making an impressive sight, the pale blue flowers often being an

D

inch in diameter. The flowering time extends from the end of May until August, especially if the plants are grown in good soil, in an open, sunny unexposed position.

Here again, propagation is by division or better still, by cuttings secured in the spring. Seedlings vary considerably in habit and colour.

C. latifolia produces spikes $2\frac{1}{2}$-4 ft. and has rather large leaves, the more or less bell-shaped blue flowers being of pendant habit. There are several forms including white and purple. It has the advantage of growing well in the shade and since the roots of this species are bigger than many of the others, it is best to propagate by securing cuttings in the autumn.

Campanula pyramidalis the Chimney Bell-flower does not always come through the winter unscathed. It does well in sheltered gardens and warm districts and can be used to great advantage as a pot plant. There are blue and white forms, growing 4-5 ft. high, and are easily raised from seed. Cleanliness in cultivation and fairly frequent change of ground usually ensures healthy growing stock.

Carnation. See Dianthus.

Catananche. Often referred to as Cupid's Love Dart, this plant has been known in gardens for very many years, although its full value as a cut flower has only recently become recognised. Effective as a border plant it produces an abundance of blooms over a long period. It has narrow grass-foliage while the flowers on 2-$2\frac{1}{2}$ ft. stems are somewhat like those of a cornflower, although the texture of the petal is after the style of the ' everlastings '. They hold well in water and are available from July until September.

Catananche caerulea major is a particularly good variety with bright blue flowers while it has a white form and one which bears white and deep purple blooms. This is known as *C. caerulea bicolor*. There is also a lavender form.

They like sun and a rather light, well drained soil and propagation is from seed sown as soon as it is ripe, or from division or root cuttings, the best time for moving the plants being in the spring.

Centaurea is the Cornflower, and although the annual forms are best known there are several perennial species worth growing. They are easily cultivated in ordinary garden soil and are usually grown because of their attractive foliage which is often silvery-grey. Propagation is by division in spring.

C. montana makes good bushy plants varying in height from 1-2 ft. and having rather thin looking violet-blue flowers in July.

It has varieties with lighter blue, pale pink and white blooms.

C. *dealbata* has thistle-shaped rosy-purple flowers on 18 in. stems, which appear from July until October, while it has a cyclamen-red variety. C. ruthenica has lemon-yellow blooms which last well when cut.

Centranthus. The common Valerian, which is of particular value where the soil is chalky and therefore the range of plants it is possible to grow is limited. The easily grown plants produce throughout the summer on 2 ft. stems, closely packed, sprayed heads of bloom. C. *ruber* is red, and C. ruber alba, white. Propagation is from cuttings or seed, although the latter have to be weeded out thoroughly so that inferior seedlings are not grown on.

Cephalaria is the giant yellow scabious. These hardy plants are of branching habit and produce blooms like those of the popular blue scabious. The plants like the sun, although they also give a good account of themselves in semi-shade.

Excellent plants for the back of the border, they will grow up to 5-6 ft. high, although they are often less than this. C. *alpina* has soft yellow flowers during June and July while C. *gigantea* (or C. *tartarica*) which is the best, also has yellow blooms which are most effective when arranged in vases, especially as the deeply cut leaves are so ornamental.

Transplant in spring when propagation by division can also be carried out. Seed can be sown in April.

Chrysanthemums are too well-known to need much description. For general outdoor use, giant flower heads are not desired as they are liable to break off, particularly if the plants are in any way exposed to the wind. Rain too, is liable to damage and discolour blooms of great size.

Chrysanthemums are plants which if the varieties are carefully selected can be made to look attractive whether planted in clumps of 3 or 4 plants by themselves, or in a mixed border or even if massed together. Seeing that there are so many subjects which flower during August it is preferable to choose varieties that will bloom during September and October, although there are sorts which flower from the end of July. Apart from their great value as garden plants their lasting qualities when cut are well-known, in fact, in a cool atmosphere and with the water changed regularly, they will often last indoors for a week or two.

Soil preparation is most important, and double digging should be done if possible, well breaking up the bottom of the trench. A really good layer of farmyard manure should be dug in the top spit, but not lower, as chrysanthemums are not deep rooting, but require their nourishment fairly near the surface. The addition of bone meal or hoof and horn manure, at the rate of 2 ozs. to the square yard, will be of great help, for chrysanthemums are gross feeders. Should bonfire ash be available, a sprinkling of this will be appreciated by the plants, as it will assist in the development of form growth and bring out the true colour of the blooms.

Unfortunately, some varieties of chrysanthemums are liable to suffer if left in the open ground during winter, particularly if the soil is on the heavy side.

Where convenient the roots of any varieties it is particularly desired to save, can be lifted in November. Place them in good soil in a cold frame giving the minimum amount of water – just enough to prevent the roots from drying out during the winter. Make sure that air is freely admitted to the frame, in fact, only during really frosty weather, need the lights be closed entirely.

These roots may be planted out of doors again the following spring, but if there are any signs of a great number of basal shoots being formed, these should be thinned for if all are left, they will become weak and drawn.

These same plants may be divided before being placed in their flowering quarters, but many gardeners having a greenhouse with a little heat like to take their own cuttings which is done in February, by selecting strong basal shoots about $2\frac{1}{2}$ ins. long and making a clean cut immediately below the node in the same way as is done with geraniums.

If it is intended to purchase plants and a cold frame is available, stock may be obtained from a nursery in March and given $3\frac{1}{2}$ in. pots to allow for greater and earlier root development, On the other hand, if plants are coming direct from the Nursery at planting time, do not arrange delivery until early May.

Place the plants at least 18 ins. apart, and always use a trowel when making the hole, for this will give the roots plenty of room and is in every way preferable to a dibber, however large. Never plant when the soil is either wet or very dry.

If the tops of the plants have not been pinched out, this should be done as soon as they settle down and in the case of the ordinary decorative sorts, a further stopping can be carried out toward the end of June but not later. This will result in the plants becoming bushy and producing a large quantity of flowers. The plants must of course be staked and tied as necessary.

If the ground has been prepared in the way suggested, no extra feeding should be necessary for blooms required for ordinary house decoration but if for any reason it is decided to feed the plants there are several good non-forcing proprietory chrysanthemum fertilisers on the market. The old-fashioned method of immersing a bag of manure in a bath or barrel of water can also be recommended. This is done by tying the bag containing the manure to a stout stick and suspending it in the water. The liquid should be used when it is nicely coloured. Soot-water maw be added or used separately.

Plants grown in the open may be successfully lifted and transferred into pots or tubs, in fact this is often done with late flowering cultivars which are first grown in the garden and then brought into the greenhouse when the colder weather comes. The soil around the roots should be thoroughly soaked a day before lifting, and to prevent the slightest risk of any possible failure in transplanting, insert the spade deeply 6 to 8 ins. from the centre of the plant and carefully cut the soil right round the plant. Half the circle may be done one day, the remainder the following day to lessen the check.

Choice of varieties must always be a matter of individual taste and in addition, every year several new kinds are put on the market by leading raisers. The following Early Flowering sorts are excellent for general garden culture providing blooms of good size and quality under ordinary growing conditions.

Cricket, incurving white; Fred Porter, red; Golden Rule, golden yellow; Jean Fell, large rich bronze; John Woolman, silvery pink incurved; Margaret Billett, cyclamen-purple; Margaret Zwager, rich pink incurved; Ogston Quickstep, golden bronze incurved; Percy Salter, reflexing apricot; Tracy Waller, large bright pink; and Woolley Charm, golden bronze incurved.

Korean chrysanthemums are great favourites for cutting. Built up from the hardy species *C. Coreanum*, which flourishes in Korea and Siberia, it took many years of patient work before they reached the standard demanded by their raisers. Their introduction has made it possible for every gardener to have attractive cut blooms of good colour, over a period of many weeks.

Those who remember the introduction of the earliest varieties such as Apollo, Mars, Ceres and Mercury will recall what a sensation they caused. Not only are the Koreans most attractive when growing, but placed in water the flowers last extremely well. They are not fussy in regard to the soil in which they grow and ought not to be omitted where cut flowers are in demand.

The flowers have a remarkable lustre in their colouring making them ideal for brightening dark rooms especially during dull autumn days, while they show up to great advantage under artificial light. Any one who has seen a display of the Koreans combined with autumn coloured leaves and berries, will at once realise the great possibilities in this connection. The plants normally retain an upright habit, although in high and exposed places some kind of inconspicuous support will be helpful.

The dwarf or cushion Koreans require no support. Growing 1-2 ft. high a bed of these scented dwarfs resembles a Persian carpet.

If care is taken over the height of each subject a marvellous show can be obtained with a wealth of bloom for cutting during September, October and even November.

The following are good varieties. Doubles—all about $2\frac{1}{2}$ ft.: Caliph, ox-blood red; Immortelle, lemon; Peach Caliph, pinkish-peach. Singles – $2\frac{1}{2}$-3 ft. high: Copper Rose, mandarin-pink; Coral Mist, coral; Coral Pink, clear pink; Cornelian, terra-cotta; Derby Day, burnt orange; Flame, brick-red; Heyday, cerise; Lammas Day, amber; Opporto, port-wine red; and Saladin, chinese lacquer-red.

Cushion Koreans: Little Tuk, yellow and bronze; Belinda, orchid pink, green centre; Red Riding Hood, terra-cotta; Bo-Peep, pinky-bronze; Miss Lockett, lemon yellow; Alice, old rose; Honey Pot, honey yellow; Little Muffett, strawberry-pink; Margery Daw, cerise-red; Polly Flinders, mandarin-red.

Chrysanthemum rubellum was originally distributed as Chrysan-themum erubescens, under which name it received an Award of Merit from the R.H.S. Culture is very simple for they are not particular as to soil, although they prefer one which is well drained, but yet does not dry out during the summer.

Of perennial habit, *C. rubellum* and its hybrids are absolutely hardy and will go on to give a bright display for years. It is possible to secure varieties which will provide a colour from early August until November.

Fresh stock can be easily produced by taking sucker growths with roots attached and planting them in well cultivated soil. In addition, cuttings secured from young growths in the spring, prepared in the usual way, and placed in a cold frame or under cloches, will root freely in a sandy soil.

The planting season extends throughout April and early May and the young plants should be placed in a sunny position being firmly embedded in the soil and watered in. They quickly establish themselves and quite small plants will give a good display the same year. When growing for cut flowers, all that is needed in future years, is to remove weak and badly placed growths, so as to ensure good sprays of long stems. The plants should be spaced about 2 ft. apart each way.

Good varieties of rubellum chrysanthemums include: Lady Brocket, apricot-pink; Jessie Cooper, chestnut-crimson; Duchess of Edinburgh, velvety-red; Prince Charles, old rose; Wild Honey, peach-yellow blended with coral; and Red Ensign, indian-red with bright yellow centres.

There are a number of hardy Pompon varieties which are invaluable for cutting purposes. They make dainty sprays and provide a wonderful splash of colour. Among the best are Andy Pandy, attractive yellow; Bob, bright red; Chick, rose; Huddle, rosy-salmon; Janet, shell-pink; Jante Wells, golden-yellow; Nipper, salmon; Paddy, bronze-red; Tommy Trout, amber edged with bronze centre.

Chrysanthemum maximum, or Shasta Daisies. The best known variety is Esther Read, and among its virtues is its earliness in flowering and its complete suitability for growing under glass. It does equally as well on heavy clay soil as in light sandy loam, which cannot be said of many plants. It sometimes dies out in the winter, not because of its poor constitution, but rather that the plants have literally flowered themselves to death, and subsequent wet conditions have given entry to disease organisms.

It is important to get the true stock, for there are actually a number of stocks being distributed which are really sports, and have not the hardiness of the real Esther Read. A distinguishing guide is that the true stock has flower stems covered with minute, yet visible hairs, whereas the stems of sports are smooth.

Given well drained and fairly rich ground this variety is hardy and reliable, although in cold damp areas, winter protection with cloches will be beneficial.

Horace Read is taller growing, often reaching 3 ft. the pure white flowers, which resemble the more usual chrysanthemums, sometimes being 6 ins. in diameter. It is not particular as to soil, but where there is an excess of nitrogen and little potash the heads may become too heavy for the otherwise strong stems.

Jenifer Read was first introduced in 1950, and is remarkable for the fact that it produces long-stemmed flowers which need no side-budding. It is very hardy and will succeed where Esther Read does not winter well. It is similar to that variety, but has outer

petals which are much broader, although of the same intense white
– the deep marigold-yellow centre being altogether striking. Long
stiff stems from 18-24 in. are produced throughout the season,
making it ideal for bunching. About 14 days later than Esther, it
carries a succession of bloom from July until September. The fresh
short foliage produced in September, provides winter cover and
prevents losses.

Wirral Supreme is another very fine large flowered hardy variety,
the fully double flowers, often 4 in. in diameter, appearing during
July and August.

Wirral Pride too, is a good cutting sort, producing a heavy yield
of white flowers with anemone centres on strong stems. It is one of
the hardiest of the Maximums.

A newer and dwarfer white is Snowball, which has double ball-
shaped blooms, which are attractive both when growing or cut.
John Murray is of lasting quality, the flowers, showing from July
until the frosts come.

The shaggy and fringed varieties are useful. Of these the old
variety Phyllis Smith and Droitwich Beauty, as well as the new
Snow Princess are all good.

Cobham Gold is of similar habit to Esther Read, but the flowers
are evenly flushed creamy yellow and when placed in bunches make
a good impression. The colour seems more intense when the plants
are growing on a heavyish fairly rich soil, than when on light,
alkaline ground. If cut when half open the blooms will expand and
colour well, and remain in good condition for a long time.

Generally speaking, it is best to avoid planting any of the *C.
maximums* in land enriched with farmyard manure, but if the
ground is treated with bone meal, bone flour, and wood ash, in the
early spring, they will provide all the feeding necessary for the well
being of the plants.

Grown under clean conditions, chrysanthemums of all kinds are
not subject to many troubles but leaf miner is sometimes a nuisance,
since it does discolour the foliage, beginning with white dots,
followed by curling white lines. The leaf miner maggot cannot be
destroyed by ordinary spraying. It is best to pick off affected leaves
before the pests gain a hold. There are one or two special leaf
miner insecticides which are most effective used on greenhouse
varieties.

Other troubles which occasionally occur, include leaves turning
yellow, which is usually due to over watering or lack of nitrogen,
red or purple coloured lower foliage, which is the effect of cold

nights, or sometimes old age. Blind shoots without buds are usually caused by capsid bugs or where the buds are damaged with brown scars, earwigs are probably the culprits. Virus diseases can attack chrysanthemums but provided healthy stock is secured in the first place, they are not likely to be troublesome.

Coreopsis. These are showy plants, many of which produce blooms which are excellent for cutting and general decorative purposes. Flowering from June to August they like sun and a fairly light, well drained soil, while to encourage continuous flowering any uncut blooms must be removed before they commence to set seed.

Of the species and varieties, *C. auriculata superba* is yellow with a purplish-brown zone around the centre. *C. grandiflora* has bright golden-yellow flowers on long stems and is excellent for cutting. It has a number of good forms, including Mayfield Giant, with extra large flowers; Badengold, with finer brighter blooms; and Perry's Variety, semi-double, deep yellow. *C. verticillata* has many quite small yellow blooms and extra finely cut foliage. Its variety, Golden Shower, is a brighter yellow and a very good plant.

Propagation is done by removing the side shoots from the base of the plants in the spring, or from seed. Avoid rich land and artificial fertilisers since these are liable to promote a lot of growth but few flowers.

Delphinium. These plants like the sun, and a well drained fairly rich soil, in which they will give a remarkable response. Disappointment is sometimes caused by the crowns rotting off during the winter, but this is usually caused by stagnant moisture around the stems. Slugs may be troublesome and they can do considerable damage to young shoots and leaves. With good drainage and suitable steps taken to keep away slugs, there should be no difficulty in obtaining best results.

Delphiniums are not used for indoor decoration as much as they deserve chiefly because they are regarded as being too stiff and formal looking. This is not really so. Particularly in large arrangements, the spikes give the essential towering line since they may be anything from 2-4 ft. in length. Even quite small specimens fit into arrangements suitable for the average room. In addition placed in containers on the floor they are most effective.

Some gardeners object to cutting the spikes for the house, since it means sacrificing the laterals which normally develop quite freely. This can be overcome by leaving the main stem and using the laterals or side growths. In addition individual florets with their long stems can be used for so many purposes. They are specially useful in posies, basket designs, buttonholes and bouquets.

There are named varieties in abundance as will be seen on referring to catalogues of delphinium growers. The Pacific Giant strain is an advance so far as colour is concerned, for apart from the many blue shades, there are purples, pinks, lilacs and whites, most with a dark central bee.

Apart from the tall massive spikes of the Large Flowering delphiniums, the Belladonna cultivars are most desirable. They vary in height from 2-4 ft. and have finely cut foliage with branching wiry stems, the florets being more widely spaced than with the larger delphiniums. Most useful for table decoration their natural beauty and lightness are coupled with long lasting qualities.

Among the named Belladonnas are: Capri, sky blue; Theodora, mid blue shadded rosy purple; Blue Bess and Cliveden Beauty, Cambridge blue; Isis, gentian-blue; and Lohengrin, deep blue. Pink Sensation is another excellent variety, while Delphinium cardinalis grows 3 ft. high and has loose spikes of cardinal red which colour makes it noteworthy.

Sow seed as soon as it is ripe, otherwise keep it in a refrigerator, to retain full germinating power. Sowing can also be done in spring, the seedlings being pricked out when big enough to handle. Transfer to their flowering quarters in September. Strong plants can be carefully divided as soon as the flowers have finished, or cuttings from young shoots can be secured. All delphiniums are best moved in the spring, since autumn transplanting often leads to black crown rot.

Dianthus. The majority of the wild dianthus species come from the limestone mountains of Southern Europe. Many hybrids of these species have spread to various parts of the world and have actually naturalised themselves in various countries. The fact that in their native homes, dianthus succeed in limestone, does give us distinct guidance as to what conditions to provide in order that the plants may flourish.

It is reckoned that there are well over 200 species but only a small number have been used for hybridising. Undoubtedly there are still other species which with great advantage could be used to bring out additional good qualities.

The majority are perennial plants with grass-like foliage, a few forming shrubby growths. Some are of dwarf growing, being ideal for the rock garden. Others are of trailing habit while there are some most attractive annual varieties. The size and shape of the flower varies too. When one considers all these qualities it is no wonder that this subject has proved very responsive in the hands of our leading hybridisers.

Dianthus caryophyllus is the well known border carnation which are among the very best flowers for garden and indoor decoration. Of the many sections suitable for outdoor culture, none is more popular and adaptable than the Hardy Border type. During the past 50 years they have been greatly improved, and although it is true that there are varieties without much perfume most have a delightful fragrance including the clove-scented varieties.

Good present day varieties are of strong constitution having stout stems without any tendency to weak neck, while trouble with ' split calyx ' can largely be overcome with good cultivation and the use of carnation rings.

Border carnations are sun loving plants so that a position should be chosen where they have the benefit of full sunlight and are not shaded by trees or buildings. Whilst a separate bed or border is best, most of us have to grow them in a mixed border. They should be placed where they are not overshadowed by tall thick growing plants or hedges, and should be planted in such a way that their evergreen grey blue foliage can easily be seen during the dull winter months.

The plants will bloom freely if given good soil which should be neither very heavy or too light and sandy. Early preparation and the addition of good manure is advisable and bone meal or a good organic carnation fertiliser should be worked into the surface soil. Acid conditions must be avoided and lime should be applied in the autumn, but not, of course, at the same time as manure. If the ground is prepared in the autumn, it will be settled for planting time in March. The earlier the plants are put in the quicker they will become established and will produce flowers during the same summer. Plant firmly and shallowly so that the collar of the plant is not buried.

Varieties are a matter of personal choice and colour will be a decisive factor for the indoor decorator. The following are among the best of the plain or self coloured sorts: Bookham Grand, crimson; W. B. Cranfield, and Fiery Cross, scarlet; Consul, orange; and Southern Mist, mauve; Sea Foam and Snowy Owl, white. Those with a real clove perfume include: Oakfield Clove, crimson and Lavender Clove, Salmon Clove and Snow Clove. There are a number of good fancies including: Downs Flame, apricot marked orange scarlet; Zebra, yellow striped maroon; Downs Souvenir, white marked scarlet; and Sweetheart, buff suffused salmon rose.

Dianthus allwoodii came from crossing a perpetual flowering carnation with a pink, the result being a splendid hybrid. This is excellent for cutting and can be grown in the front of the border or in an unexposed pocket in the rock garden. Plant firmly either in April or early October in a good soil mixture containing limestone and bone meal with if possible a little well decayed cow manure. If where slugs are troublesome the plants are surrounded with weathered soot it will both deter the pests and help the plants.

It is advisable to grow varieties which are naturally of a bushy habit and not inclined to be flattened by the wind although small split canes provide suitable inconspicuous supports.

The lightness and daintiness of the *D. allwoodii* varieties makes them excellent for all decorative purposes. Many of them are in shades of pink and red having a delightful perfume. Among the best doubles are: Monty and the orange-scarlet Rupert; Betty, Bridget, Derek and Eva are also worth growing. Good singles include: Winston, which is very highly scented. Yellow Hammer is noteworthy because of its colour.

The Allwoodii alpinus varieties are smaller but still useful for cutting. Nymph, Oberon and Mars, with crimson double flowers, and the tiny Tinker Bell and Dewdrop are first class in every way.

Propagation of carnations is by layering in July selecting strong shoots from healthy plants. Remove the leaves from the part of the stem to be pinned down. Then make a downward cut just below a joint. The tongue so formed should be cut off for it is at this point that the roots will form after the cut has been pegged down and covered with fine soil.

Dianthus plumarius, better known as ' Pinks ' are among the easiest and yet most attractive of flowers to grow for decorative purposes. They are hardy and the only reason they sometimes fail to come through the winter is due to wet rooting conditions. They like lime and in established beds it is a good plan to give a top dressing of hydrated lime early each winter. This is especially the case when a mulch of peat is given before the plants commence to bloom in June.

Little attention is needed by Pinks, excepting to keep down all weeds and the removing of dead flowers. There is little trouble from ' split calyx ' as sometimes occurs with carnations.

As to varieties, the lily-white Mrs. Sinkins is still good, while White Ladies is larger and cleaner looking; Inchmery, is a lovely pale pink, while Dad's Favourite is white with chocolate edging.

There are many other varieties all of which give a pleasing effect when used alone or with other flowers.

Propagation of Pinks is simple, and cuttings may be secured from June to September, or pipings can be pulled out, both being inserted in sandy soil either in a shaded cold frame or cloche, or in the open ground. Roots form quickly and the plants can go into their flowering positions in the autumn or they may be moved in March.

There are a few dianthus hybrids that come true from seed, but it is certainly possible to obtain really good mixtures. Sweet Wivelsfield was actually a secondary hybrid, raised in 1920 by Mr. Montague Allwood, having Dianthus allwoodii and *D. barbatus* as its parents. The flowers are all well marked and a wide colour range is represented, only yellow and blue being absent.

Dianthus x Rainbow Loveliness is another first class hybrid, being the result of crossing Sweet Wivelsfield and Dianthus speciosus. It is fairly hardy and nicely fragrant, the good sized flowers having laciniated petals. The plants make a good show over a period of several years, in fact, are usually at their best when they have been established for a year or two. The colour range is wide and varied.

Dianthus x Delight is a hybrid between Sweet Wivelsfield and an alpine species, *Dianthus roysii*, and first appeared in 1935. It grows about 9 ins. high, and resembles both of its parents being perfectly hardy. The flowers show from June until frosts come in the autumn. Very many pleasing colours are in this strain, including some vivid reds and crimsons.

Dianthus x Sweetness is very fragrant and hardy, and will usually be available in a good range of colours.

Dicentra. The Dielytras as they were formerly known, are returning to favour. At one time, they featured in every border worthy of the name and for apart from the flowers the large fresh looking, well cut ferny foliage is altogether attractive.

The plants like a cool, semi-shady position. They object to a waterlogged cold condition in winter, but like plenty of moisture during the spring and summer. For the front of the border, *D. eximia* and *D. formosa* are first class, their attractive fern-like foliage grows 6 or 7 ins. high acting as an excellent foil for more colourful subjects growing nearby. The arching 1 ft. spikes of both varieties, with pendant mauvy-rose-pink flowers remain decorative for a long time.

Dicentra spectabilis which has received an Award of Garden Merit from the R.H.S. grows nearly 2 ft. with correspondingly larger foliage. The well arched stems are furnished with heart-shaped deep pink flowers from which a protrusion hangs with a crimson spot at the base. It is this appearance which gives rise to the common name of Bleeding Heart. Other attractive names given to this plant are: Lady's Locket, Lady in the Bath, the Lyre Flower and St. David's Harp.

Dicentras make good pot plants and it is possible to force them into bloom early in the year. Out of doors flowers appear from the end of May until July. Propagation is by division in autumn or spring, while root cuttings can be taken in early spring.

Dierama. This is a small genus of plants which may be grown out of doors in southern England, but elsewhere is not reliably hardy. Once fairly well-known as Sparaxis pulcherrima, the dieramas have the common name of Wandflower, which is an indication of the gracefulness of the pendulous flower stems which grow more than 4 ft. high. According to variety they appear from July to October.

Transplant in November, as soon as the ribbed foliage has died down. A well drained loam is desirable and straw or bracken placed over the planted roots is advisable during severe weather. The species *D. pulcherrima* has purplish flowers and reliable varieties include: Heron, wine-red; Magic Wand, lavender-pink; and The Dove, shell pink. Propagation is by separating offshoots in spring.

Dimorphotheca barbariae or *lilacina*, is a herbaceous plant which can be grown out of doors in favourable southern and western districts without any trouble. The graceful single flowers are a silky shade of rosy-lilac the reverse side of the petals being a darker tone. It grows in the open in a light sandy, peaty soil which does not become waterlogged. Although known in this country for over 90 years, it has only recently been regarded as a good cut flower. The blooms appear from the end of May until October on stems of 15-18 ins. long. Propagation is by seed sown in warmth in spring.

Doronicum. Any plant which flowers early in the year is bound to be valuable. In this category comes the doronicum, which produces yellow daisy-like blooms and bright green toothed leaves very early in the spring, before the usual run of perennials, and therefore makes a welcome change from bulbous flowering subjects which so often are the only type available.

This subject, having long graceful stems, is ideal for cutting. To ensure they last well plunge the stems into water immediately they are cut before the ends seal.

Doronicums will grow almost anywhere doing well in sun or partial shade. Perhaps the best position is where the soil is on the heavy side and yet does not become wet or sour. The rhizomatous-like roots prefer to be near the surface.

There are new varieties of doronicum to consider, which perhaps is an advantage. The best are probably *D. plantigineum* 3-4 ft., and D. excelsum often known as Harpur Crew 2-2½ ft. Both being very early, and have large bright yellow flowers.

Propagation is simple, the plants being lifted either immediately after they have finished flowering or in September or October. Avoid chopping the roots with a spade, which leads to the entrance of disease. Simply remove the soil from the roots and either pull the crowns apart or carefully split them with a sharp knife, alternatively, use two trowels or forks, place them back to back and lever the sections apart.

Echinaceas are closely related to the rudbeckias, in fact, the old type *E. purpurea* used to masquerade under the name of the latter. The cause of the confusion, or partly so, is that the echinaceas have the common name of Purple Cone Flower, and the rudbeckia is the Cone Flower, the reason being that the last named has a cone-shaped centre, while that of the echinacea is somewhat like a curved disc.

Echinacea. The King is the best known variety. This has dark crimson or red-purple flowers often as much as 5 ins. in diameter produced on stems of 5 to 6 ft. The flowers are unmarked with green or pale yellow, as occurs in E. purpurea, and this is another improvement. E. colwall is rose-purple, and in common with most of the best hybrids has petals which remain outstretched instead of bending back, which gives to E. purpurea a rather drooping, fading effect. E. Ballard's Improved, is another good form, and Earliest of All, a good deep crimson. The flowering time of echinaceas is during July and August.

Echinaceas should not lack moisture, but must be protected from water actually settling around their roots, in fact, it seems that where such a condition occurs, the roots are prone to decay and the foliage becomes susceptible to some kind of damping off disease. Transplant either in the spring or autumn. Propagation is by division or root cuttings in the spring.

Echinops, or Globe Thistles, are not difficult to grow or propagate. Plant them in a sunny position in a good deep soil since the thong-like roots often penetrate widely. With this condition fulfilled and good drainage provided, no other special requirement is necessary. Echinops invariably provide a remarkable show and it is surprising that they are not seen in gardens more frequently. The thistle-like heads are handsomely formed with evenly placed points so typical of the thistle. These heads have a metallic lustre which makes them showy in the garden and most decorative in their dried state when they are used for indoor decoration during the winter.

E. ritro is probably the most widely grown sort. This grows over 3 ft. high, its bright blue polished-looking heads being much in demand as 'everlastings'. A darker cultivar known as Taplow Blue, growing 4-5 ft. high, produces bright blue flower heads in July, while the large E. giganteus, 6 ft., has greyish-white heads. Less common is *E. sphaerocephalus* the silvery-white form, which is sometimes seen at flower shows although it has not the same appeal as the coloured forms.

Propagation is done by cutting up the thong-like roots or by removing the freely produced eyes or buds which appear on the roots. Where not required for propagation and left undisturbed for 2 or 3 years or more, the plants will produce flower spikes in abundance.

Erigeron. This most useful family of perennials has the common name of Fleabane. There are a number of good species, and many varieties, all of which grow 1-2 ft. high in good soil, preferably in a sunny situation.

Of the older sorts, *E. aurantiacus*, orange, is a good plant but inclined to be floppy and may die out in the winter. *E. speciosus* has produced many garden varieties having fine cutting qualities, including Quakeress, pinky-blue.

E. hybridus. Under this heading there are many garden varieties of uncertain origin, including the rose pink E. Ladhams. The following newer cultivars are outstanding: Dignity, violet-mauve; Felicity, clear pink; Integrity, rose-pink, yellow centre; Serenity, deep mauve; and Sincerity, light mauve. The main flowering period is June to August but excepting in poor dry soil there is often a later flush of bloom.

Propagation is very easy, and the plants can be divided in the spring when the new growth commences to show, while seed is a ready means of working up a stock of the hybrids.

Eryngium. Commonly known as Sea Holly, the flowers are useful in a dry form for Christmas decoration, when apart from their natural colour which varies according to variety from silver-grey to steel blue, they look well when painted or gilded.

A corner of a cut flower border

Stock, Column Cascade

Give the plants a sunny situation and a really good deeply moved soil, since their thong-like roots go down deeply, but they are adaptable, in that with plenty of room for their roots they will grow in almost any type of soil.

Of the species available *E. alpinum* grows 2½ ft. high, and is particularly fine with steel-blue, cone shaped heads, having many well divided, attractive bracts at their base. *E. oliverianum* which grows between 3 and 4 ft. has well branched stems and large bright steel-blue cones. *Eryngium planum* has rather smaller cones, while *E. tripartitum* is a vigorous free flowering species producing an abundance of 4 ft. well branched stems, which are most attractive with their shiny blue cones.

Propagation is in spring, by root cuttings 2 or 3 in. long, inserted in sandy soil, either in boxes or under the cold frame.

Gaillardia. For these plants select a sunny situation, where the soil is of an open texture without being too sandy and avoid water-logged conditions during the autumn and winter, otherwise the crowns may damp or rot off. If it is possible to purchase plants which have been grown in pots, so much the better, for sometimes stock secured from the open ground is slow to settle down, especially if it has been necessary to procure from a distant place, where the growing conditions are different.

Whether new stock is required or not, established plants should be divided every 3 years, and the healthy outer portions replanted. Whilst it is unnecessary to grow a large range of named varieties of gaillardias, there is always a demand for those which are predominately yellow or mainly red, some of which have outer frilly petals.

Named varieties include *G. grandiflora* which is the type plant, with yellow petals stained maroon; Burgundy is reddish-brown; while Ipswich Beauty which often grows from 3 ft. is yellow and crimson. Wirral Flame is mahogany, with yellow tips. There are one or two all yellows, but on the whole they are not so popular.

Cut the blooms before they are fully opened, and stand the stems in deep water for some hours before they are arranged.

Propagation can be carried out by taking cuttings of sturdy basal growths in March or April, or again in the summer. Plants can be carefully divided in the spring when seed can also be sown.

Geum does not present any cultural difficulties since it will grow and flower freely in any good soil whether in sun or partial shade, although the roots must never lack moisture. The species *G. chiloense*, from Chile, better known as *G. coccineum*, has given us

E

several varieties having flowers which are ideal for cutting, although this is not a long lasting flower. Lady Stratheden, is deep yellow; Mrs. Bradshaw, bright scarlet; Orangeman and Red Wings, orange-scarlet; all growing about 18 in. high.

Propagation is from seed sown in the cold frame in April or May or out of doors later. All seed raised plants are liable to vary so it is necessary to cull the plants retaining only the finest specimens. Extra good stock can be propagated vegetatively by carefully dividing the roots of established plants in September, and firmly replanting the divisions in sandy soil.

Gypsophila. The perennial forms are greatly valued not only for their own dainty flowers but because of the ways in which they can be used to mix with other blooms.

G. *oldhamiana* grows up to 3 ft. and produces sprays of pink flowers in August and September. G. paniculata and its double forms are much in demand both as garden plants and for cutting. Bristol Fairy, white, is probably the best known of the doubles, while Flamingo pale pink, is also valued. Generally speaking the doubles are less strong growing than the singles.

Gypsophilas do well on most soils so long as they are deep and free from perennial weeds. Do not give the plants too rich fare or growth will be rampant to the detriment of the blooms. The name gypsophila is derived from the Greek, meaning ' chalk loving ', an indication that the plants should not be grown on acid soils.

Propagation. Most sorts can be raised from seed but Bristol Fairy must be propagated vegetatively. The usual method is to graft on to the root stock of the single. For this purpose the roots to serve as scions and stocks should be lifted in the autumn and kept in soil in the cold greenhouse for winter protection. After the cuttings required have been secured in the spring, these plants can be put outside again.

Several other varieties of gypsophila can be grown from cutting, especially Flamingo, rosy-pink 3-4 ft. and Rosy Veil, 15-18 ins. Neither of these require grafting.

Helenium. Not by any means the choicest of cut flowers, heleniums are easy to grow. According to season and variety, they are available from June until September. They like the sun and established plants may be divided either in spring or autumn.

There are many first class named varieties with many colour tones of yellow, orange and brownish-red. Among the best of the cultivars are the following: *H. pumilum magnificum* and *H. bigelovi aurantiacum*, rich golden-yellow. These are succeeded by Moerheim

Beauty, rich brownish-orange flowers on $3\frac{1}{2}$ ft. stems; Chipperfield, orange 5 ft.; Madame Canivet, rich gold yellow 3 ft.; Riverton Beauty, brownish-yellow and Wyndley, chestnut-orange $2\frac{1}{2}$ ft.

Once cut, heleniums are long lasting if the water is changed frequently. It is possible to raise a stock from seed, but so often inferior plants are secured in this way. The best method is to divide the plants every 2 or 3 years so that young free flowering stock is always available.

Helianthus. This member of the compositae or Daisy family, derives its name from two Greek words helios – sun and anthos – flower, which accounts for the common name of Sunflower. Not now so popular as it once was, there is still a limited demand for the flowers which are useful in bold arrangements.

The planting season extends from November to March whenever the soil is workable. A mulching of stable manure or compost in the late autumn will do much to give both protection and enrich the soil, thus ensuring the production of really fine flower heads. Some gardeners give a few applications of liquid manure when the flower stems begin to develop, believing that this feeding prevents the stems from hardening so early without making the growth too soft.

Species and varieties worth growing include: H. soleil d'or, rich yellow flowers with double quilled petals on 5 ft. stems; H. scaber or rigidus, yellow with brown central disc 6 ft.; and *H. sparsifolius*, semi-double, orange flowers, 6 ft. high.

Cut the flowers before the petals are fully opened and plunge the stems in water for some hours immediately after cutting.

Propagation is by division in spring or autumn.

Heliopsis. A sunflower-like perenniel needing the same culture as helianthus. The strong erect stems, grow about 3 ft. having one central bloom and a number of laterals. The flowers last well in water in which they should be placed immediately they are cut. If they wilt after being gathered, they have difficulty in taking up water again.

Of compact growth they rarely occupy more space than 2 ft. square. They flower from July to September, and among the best to grow, are varieties of *H. patala* and *H. gigantea*, including Orange King and Light of London.

Propagation is by division in spring or autumn.

Helleborus. Although usually known as the Christmas Rose, *Helleborus niger* does not belong to the rose family, but is in fact, related botanically to the Buttercup. However, the name Christmas

Rose sounds attractive and undoubtedly is one of the reasons why the flower is so popular.

There is no difficulty in securing from established plants really pleasing pure white flowers, and if they can be covered with cloches or hand lights from the time the buds begin to develop the pure whiteness of the blooms is preserved. It is this clean appearance which adds to the value of the flowers. With this protection there is no difficulty in obtaining blooms at Christmas.

The plant should be given a fairly rich deep loam with a good leaf mould content. Grown in a partially shaded site under the shelter of trees, shrubs or a wall, they will thrive and luxuriate without difficulty. They like moisture when in growth, so it is useless planting helleborus where they will have to put up with drought.

Where the blooms are required for indoor decoration the stems should be placed in water immediately after cutting and if this is done, they will usually last in good condition for 14 days or more.

Apart from *Helleborus niger*, forms which demand attention include *H. altifolias* or *maximus*, of which the large white flowers, appearing from December until March, are more or less tinted rose on the outside of the petals. Although less easy to obtain than H. niger itself, it is well worth hunting for.

Another form of Helleborus niger is the Bath variety, which many years ago was actually grown at Bath especially for market work. It is a robust growing plant with handsome foliage and really large pure white flowers appearing during January and February. H. corsicus is another good species. In all cases the stems are between 5 and 8 ins. high.

Helleborus orientalis is the Lenten Rose, which flowers from February to May according to variety. Growing from 6-12 ins. high, the colour range, while not bright, takes in white, purple, pink and green, while there are spotted sorts. Not suitable for every purpose, green or purple blooms are of great value in certain arrangements.

The blooms of *Helleborus orientalis* are inclined to droop quickly, unless the stems are plunged into water immediately they are cut. If severed while actually being held under water so much the better. It is also possible to use the flower heads themselves in floating bowls. The time to move the plants is after flowering, or in September.

The dividing of plants can be done in the spring when they are in full growth, each division replanted having a good root-stock with two or three buds. Where beds are being planted up anything from 18-24 ins. should be allowed between plants and rows. Propagation can also be effected by seed which should be sown in pans or boxes under glass as soon as ripe. When big enough to handle the resultant seedlings should then be pricked out on to a shady border.

Heuchera. This will grow in almost any soil, excepting stiff clay, although a good, deeply cultivated site with plenty of sun and good drainage is best. To keep the plants in free flowering, healthy condition, occasional division is advisable, even when plants are not being propagated to increase stocks. If the crowns are replanted fairly deeply and firmly they will soon become established, otherwise they have the tendency to grow out of the ground. Then they look insecure and become blown about.

Dry weather conditions will not prevent them flowering although occasional applications of liquid manure help to maintain a plentiful supply of charming blooms giving a unique brightness to a border or rock garden as well as providing cut flowers.

Some Heucheras such as *H. tiarelloides*, having carmine-pink flowers, commence to bloom at the end of May and go on giving colour for many weeks. Other species include *H. pubescens* 12 ins. high with crowded panicles of dainty pink flowers, the plants being covered with a powdery down. H. villosa has small, loosely arranged spikes of violet flowers appearing in August and September. It is from brizoides, clear rose-carmine, and its forms, that the best displays are secured. Of these *H. gracillima* freely produces rosy-crimson blooms, while the fine Pink Spray, is a charming, bright carmine-pink, on stems of 18-24 ins.

H. brizoides, Bloom's variety, bright red, is undoubtedly one of the best, while other excellent sorts include Pluie de Feu, brilliant fiery-red, and Sanguinea Edge Hall, pale pink flowers on 2 ft. stems. Freedom is bright rose-pink, and Oakington Jewel, deep coral-rose, with a coppery tinge. The Bressingham hybrids include a wide colour range, varying from pale pink to intense crimson, and contain both tall and dwarfer growing sorts.

Although these are days in which there is usually a demand for size in flowers, the Heuchera is a subject which by its gracefulness and almost fragile appearance, has made a place for itself, being particularly valuable for table decoration. In addition the foliage colours up well during winter.

Propagation is by division of crowns in the spring, whilst seed of some is available.

Inula. This subject is deserving of greater use as a cut flower. An easily grown herbaceous plant it likes good soil and a sunny situation, which encourages sturdy growth and the production of long lasting flowers. The yellow, fine petalled, daisy-like flowers lend charm to a bowl of mixed blooms.

For cutting, the best species is *I. orientalis* (or *glandulosa*) with large shaggy orange petals. *I. royleana* also has large orange blooms with long drooping petals. *I. magnifica*, yellow, grows 5 or 6 ft. high, the blooms being up to 6 ins. in diameter.

Propagation is by division of roots in October or March or by seeds in April.

Isatis glauca is the perennial Woad. It produces on 3 ft. branching stems, narrow pointed blue-green leaves and during the summer has graceful panicles of quite small yellow flowers. This plant will grow in any soil and does not seem to mind a fairly dry position. Although quite interesting it is not very long lasting as a cut flower.

Propagation is by division in autumn.

Kniphofia often known as Red Hot Poker, or Flaming Torch, these plants are not nearly so difficult to grow as is often supposed, and they have considerable decorative value when cut.

They like a position where they never lack moisture so the humus content of the soil should be increased. Dryish conditions during winter are desirable. If the foliage is retained instead of being cut off it will provide sufficient winter protection, more so if the leaves are tied together over the crowns, so as to form a kind of thatch.

Species and varieties vary in height from $1\frac{1}{2}$ to 6 ft. The old species Kniphofia aloides produces from July until September, orange scarlet flowers on 5 ft. stems. *K. caulescens* 4 ft. has spikes of pale pink passing to yellow; *K. goldelse*, 2 ft. is soft yellow; *K. nelsonii*, 2 ft. coral red; and *K. tuckii*, 3 ft. red shading to yellow.

Of the dwarfer kinds, K. macowanii has dainty 2 ft. coral red spikes, *K. galpinii* $2\frac{1}{2}$ ft. apricot orange, showing from September to November. All of these will live up to their other common name of Torch Lilies and are dependable for cutting.

Although plants can be raised from seed, named varieties must be propagated vegetatively, to maintain a true stock. Planting is best done in spring and a mulching of peat or moss litter during hot weather will help new roots to form.

Lathyrus latifolius is the Everlasting Pea which is easily raised from seed. A climber, it grows up to 6 ft. high, bearing from July to September sprays of pink or white flowers according to the variety being grown. Although liking the sun, lathyrus will succeed in partial shade and the presence of the leaves and flowers in any arrangement leads to a less formal appearance. Growth can be pruned back to soil level in October. Other informal species include: *L. grandifloris* rosy-crimson; *L. magellanus*, Lord Anson's Pea, purple and *L. rotundifolia*, rosy-pink.

Hosta. Named in honour of N. C. Host a physician of an Austrian Emperor, this plant is also known as funchia and plantain lily. It is a versatile labour saving plant being suitable for border, shrubbery or as a specimen plant, while it can also be grown in tubs or in the greenhouse. The plants are of stately appearance with pleasing foliage. The leaves assume their beauty as soon as they begin to unfurl after emerging from the soil.

They like good fairly rich soil not liable to dry out and both leaves and flowers are excellent subjects for cutting lasting well in water. Another of their values is that of ground covering where they blockout weeds. They can be kept in good condition by a mulching of decayed manure or peat at the end of May. The variegated forms are particularly useful for planting in semi-shaded places where they show up well.

Among worthwhile species are the following: *H. albo marginata*, with white margined leaves; *H. crispula*, dark green leaves with white border; *H. fortunei albopicta*, yellow leaves with green edge; *H. glauca*, blue-green; *H. undulata*, wavy leaves and H. ventricosa, dark green, oval to heart-shaped leaves.

When gathering the foliage it is best to pluck a few leaves from each plant rather than stripping individual specimens.

Dwarf Iris. While the tall flag Irises are so impressive because of the length of stem the shorter growing iris species have a charm of their own. They are particularly useful for indoor decoration used alone or in conjunction with other showy blooms.

Iris graminea is a pretty beardless European species growing 15-20 in. high. In May and June it produces its violet purple flowers, the lower petals being heavily marked bluish purple on a white ground. Sometimes the elegant foliage grows rather taller than the flower stems and on occasions the leaves are quite broad, but if the narrow leaved form is secured, the quite large flowers can easily be seen.

As a cut flower *Iris graminea* is attractive, and although it is normally described as being deliciously scented its perfume certainly varies being, if anything, more pronounced on dull days.

Of most easy culture, it thrives in good soil, in fact it does not need a rich site for in such a place the plants will produce an abundance of foliage but few flowers.

Another excellent but little known iris is *ruthenica*, sometimes known as *I. caespitosa*. It has tufts of dark green foliage and bears on stems varying from 6 to 9 in. fragrant violet-blue flowers of fine form. Although sometimes a little shy in blooming it will when established flower from April until June, especially when planted in a well drained sandy loam in a sunny position.

Suitable for both the rock garden and the herbaceous border, Iris tectorum, sometimes called the Japanese or Chinese roof iris produces loose sprays of blue flowers flecked with mauve. These striking flat blooms are often 4 or 5 in. across, the flower spikes growing up to 2 ft. A white form *I. tectorum alba* grows about 18 in. high and both flower in May and June.

Iris longipetala is a beautiful Californian species with narrow glaucous green foliage and freely produced strong growing stems up to 2 ft. high each carrying large lavender blue flowers which are prettily reticulated with white. A much less common form of I. longipetala known as montana, grows about 18 in. and makes an admirable cut flower. The blooms which are produced during May and June are a delightful shade of cool lavender. Given a sharply drained site in the full sun, these two varieties will carry on flowering for years without cultural attention, although they are not difficult to divide when necessary.

Requiring the same cultivation as *Iris longipetala I. innominata* grows 8 or 9 in. high and produces a tuft of rather grass-like foliage. The blooms are buttercup-yellow although I. innominata seedlings are available in various shades of colour.

Iris hyacinthina does well in poor soil so long as it has good drainage. Introduced into this country by Reginald Farrar this species has attractive grass-like foliage and delightfully hyacinth scented soft blue flowers which on 15-18 in. stems appear during June.

Preferring a fairly moist position in a sunny situation *Iris bulleyana* from China has rich blue flowers during June on 18 in. stems which rise amid narrow foliage.

Many iris species are of elegant habit, some having a delightful scent, a point which is often overlooked when the value of irises is being considered.

Limonium. Long known as perennial statice this is one of the plants which have had a name change, although it is still widely referred to as statice. The common name is Sea Lavender which is appropriate in that some of the species can be found growing naturally on cliffs and other places near the sea. They are quite suitable for garden cultivation, where they like sunshine, good soil and free drainage.

There are several species *L. incana* being a favourite for drying. The wiry stems grow 15 to 20 in. and in summer, produce densely branched, flattish heads of flesh-pink flowers, surrounded by bract-like white calyces which retain their decorative character in winter. There are several forms of this species.

L. latifolia will often grow 2½ to 3 ft. high, and this is the real Sea Lavender. On wiry stems, it forms spreading heads of lavender-blue flowers from June to August. These retain their colour when dry. The foliage which is almost evergreen, is useful when individual leaves are needed to include in floral arrangements.

Propagation is by root cuttings; careful division in spring, or by seed. There are several named varieties which have been produced from seed, but these can only be propagated from root cuttings, since they do not come true from seed.

Liatris. A genus of North American perennial plants with tuberous rootstocks, commonly known as Snakeroot. Other common names are Kansas Feather, and Blazing Star. The erect growing flower stems, are clothed with smallish leaves, many being excellent for cutting. Liatris will grow in any good garden soil, but seem to object to being planted deeply. The flowers appear during August and September, the spikes opening from the top downwards instead of the usual, opposite way. Make sure the soil does not dry out in dry weather.

As to the species, *L. callilepis* has showy 3 ft. spikes of purple-magenta, often as early as July; L. elegans, 3 ft. is purple; L. punctata, 2-3 ft. is violet-purple with spotted brown leaf stems. L. pycnostachya, in spite of its name, is popular with florists, often growing 4 ft. with attractive spikes of pale purple. Other species include: *L. scariosa*, 3 ft. purple; *L. spicata*, 2-3 ft. mauve; and *L. squarrosa*, 2-3 ft. bright purple.

Propagation is by careful division of the tuberous roots in spring and autumn, or in most cases, by seed sown in the usual way with hardy perennials.

Lychnis. These are plants which often grow 3-4 ft. and are of special note because of the bright colour of the flowers during the summer. Not difficult to grow lychnis like plenty of moisture during the growing season, but to be rather drier at the roots during the winter.

L. chalcedonia is the best known species having bright scarlet flowers and is sometimes referred to as 'Jerusalem Cross'. It is good for cutting and takes up water easily. Do not let the roots dry out, otherwise the stem leaves will wither detracting value from the flowers.

Other species and varieties, all of which produce their flat flowers at the top of the stem, include the dwarf *L. haageana*, 1 ft., and *L. viscaria plena*, 2-2½ ft. which has semi-double rosy-carmine flowers.

Stock may be increased from seed, or by division of roots either in early autumn or spring.

Lysimachia. Although there are numerous species and varieties few are of real use for indoor decoration, although even the prostrate stems of *L. nummularia* (Creeping Jenny) with their yellow flowers can be effective in some decorations. It is, however, *L. clethroides*, with its 2-3 ft. arching spikes of white flowers which are so useful for cutting purposes, although not very long lasting.

Propagation is by division of plants in spring.

Lupins commence to flower from the end of May, and thus fill a gap which often appears after the earliest flowering hardy subjects are over, and before the summer blooming sorts show colour. The flowers are most effective in the right type of container, and perhaps their only fault is the tendency of the blooms to drop early, when placed in a very close atmosphere.

To do really well, lupins should have a well drained soil in which there is a good quantity of well rotted manure. First class results can be had by using land which was well manured for a previous crop. When the plants are in position, an annual mulching can be given after growth dies down in the autumn. A good amount of humus in the soil is desirable, for on thin, dry land the flower spikes are both small and of poor quality. Failing manure, a dressing of bone meal or hoof and horn meal, 3 ozs. to the square yard, is most helpful. Autumn and spring are good planting times.

Cut the spikes when a few pips are open and stand them in water before bunching or arranging them. Some gardeners make a short slit at the bottom of the stem to encourage a good intake of water which greatly increases the lasting quality of the flowers.

While lupins can be raised from seed the plants so produced do not come true to type. The only sure way of increasing a particular stock is from cuttings or division. For this purpose stock plants should be given protection during the winter and spring, young basal shoots 2-3 ins. long being taken in February or March. If secured with a heel, they will normally root quickly. It is also possible to detach some young shoots with roots from developing plants and put them out at once.

Macleaya cordata, better know as *bocconia*, has the common name of Plume Poppy, although it does not resemble a poppy in any way.

An ideal plant for the centre or back of the border it produces spikes 5-6 ft. high. It is important to space the plants so the foliage can be seen, for the leaves are highly decorative. They are well cut and of a greenish bronze shade, being white underneath, so that individual leaves may be used when arranging flowers of many kinds.

The colour of the spikes is a lovely buff apricot, while a form known as Coral Plume is a distinct coral pink shade. These flowers give height and distinction to large arrangements and as far as the plants are concerned, if kept in their allotted space, they become a most valuable feature.

Propagation is by root cuttings taken in the spring, by suckers in summer or by soft cuttings in June when they should be rooted in the cold frame.

Mertensia virginica often known as the Virginian Cowslip, is most attractive, the flowers lasting in good condition for a week or more when cut. The graceful arching spikes appear from April to June, on 18-20 in. stems, the lovely blue flowers standing out well among the greyish-blue foliage.

Care is needed when clearing the ground during the winter so that the roots are not damaged for the foliage dies right away during the autumn. Propagation is by division of foots in spring or autumn.

Monarda. Sometimes known as Bergamot or Bee Balm. These are hardy perennial plants which will grow almost anywhere excepting in deep shade. They provide colour from July until September when many other herbaceous plants are passing out of bloom. The species *M. didyma*, and its variety Cambridge Scarlet grow 2 to 3 ft. high having square-shaped stems with pointed lance-like leaves which are rather hairy. The plants are of branching habit, the long lasting flowers appearing on heads at the end of each stem.

The leaves are fragrant, being sometimes used in salads, while the young foliage is used for making a herb tea. *M. fistulosa* is lilac-purple and there is also a white form. Croftway Pink is extra good.

A particularly fine series of monardas has fairly recently been introduced including shades of pink with such attractive names as Clover, Melissa, Pink Ponticum and Valerian. In addition, there are blues, purple, red, dark ruby, mahogany and magenta.

The best means of increase is division of roots in spring or autumn, retaining for best results, the outer portion of the clumps. Seeds can also be sown in the open in June.

Onopordon arabicum. This is the Scotch Thistle always in great demand by flower arrangers. It is a first class foliage plant with pinnate leaves often 15-18 in. long. A biennial it is easy to grow and once in the garden and allowed to flower, its self sown seedlings usually appear regularly.

It is in its second year that the plant reaches its full size when it makes a stately specimen 6 ft. or more high. The deep purple flowers are pleasing but it is for its foliage that this subject is grown, both the stem and leaves being useful for indoor decoration as well as for exhibition purposes.

Sow seeds where the plants are to flower, for seedlings usually form tap roots quite early. If these are broken or damaged in transplanting, the plants may not recover from the move.

Potentilla. Sometimes known as Cinquefoil, many of the species are of shrubby habit. There are some however, of both shrubby and herbaceous growth which are valued for their foliage which shows off more colourful subjects.

Among these is *Potentilla argenta*, which has well divided greyish leaves, often with a silvery ' wool ' underneath. *P. argyrophylla* has silvery, strawberry-like leaves on neat bushes and also produces yellow flowers.

The well known *P. fruticosa* makes a shrubby specimen and has several forms, including *vilmoriniana* which has silvery-grey foliage on upright branches of 2½-3 ft. The pinnate leaves have cut edges and are usually coloured on the underside.

Sprays of any of these are useful for including in vases of cut flowers. All potentillas prefer a sandy situation and will grow in ordinary good soil which does not dry out.

Pansies. While it is true that there are many plants with larger and more imposing flowers, there are few which have the same appeal as the pansy. Many quaint and intriguing names have been given to this plant because of its unusually marked blooms. When one considers for a moment the particular colours of many of the varieties, the reason for their having been given such titles as Heartsease, Three faces under a Hood, and Tickle my Fancy will not be difficult to understand. The fact that many of the flowers look like a pensive human face has given rise to the expression, ' pansies for thoughts '.

The finest strains of seeds must be sown for no amount of subsequent culture can make up for any deficiency on this score. It is possible to obtain bedding and exhibition pansies in separately coloured varieties but for general purposes, a choice mixture provides an interesting display for cutting.

The newer Felix strain has large slightly waved blooms, with radiating dark ' wisker ' marks. The Majestic Giant strain is first class with well marked flowers, while Holland's Festival pansies produce enormous blooms with very rich colourings and long stems, making them ideal for cutting. Read's Scented pansies are attractive both in colour range and perfume. Mixtures of red shades which include orange-red and crimson-red tones always attract attention, being both uncommon and effective.

Then there is the Clear Crystals type in separate colours, all without blotches, and very free flowering. There are several F.1 hybrids of great value including Sunny Gold, a pure yellow and Azure Blue a most effective colour.

Apart from the Large flowered strains, the winter flowering pansies should not be overlooked. These will bloom from November until March and come through the hardest of weather without any great harm. Blue Velvet, violet-blue; Snowstorm, pure white and Yellow Queen are particularly pleasing and look well either in separate beds or as edgings to other subjects.

For early spring flowering, the seed should be sown from the middle of June until August, either in a cool, partially shaded position or in boxes in the cold frame. The latter method enables the seedlings to be watered and attended to more easily and is likely to provide an earlier display of colour.

Sow thinly and shallowly and cover the receptacles used with paper until after the seeds have germinated. This prevents the top soil drying out with subsequent bad effects.

Once the third leaf has developed, prick off the young plants into other boxes. Seed can also be sown out of doors with great success in a favourable semi-shaded place and prepared site. The subsequent plants are best thinned out to about 8 in. apart in October.

Always cut the flowers with a long stem and just before they are fully opened.

Nepeta is well-known as a border edging plant, but there are some taller growing sorts which are of value for cutting. The secret of securing a regular abundance of spikes is to divide the clumps every third year.

The species usually referred to as Catmint, is *N. fassena*, although it is a hybrid, *N. Mussini*, which is usually distributed as such. The variety Six Hills Giant, will reach 18 ins. and the flowers are larger, although they are inclined to drop more quickly. Lavender-blue flowers appear in profusion from May until September.

Propagation is by division or cuttings taken from July until September and inserted in sandy soil in a cold frame.

Paeonia. These hardy plants will succeed both in fairly low temperature and under warm, dry conditions which shows how adaptable they are to all conditions. The value of paeonies is further enhanced by the suitability of the blooms for cutting since they have extremely long lasting qualities. Provided with large jars or vases they will give tremendous pleasure proving entirely satisfying to the most fastidious of flower arrangers. Many varieties have particularly beautiful foliage, some of which colours up well in the autumn, adding to the display if they are cut and used with the blooms.

The planting season extends from September until the first few days of March although early autumn planting is undoubtedly best for quick establishment. Paeonies should not be disturbed more than necessary since once they are moved they usually take a season or two to flower again.

Soil requirements are not difficult and a situation can be prepared to enable the plants to give of their best. Move the soil deeply, providing drainage where necessary. Add old cow or stable manure which however, should not contact the roots. The addition of bone meal at the rate of 2 oz. to the square yard, will provide the phosphates which paeonies require to do really well. Deep planting is a mistake and the crowns should not be buried more than 2 ins. on heavy soils even less is advisable.

For May flowering, the single sinensis or Chinese Paeonies are invaluable. Particularly useful for house decoration, the flowers have masses of conspicuous golden anthers and among the finest sorts are: The Moor, dark chocolate red; Whitleyi-Major, a vigorous pure white; Beatrice, blush pink; and Gay Ladye, an attractive free blooming deep rose.

As for the doubles, the array of tip top sorts is amazing. The following are all specially recommended because in addition to their good growth and colour, they are superbly scented. Baroness

Schroeder, pale flesh to snow white; Duchesse de Nemours, sulphur white to pure white, incurved petals; Festiva maxima, white with central blotch of blood red; and Sarah Bernhardt, handsome apple blossom pink with silver tipped petals.

In addition to the varieties mentioned, the Imperial section of paeonies flower in June, and have strong shell-like outer petals forming a wide saucer-shaped flower which is half filled with smaller narrow petals thus making a rosette, reminding one of a choice water lily. They are just as hardy and easy to grow as other herbaceous paeonies.

Paeonies are rarely affected by disease, the only likely trouble being die-back, sometimes known as wilt or rot. This is a form of botrytis which sometimes attacks shoots at soil level in the spring. The young foliage wilts and turns brown, subsequently becoming covered with a grey mould. Occasionally, the disease extends to the underground growths, although plants are rarely killed.

Suspected plants should be sprayed with a copper fungicide and all discoloured foliage destroyed. When replanting, avoid a site where the disease is known to have occurred so as to minimise its spread.

Spring frosts sometimes cause the flower buds to turn brown and fall off. If plants are shaded from early morning sun such a happening, brought about by a quick thaw, will be avoided.

Propagation is done by division of the roots in the autumn. A root with 2 or 4 eyes, is greatly to be preferred to a large clump, since the latter will probably be hard and woody and less likely to establish itself quickly.

Papaver nudicaule the Iceland Poppy, is a first class cut flower and available in a wide colour range, including shades of orange, red, salmon, yellow, chamois and white. The result of careful and patient breeding has brought about much more vigorous growth and longer, stronger stems than the older types.

It is essential to gather the flowers whilst they are in the bud stage, and just as the petals show through the green sepals. The morning or evening is the best time to cut the blooms and to ensure that they do not flag, it is wise to dip the end of the stems in boiling water for a few moments, so as to seal them, alternatively, the ends may be held over a flame for a moment.

Propagation is from seed sown in the spring in a sunny position in the open or in the cold frame. Use soil which has been brought to a fine tilth and is fairly rich in organic matter. Whilst the plants like the sun, there must be no lack of moisture at any time. Transplant the seedlings while small and give shade in the event of very sunny weather. Bushy sticks laid over the ground are sufficient for this purpose. Particularly good strains are the Giant Coonera, 18-24 ins. and Sandfords Giant Mixed 2 ft.

Papaver orientalis is the Oriental Poppy which produces its showy flowers during May and June. Avoid a rich soil and one which remains wet, otherwise the stems may not be strong to hold the flowers firmly and the large petals may flop.

Among the most reliable varieties are Enchantress, rose pink; Indian Chief, mahogany; Jeannie Mawson, geranium pink; Lord Lambourne, orange-scarlet; and Mrs. Stobart, salmon pink. Here again, the blooms must be gathered whilst very young, preferably just as the buds are opening, when the petals look like crinkled satin.

Plants may be raised from seed, or propagated from root cuttings.

Penstemon. This is a very large family of both hardy and half-hardy plants. We are concerned now with those which are reasonably hardy and which produce flowers suitable for cutting, although they do not travel well.

Penstemon heterophyllus grows from 12 to 18 ins. high, and from June until August, freely produces brilliant blue tubular flowers. *P. barbatus* (*Chelone barbata*) has grey-green leaves and spikes of pinkish-red blooms. *P. newberryi rupicola* is a rather prostrate growing plant, being covered with showy carmine-red flowers from July until September.

Some years ago, a hybrid distributed under the name of Six Hills, made its appearance, this has pinkish-lilac flowers on 6 in. stems from June until September. One of the good qualities of P. rupicola or davidsonii, is its ability to withstand hot, dry conditions, which is why it is so useful for the upper parts of a rock garden.

P. scouleri a shrubby evergreen plant has 12 in. stems of purple-mauve flowers from May to July. Among the other more or less hardy penstemons are included the somewhat shrubby growing P. isophyllus varieties, which are serviceable and gay during the summer.

All are of easy propagation, and young growths secured in the late summer, and inserted in sandy soil under a frame or hand light will soon root well making sturdy plants. This glass protection should be retained through the winter. This not only encourages roots to develop, but prevents frost damage by providing necessary protection while the plants are becoming established.

Narcissus, begonia foliage and Driftwood

Aquilegia Mckana hybrids

Antirrhinum, Hyacinth Flowered

Candytuft Fairy Mixed

Phlox decussata will grow in any ordinary good soil which for preference should be deeply moved before planting time. They will grow in partial shade but they give of their best in an open, sunny situation where the ground does not dry out.

Land rich in humus material is advisable, otherwise during hot, dry spells, the plants cease to look perky. Any kind of bulky manure is preferable to artificials when feeding material is being added, to the ground before planting is done.

Once established in the right position, watering is rarely necessary but if it is, thorough soaking should be applied rather than dribbles, which bring the roots to the surface, and really make matters worse. They are not the best of flowers for cutting since the petals tend to drop quickly especially in hot weather.

One of the reasons why phlox are not grown as much as they once were, is because of eel worm which causes growth to become stunted and distorted. When a plant shows these symptoms or has brown patchy stems and prematurely yellow leaves, the presence of eel worm is indicated. This minute pest gets inside the stem and all affected plants should be destroyed. Experience has proved that stocks are more likely to remain free from this pest if propagated from root cuttings rather than the old-fashioned method of chopping up established clumps with a spade. When this is done, there is inevitably much damage and it is far better to pull the root portion apart with the hands than to use a spade. In addition, experience has shown that plants grown from root cuttings are of better constitution, than those from division, however well the latter may be made. Named sorts are available in many shades of orange, scarlet, crimson, puple, lilac, rose and white.

Phygelius capensis or the Cape Figwort, has established itself as a firm favourite among gardeners who like something a little out of the ordinary. Although sometimes damaged in a severe winter it can be grown in the open, excepting in exposed and northern districts. Even when cut by spring frosts, it will subsequently make new growth and soon replace the stems which have been cut back.

In the open border, the plant normally attains a height of about $2\frac{1}{2}$-3 ft. but given the protection of a wall or fence, it will grow up to 5 or 6 ft.

A moderately rich, well drained site should be provided and if feeds of liquid manure are given at 14 day intervals, the graceful, attractively shaped tubular, crimson-scarlet flowers, will appear from June until September or even later.

F

The form now usually grown is coccinea, the flowers of which have less orange than the type *P. capensis*.

Propagation is from cuttings, division or seed, while rooted plants can easily be secured from the suckers.

Pinks. This is a group within the large dianthus family, and apart from the well known varieties such as Mrs. Sinkins, white; and Inchmery, pale pink there are many pleasing varieties in different sections.

One of the oldest types are those known as Laced Pinks, all of which have unusual markings, and are most popular for cutting. These include Laced Joy, crimson lacing on a rose pink ground; London Poppet, white ground, pink flush, red eye; Dad's Favourite, white ground laced chocolate with a dark eye.

The group known as Old World Pinks are most hardy, with a strong clove perfume and are available in several colours.

The Show pinks are reckoned to be the aristocrats of the family, the flowers of perfect shape in exquisite colours being extremely double. They are hardy, free flowering, and most reliable. Named varieties include: Show Aristocrat, pale pink, buff eye; Show Distinction, crimson-cerise; Show Ideal, creamy-pink; salmon central markings and Show Pearl, perfectly formed pure white flowers.

All Pinks require well drained land and fairly rich rooting conditions, a slightly raised bed being ideal. They can be planted either in September or in early spring. Propagation is by making cuttings or pipings. The latter are produced around the base of the plants of most varieties and should be taken soon after the plants have finished flowering, being detached by a sharp pull instead of cutting. A few lower leaves are removed and the pipings are then inserted in boxes or pots of well drained compost preferably in a cold frame.

Physalis franchetti is better known as the Chinese Lantern or Bladder herb and is valuable for winter decoration. It is extremely easy to grow, in fact, it is one of those plants which must be kept in check, otherwise it will soon occupy more than its allotted space.

When the 'lanterns' are well out the stems should be cut and hung upside down in an airy place so that they dry off well. It is, of course, possible to make use of them in arrangements as soon as the stems are cut, while the individual flowers or lanterns can be removed and wired to make various kinds of decoration.

Propagation is by division of roots in spring or autumn or by sowing seeds in spring.

Polygonatum (solomons seal)

Physostegia. Sometimes known as dracocephalum, this is an interesting subject flowering from September onwards. The plants produce 2½ ft. spikes, thick-set with dark green leaves and tubular, lipped flowers. The best known species is *P. virginiana* which has several excellent forms, Vivid, pink being particularly good. All grow well in ordinary soil and need to be kept in check so that they do not spread too much. A curious feature of all the physostegias is that the individual flowers will remain in whatever position they are moved to on the stem.

Propagation is by division, or root cuttings, or by seed sown in spring.

Polygonatum (Solomon's Seal). This too, is a fairly rampant grower. It is ideal for a cool, shady position. The leafy arching stems are laden with greenish-white bells not unlike a large Lily of the Valley. It is, therefore, most useful in all manner of floral decorations providing informality to otherwise stiff arrangements. *P. multiflorum* is the best known and varies from 2-3 ft. or more in height. *P. officinale* grows to about 16 ins. The plants like cool root conditions and they are useful for planting in a shady corner.

Propagation is simply division of roots in spring or autumn.

Polygonum. Useful if not rare plants for cutting purposes are the species *P. bisorta* superbum 18 ins.; affine, 9 ins.; and amplexicaule 2½-3 ft. all with brush-like heads of reddish flowers on wiry stems. Easy to grow and long lasting as cut flowers.

Stock can easily be increased by dividing the roots in the spring.

Polyanthus. There are several modern strains which are ideal for cutting. As the result of patient work by hybridists, there are a number of strains, producing on really long stems flowers having a tremendous colour range.

To do their best polyanthus need a site rich in humus content and during the summer regular sprayings of water in the evening will prove beneficial.

Plant in October. Propagation is by splitting the roots after flowering or by sowing seed in spring or early autumn.

Primula denticulata is occasionally known as the Drumstick primula, and is one of the easiest members of the primula family to raise and most useful for cutting. Seeds germinate fairly freely in the J.I. or a similar compost, in a temperature of 60 deg. F. The seedlings are pricked out and hardened off in the usual way, and the roots kept well supplied with moisture during dry weather. Plants are moved to their flowering quarters in November. Flowers are cut with long stems when about two-thirds of the individual florets are fully developed. If they are placed in water a day or two before being arranged in vases, they will soon plump up. Propagation is subsequently done by division or more seeds.

Pyrethrums. Almost all daisy-like flowers are popular for cutting. The pyrethrum is important because it follows soon after the early tulips and daffodils and is at its best from the end of May to the end of June. It is often possible to obtain a second flush of flowers in September. The plants like a well drained fairly light soil well enriched with sufficient humus to retain moisture during spring and summer. When preparing the site work in well rotted compost or decayed manure and just before planting fork in a dressing of fish manure 2 or 3 ozs. to the square yard. Each autumn apply a dressing of lime which will not only improve the soil but deter slugs.

When planting spread out the roots evenly allowing 21 to 24 ins. between the plants. Although early spring and autumn planting is sometimes recommended the best time is in July after the flowering period, although in a very dry season, unless water can be regularly supplied, it is best to wait until the next spring.

A normal healthy plantation, used for cut blooms can be left down for 4 years before replanting with fresh offsets. Long stemmed flowers cut during the early part of the day and given a long drink in deep water are those which will remain in good condition a long time.

Good varieties include: Eileen May Robinson, salmon pink; Kelway's Glorious, crimson-scarlet; Avalanche, white; Scarlet Glow and Queen Mary, double pink.

Propagation is by division in July each piece consisting of a vigorous portion, dry woody parts being discarded. Another method is to take cuttings at the end of May planting them in boxes in the cool greenhouse. Plants can be also raised from seed but only in mixture.

Primrose. This strictly speaking is Primula veris, a flower which has been grown in Britain for centuries. Primroses like shade and cool, moist conditions, although some will grow quite happily in full sunshine. If they can be grown where there is plenty of peat or leaf mould in the soil they will produce the best results.

Apart from the wild yellow Primroses there are now many coloured hybrids of great beauty, among these is the Jewel Box mixed, the result of years of patient breeding and selection. This strain is of uniform habit, freely producing its brilliant flowers in a wide colour range. Whilst they are excellent as border edgings, and pot plants, they are really exceptional as cut flowers and never fail to create attention.

Seed forms a ready means of propagation and although sometimes germination is slow, once they are growing well, they soon form really sturdy plants. Separate colours can be kept true by propagating from division or by rooted offsets.

Primula auricula is another ancient species. Here again the flowers were originally yellow, but today they can be obtained in a wide range of separate colours, some having mealy foliage. Auriculas like fairly rich soil and as with the primroses, produce their main flush of flowers from February to June, although the coloured hybrids will often go on much later.

Ranunculus. Although the bulbous species and varieties are best known, there are several herbaceous species that are useful for really good cut flowers. *R. aconitifolius plenus* has double button-like white flowers on branching stems from May onwards. It is a little particular as to soil, preferring one which while on the light side, does not dry out during the summer. *R. acris plenus* has sprays of double yellow buttons which are not very long lasting. R. speciosus plenus looks like a large double buttercup.

Propagation. To keep the plants in good free flowering condition, they should be divided every two or three years, preferably in the early autumn.

Rudbeckia. First class as a border plant the rudbeckia is of some value as a cut flower. Their common name of Cone Flower gives an idea of their appearance. They are sun lovers and like good well drained soil. During the growing season they should not lack moisture while when established a few soakings with liquid manure will increase the quality of the flowers.

Some varieties are known as Black-Eyed-Susans. R. laciniata is a tall growing species with yellow flowers and green cones. The double form known as Golden Glow is good as is the dwarfer growing Goldquille.

It is *R. speciosa* (or *newmanii*) and its varieties that are so useful for cutting. This grows $1\frac{1}{2}$ to 2 ft. high producing from July to September rich orange flowers with small purple discs.

Salvia. There are several hundred species in the large Sage family, but only few can be regarded as cut flower subjects. They grow in ordinary good soil and like sunshine.

S. argentea, the Silver Sage, is grown for its greyish-white leaves rather than its spikes of pinky-white flowers. *S. grahami* is of shrubby habit, growing up to 3 ft. high, and bearing spikes of red flowers although these are not very freely produced.

S. superba, best known as S. virgata nemorosa, is an excellent border plant, producing 2½-3½ ft. high branching spikes of violet-purple, whch give way to reddish-brown, seedless calyces these remaining decorative after the actual flowers have disappeared. This means that the plants are ornamental from summer to autumn.

Propagation is by division or separation of the freely produced rosettes of basal growths.

Sedum. In this very large family of plants there are a few which are suitable for cutting. *S. spectabilis*, growing 12-15 ins. high, has heads of shining rosy red flowers in September and October, the grey-green foliage being attractive throughout the summer.

It is easy to grow and lasts well in water. While not among the daintiest of flowers, this sedum is useful for using in wide shallow bowls and makes a reasonably good pot plant because of its glaucous-grey foliage. There are several cultivars, including Brilliant, rose-pink; and Meteor, a rather deeper shade of pink.

Propagation is by division or from cuttings in spring.

Scabiosa caucasica sometimes known as Blue Bonnets. This subject likes an alkaline soil, so that an annual top dressing of hydrated lime, 4 ozs. or more, to the square yard, will be of help in securing good quality blooms. The first year of planting it may be necessary to use overhead irrigation during dry spells although much will depend on the type of soil being dealt with. The extra moisture will certainly increase the size of the flowers and length of stem. Spring is the best and safest time to move the plants.

Watch must be kept for slugs which often go for the young shoots as they begin to develop. The modern slug baits will be found to be effective killers. Both greenfly and thrips must be cleared off the young growth before they gain a hold.

The variety Goldingensis was for long the favourite, but now there is Clive Greaves, with its large lavender-mauve flowers. There are several others, including Penhill Blue, a real beauty, taller than Goldingensis and Clive Greaves, and the new Malcolm, dark blue; Purple Prince and Vincent, cobalt blue. *Scabiosa caucasica* is also to be had in white, the variety Miss Willmott being reliable.

The cutting of the blooms is important, and is best done as early in the morning as possible when the petals are just fully open; before the centre florets flatten. Stand the stems in deep water as soon as they are cut. This will keep them turgid and ensure the colour is retained.

Spring is the only satisfactory planting time for scabious never do well if disturbed in the autumn or winter. Young plants should be secured and planted in the early spring, but when increasing stock great care should be taken in dividing the roots, for if divisions are torn away carelessly, they are liable to rot. Use the outer crowns only discarding the centre of the old plants.

Propagation can also be effected by seed, which is best sown as soon as it is ripe in pans or boxes of light porous soil to which plenty of silver sand has been added. Shade the pans until after germination. Subsequently prick off and plant out in the usual way. Seeds will not come true to type so that to gain a stock of a particular variety cuttings must be taken.

These should be from strong firm basal shoots taken in the early summer and inserted in a compost of good loam, to which plenty of silver sand and granulated peat has been added. Give the cuttings shade in the early stages with sufficient, but not too much moisture, and they will soon root and make sturdy young free flowering plants.

Sidalcea. There is something distinct about a plant which carries its flowers in spikes and this is particularly so in the case of the sidalcea which produces its colour just as the delphiniums are passing over. They are therefore, very useful during July and August. There are 2 or 3 dozen species, although few are of real use for the average gardener. Sometimes known as Greek Mallows or ' dwarf hollyhocks ' which gives a clue to their appearance, sidalceas do not ask for any special cultural conditions. They flourish in an open position and in any good soil, provided it is not too wet or cold, although moisture must never be lacking during the growing season. The flowers are valuable for cutting, while the plants are ideal for a good herbaceous border where they will give a creditable display over a long period.

The plants can be moved in the spring or autumn and among good varieties, all growing 3 ft. or so high, are Candida, white; Rev. Page Roberts, rose-pink; Sussex Beauty, bright rose; Crimson Beauty and Wensleydale, rosy-red.

Propagation. The plants are best lifted and divided every 3 or 4 years, for by so doing, they will be kept healthy, vigorous and enabled to produce plenty of flowers.

Solidago. As an autumn cut flower Golden Rod is not to be despised although it is so often referred to slightingly. Growing well in ordinary soil and in full sun or partial shade, the plants do not require any special situation. It is wise to thin out growths and so obtain better spikes of flowers.

Sidalcea (greek Mallow)

Flowers are available from the end of July until October and good varieties are: *S. canadensis*, 5 ft.; *S. shortii*, pyramid-shaped spikes of 4 ft. or more. Recently several new sorts have been introduced which generally are considerably shorter than the older varieties.

These include Goldstral, bright yellow, $2\frac{1}{2}$ ft.; Golden Gates, Golden Falls and Lemore, all 2 ft. *S. missouriensis* was once widely known under the name of *Aster hybridus luteus*, growing about 2 ft. it has panicles of star-like yellow flowers. Some of these Golden Rods are useful for drying.

Propagation. The ideal way to maintain a first class stock is to place some plants in the cold frame in the autumn when flowering is over and make small divisions of 1 or 2 crowns each in the early spring. These are planted out at 18-24 in. apart which will give room for good blooms for cutting to develop.

Sanguisorba. This hardy perennial plant is sometimes known as poterium. It grows well in ordinary soil although it does best in sandy loam and peat, while it likes sun and plenty of moisture during the growing season. The attractive flowers are produced on wiry stems up to 3 ft. high.

S. canadensis (*Poterium canadense*) is the best species, the white flowers showing from July to September.

Propagation is by division of roots in spring or seed sown under glass in February or March.

Stokesia cyanea or laevis as it is sometimes called, is an interesting perennial plant. It has large lavender-blue flowers, which resemble the well-known annual China Aster and are often 3 ins. in diameter. They commence to appear in late August and under ordinary conditions continue to do so until early November.

The plants are of a branching habit with leafy stems from $1\frac{1}{2}$-2 ft. high. They like a sunny position and well drained ground. Excellent as a cut flower, it remains in fresh condition for a long time.

There are several good forms of this plant including S. cyanea alba, a fine white; *S. cyanea lutea*, creamy-white; *S. cyanea rosea*, pink and praecox, the latter form being the earliest to flower. Because of their free flowering capabilities and suitability for cutting, stokesias deserve to be much more widely grown than they are at present.

S. cyanea can easily be raised from seed, while plants divide well in the early spring.

Thalictrum. This subject should be included in every border of herbaceous plants for they are unusual, interesting and valuable for cutting. They are not difficult to grow, and while enjoying full sunshine, they do well in partial shade.

The best and most popular of all the taller growing species is undoubtedly *T. dipterocarpum*. According to local conditions, it varies in height from 4½ to 6 ft. or even more, and the tall well-shaped bushy plants, have graceful sprays of mauve-coloured flowers with yellow stamens and attractive finely cut foliage. It also has a white form.

There has now come into well deserved prominence, a variety of T. dipterocarpum, known as Hewitt's Double. This has rapidly become popular, both as a cut flower and a border plant. Being double, it does not produce seed, and therefore can only be propagated by root division. It is a vigorous grower, attaining a height of 5 ft. or so, and producing sprays of very small violet-pink double flowers. These are carried on dainty, yet strong, stems the whole plant giving a most desirable effect.

All the taller growing sorts should be given some inconspicuous supports. In a deeply moved and fairly rich soil, the unusual flowers, which are in reality composed of sepals and prominent stamens, keep on giving a good show over a period of many months. They are ideal for mixing with other flowers and produce a light, graceful effect.

Propagation can be effected by division of the roots, this being better carried out in the early spring, thus avoiding any possible loss during the winter, although it is not wise to disturb the roots more than is necessary. Seed too can be sown in boxes of sandy soil in the spring.

Tellima grandiflora is a hardy herbaceous perennial of North American origin and known in Britain for 150 years. It will flourish in ordinary garden soil and grows well both in partial shade and in open positions.

From May onwards, it produces stems 18 to 24 in. high, bearing little bell-like, creamy-greenish flowers which when open, show a rim of a purplish shade. *T.g. purpurea* forms a dome of scalloped heart-shaped leaves which assume reddish brown tints in autumn. Both are excellent for cutting and are welcomed for the unusual colour they supply as well as for their foliage.

Plants can be moved in autumn or spring and as necessary, propagation can be done by dividing the roots in early spring.

Tiarella. Often known as the Foam Flower. This is not a robust growing plant but is very useful where small spikes of blooms are required. The sprays are not unlike those of the heuchera. These flowers look superb arranged with bluebells and forget-me-nots early in the year.

The plants thrive in good soil on the lightish side and do well in partial shade. *T. wherryi* produces starry scented blush-apricot flowers on 12 in. stems, and shows colour from early summer to autumn. The leaves too are prettily tinted. Propagation is by division.

Trollius the Globe Flower is a plant liking peaty soil where the moisture content is fairly high, since the roots must not be allowed to dry out. They produce their beautifully rich yellow blooms in May and early June, and are first class for cutting. It is best to gather the stems just as the central flowers are opening. Plunge them in water immediately they are cut. They will then last a considerable time.

Trollius Orange Princess and Golden Wonder are two of the finest varieties for cutting, although there are several others readily available from nurserymen.

Propagation is by division in the spring.

Tradescantia. Although not reckoned among the usual cut flower plants this subject is useful when stems of broad rushy foliage are required. They make no outstanding show but flower continuously from June to late September.

Of easy culture they grow well in almost any soil which does not dry out. The clusters of buds produce three petalled flowers giving them the name of Trinity Flower or Spider Wort.

T. virginiana is variable, the colours including rose-red, mauve, blue and white. There are separate named sorts having distinct colours. Propagation is simple by division in spring or from self sown seedlings.

Violets. These are plants with an ancient history and about which many stories and legends have been written. At one time the roots, leaves and flowers were all used for medicinal purposes, while the seeds were said to ' drive away scorpions '. Violets are still greatly valued and always appreciated whether used by themselves or with other flowers for floral arrangements.

Poor violets can be grown by anyone but good flowers require the right conditions. Few plants respond so quickly to attention as violets. They like to be grown in airy conditions and do not give of their best in smoky industrial areas.

They also like plenty of sun, although under continual dry weather a watch must be kept for red spider and the roots must not be allowed to dry out during the summer.

Well drained soil is necessary and one containing plenty of organic matter, such as leaf mould is helpful, lime being a useful addition on clay soils. When preparing the site, decayed manure will be a useful addition and when the plants are established, a top dressing of fresh manure each autumn, lightly worked in, will increase the size and number of flowers.

For preference, plant in the autumn, keeping the crowns level with the surface soil. The flowers are best gathered early in the morning or the evening, the stems being placed in water immediately before they are bunched or arranged in vases. Regular picking will prevent seed pods from setting and encourage more flowers.

Among the best sorts in cultivation are the following: Single flowering: Admiral Avellan, reddish purple; Governor Herrick, deep purple but scentless; and Princess of Wales, a favourite very sweetly scented blue sort. Double varieties include: Comtesse de Brazza, white; Duchesse de Parme, pale mauve and Marie Louise, a beautiful strongly scented mauve.

CHAPTER 7

FLOWERS UNDER GLASS

ANTIRRHINUM. Well known very showy and reliable bedding plants, antirrhinums can also be used as a cut flower and pot plant.

Winter blooms can be produced in the greenhouse. For succession, the seed should be sown in batches from July onwards. The first batch of seedlings will be ready to plant in the greenhouse from September and will normally flower from December to February.

The late cultivars are sown in August and September, the young plants being put into position in November and December for blooming from March to May.

The sowing procedure is the routine one the seeds being sown very thinly in boxes or pans of the John Innes or similar compost and pricked out into trays and stood for preference under frames, Dutch lights or cloches. Care in watering and attention to ventilation is necessary so that the plants are kept growing without a check. The object should be to ensure good soft plants during the autumn for if they become hard and woody they may produce an unwanted early spike.

Antirrhinums like a rooting medium on the acid side. They appreciate an application of bone flour or fish meal worked into the soil well before planting out is done.

Space the plants 9 in. apart each way and where a quantiy is being grown leave a path after every 6 or 8 rows to make it easy for cutting and other necessary attentions. Once the plants are a couple of inches high, the growing points can be pinched out. This will lead to the production of several strong side shoots.

If the plants are not stopped they will produce a central spike. This will be early but the several not so early spikes from each plant will prove more pleasing. The aim should be to keep the temperature at not less than 45 deg. F. at night.

American forcing varieties are better for glasshouse growing than the usual bedding sorts. These hybrids are early and among the best are Cherokee, Golden Spike, Snowman, Lavender, New Tunes and Ticasure Chest.

Antirrhinum nanum varieties are useful for cutting and there is a wide colour range. Especially popular are the flame, orange, yellow, pink and red varieties.

Alstroemeria. These have long been used as cut flowers from the outdoor plants but recently, a strain known as the Parigo Super Hybrids for greenhouse culture has been evolved. This produces flowers in a variety of subtle shades ranging from delicate pink through rose and light red to deep rose-pink. With good culture, the plants can produce flowers from early March through to late October.

The straight springy stems with narrow attractive leaves, grow 4 ft. or more in height. The stem branches at the top, each branch having at least 4 flowers or buds at different stages. The individual flowers are much larger than those of the well known outdoor *A. aurantiaca* varieties. The normal life of these stems is 3 weeks without any fading of the foliage and even the smallest buds will open.

Work on this newer strain is continuing and undoubtedly further improvements will be made. There are as yet few named varieties available but taken, in addition to Charm, yellow; and Pride, carmine-red, there are also white, pink and other shades, as there are in the *A. ligtu hybrids*. These indoor alstroemerias will certainly become in great demand as cut flowers.

Freesia. Not only are the tubular flowers pretty and fragrant, but the fibrous coated corms which come originally from South Africa, produce wiry stems about 24 in. tall, and attractive narrow leaves which make freesias so useful as cut flowers.

Freesias required for early blooming from the end of January until April, should be planted by the end of September. The most suitable planting mixture is ordinary good garden soil and sandy loam in equal parts, with a dash of sharp sand. Cover the corms with about an inch of this mixture; a 5 in. pot will accommodate 5 or 6 corms, and plunge the pots in the ground in a cold frame covering them with 1 in. of sandy garden soil or peat. This covering should be syringed occasionally, in hot weather once a day, in ordinary dry weather about 3 times a week, to keep the pots cool and moist.

The new top growths will appear after about 3 weeks, first split into 2, and then more leaves appear gradually. When there are about 7 leaves to a corm the pots may be moved into the greenhouse and placed in an airy position with full light and a temperature of 50 deg. F. Gradually, in a fortnight's time, the temperature may be increased to 60 deg. F. but extra heat must be applied with care, for if too much is given the plants will become spindly and the flowers will not last as long as they should when cut. Water should be given from time to time to keep the soil moist.

Bulb specialists offer mixed selections of freesias, but you can also purchase named varieties in separate colours.

Gerberas. This is a most attractive flower, but not as widely cultivated as it deserves because it has the reputation of being difficult to grow. Of South African origin, some of the best modern strains come from the United States and Holland. Since the introduction of *G. jamesonii*, have come the jamesonii hybrids which take in such colours as orange, salmon, terra cotta, peach, apricot, yellow and white.

One of the secrets of success is to use really fresh seed, for it soon loses its ability to germinate freely. Another is to provide an equable day and night temperature. As most of the seed is imported, it is not always possible to sow as early as one would wish, but where possible, February is a good month otherwise April and May are satisfactory times.

For preference, sow where there is bottom heat and in an even temperature of 65 deg. F. Use a good light sowing mixture composed of sweet fibrous loam and silver sand, into this insert the seeds individually and firmly, but leave the top exposed to minimise any possibility of damping off. When the seedlings can be handled, prick them out into sandy compost and subsequently transfer to 5 or 6 in. pots.

Gerberas make a big root system and like a deep rich peaty soil. They should be planted with the crown of the plant raised slightly above soil level to prevent crown rotting caused by damp conditions. Where grown for cut flower purposes, plants can be cultivated in a well drained, sunny glass house border the planting distance being 12-18 in. apart to allow for the normal bushy growth.

Full cropping will not commence until the summer of the year following sowing, although when it does start flowers will be available for several months. In addition, with quite ordinary treatment, plants will bloom annually for several years. Apart from seed sowing it is possible to divide good plants although the divisions grow rather weakly in the first season after division. This method of propagation is the only means of increasing stock of

Bartonia aurea

Chrysanthemum tricolor

Calliopsis mistigri

Chrysanthemum, Sunset Mixed

Venidium fastuosum

Carnation, Chabaud Mixed

a particular form or colour, since hybrids cannot be raised true from seed.

The plants require plenty of water in summer and leaf spraying will prevent red spider. Shade is needed during bright sunshine. If the plants are grown in cold structures, watering should stop in September and the plants kept dry during the winter, since it is cold dampness which causes losses.

Coloured leaved pelargoniums have an attraction beyond their flowers for the foliage is very ornamental and has a variety of uses. Apart from the ornamental effect created in greenhouses and living rooms and when used in window boxes and hanging baskets during the summer individual leaves suitably placed in an arrangement of flowers can make a great deal of difference. The removing of one or two leaves from individual plants will not have a permanent harmful effect, and in so doing leaves of various colours and size can be used.

It would not be possible to refer to all varieties, but among the most showy and attractive are the following: A Happy Thought, creamy-yellow markings in centre of leaf; Bronze Queen, golden leaves with chestnut zone; Caroline Schmidt, white variegated foliage; Chelsea Gem, silver white marked leaves; Crystal Palace Gem, golden leaves with deeper markings; Distinction, olive green with almost black picotee edge; Dolly Vardon, silver tricolor; Golden Harry Hieover, golden leaved; Madame Butterfly, pale green with deeper butterfly-like markings; Madame Salleroi, silver variegated edgings; Marechal MacMahon, rich bronze zone; Miss Burdett Coutts, an outstanding tricolor having a creamy-yellow base; Skies of Italy has deeply toothed leaves with yellow edges, zoned crimson-orange; Bronze Queen has large foliage with a prominent chestnut zone.

A famous old variety Red Black Vesuvius is a miniature with nearly black leaves. Mephistopheles is also heavily zoned black. Mrs. Henry Cox is a brilliant tricolor, the colour being bronze red and creamy-yellow variegations. Flower of Spring is a strong growing sort with an unusual wide irregular deep ivory border.

There are a number of scented leaved varieties which at the same time have variegated foliage, such as Pelargonium crispum variegatum and Lady Plymouth.

Where plants are being grown for their foliage it is usual and advisable to keep the flowers removed since such action encourages the foliage to remain stronger and the colouring to be more intense.

Stocks are among the most popular of our annual flowers. Ease

G

of culture, bright colours, combined with their fragrance, account
for their being so well liked.

Summer flowering stocks can be ground out of doors excepting
in the seed raising stage, but where there is a small amount of glass
which is only just heated, stocks for spring cutting can prove a
very useful crop.

Although there are various strains that respond well to early
culture, the normal Summer-flowering types are the most satis
factory, since their growing period is shorter. Hansen's double
strain is valuable, for it is possible to plant out only those which
will produce double flowers.

So that only double flowering plants are used the seedlings should
be raised in warmth and when they are $\frac{1}{2}$ in. high move them to a
temperature of 45 deg. F. for 2 or 3 days. Some of the plants will
then have dark green leaves, others light green. The latter are those
which will produce double blooms.

For spring flowering seed is sown in November and December in
either a heated frame or greenhouse where there is a temperature
of around 65 deg. F. A well drained loamy compost not lacking
in lime should be used, and after sowing the seed thinly, cover it
with a very thin sprinkling of sand. Once the seedlings break
through the surface, another sprinkling of sand is applied. This
action prevents the appearance of fungal diseases. Moisture must
be available during the germinating stage, but afterwards the young
plants should be kept rather on the dry side with plenty of
ventilation. This will result in sturdy growth resistant to disease.

Once they have really settled after their move they are kept in a
lower temperature of, say, 50 deg. F. where they remain for at
least 3 weeks. By the first few days of March they will be ready
for moving to their flowering positions in the glasshouse or Dutch
light structure which will have been enriched and well prepared
in advance.

Cutting can be commenced fairly early in April and will go
on throughout May. Stocks are inclined to wilt quickly. The
flowers should therefore be placed in deep buckets of water and
kept in a cool place for some hours before they are arranged in
vases.

Thunbergia. These are really tender perennials of climbing habit
but there are at least two species which respond to half hardy
annual treatment – *T. alata* and *T. gibsonii*, both varying in height
from 2-5 ft. Excellent for the cool glass house they can be grown
in pots or hanging baskets, while seen flowering against greenhouse

pillars or other supports, they immediately attract attention. Sow the seed from February onwards using a sandy compost. Prick out the seedlings early and pot up singly into light, rich soil according to growth.

T. alata is often known as Black Eyed Susan having buff coloured flowers with a deep purple throat. The foliage is an attractive heart shape which is why both the leaves and flowers are valued by floral artists, particularly since the growths are of trailing habit. There is also a mixture producing white, orange or lemon flowers. *T. gibsonii* is an excellent species, its orange coloured flowers being 1½ in. or more in diameter.

Zantedeschia aethiopica. Although this is now the correct name of the white arum lily, many of us will continue to think of it by its long used names of calla or richardia.

Although it is possible to grow arums in the greenhouse border with success it is usually more convenient to grow them in pots, where they can remain for two seasons. It is wise to depend on the 8 or 9 in. size, for anything smaller is liable to dry out rather quickly and this is just what arum lilies will not tolerate.

In regard to soil mixture 3 parts good loam and 1 part each of rotted manure and peat, plus a good sprinkling of sharp silver sand with a 7 in. potful of bone meal to each bushel or so of soil has proved an ideal rooting and feeding medium.

The rhizomes are of irregular shape but the soil must be firmly pressed around them, although it is really important to leave the top uncovered. Time of potting and subsequent treatment largely depends on when the blooms are required. Where they are wanted to cover the Christmas period, and from then until February, the rhizomes should be planted in July and at monthly intervals, for a succession of blooms.

After potting stand the rhizomes outdoors in a partially shaded place where they can remain until well into September. During this time water as necessary without overdoing it, but make sure that at no time is there a lack of moisture. Stand the pots on a hard base to prevent the entrance of worms or other pests.

When taking the plants indoors place them in full light. If kept in the shade the leaf stalks may not grow upright and there may be trouble with the flowers failing to open properly.

A temperature of anything around 60 deg. F. by day and 5 deg. lower at night seems to be what these plants like. For early blooms it is necessary at the end of October to provide a temperature of not less than 60 deg. F. at night and up to 10 deg. higher by day.

Avoid great variation for it is preferable to have rather less heat all the time than to have any great fluctuation.

Good ventilation is important but draughts must be avoided and as the growths attain good size, supports may be necessary. Constant moisture is required at the roots, while overhead sprayings will help to provide the right conditions for the proper unfolding of the spathes.

The plants will be helped if fed with liquid manure every 4 or 5 days for this will encourage good sturdy development. A watch must be kept for aphis which will sometimes prove troublesome if they gain a hold. Either a nicotine insecticide or a good fumigant is required to deal with this trouble.

So that the rhizomes remain in good condition, the plants should be watered and fed even after the blooms are cut or have ceased to be ornamental. Subsequently, the plants are dried off and if the pots are left on their sides which is so important for future results, this will greatly assist the ripening process.

CHAPTER 8

FLOWERING SHRUBS, TREES AND ROSES

SINCE they are more or less permanent occupants of the garden flowering shrubs and trees need to be chosen and planted with care. They are in effect, the backbone of the garden providing an outline from which other sometimes more temporary features can be developed.

They are labour saving in that once planted they remain in position for many years, perhaps a lifetime and their initial cost is the final expense. The removal of individual flowers or sprays of blooms can often take the place of the more general pruning which is one good reason for always cutting flowers with great care and in such a way that the shape of the shrub or tree is not spoiled.

The type of soil available will usually dictate what can be grown for rhododendrons, azaleas, camellias and other lime haters should be grown where there is an abundance of peat, leaf mould and other humus matter. Very light soil can be improved by adding the same ingredients.

To encourage shrubs or trees to become established quickly plant deciduous subjects from late October to early April and evergreens from mid September to early November and from March to early May. Many nurseries now supply container grown plants which means they can be transplanted at any time of the year.

Pruning is an important matter with flowering shrubs and trees and should not be neglected. Remember that subjects that bloom early in the year should be pruned when the flowering season is over.

Camellia. It was once considered that this beautiful flowering shrub was suitable only for greenhouse culture. Experience has proved that some species and cultivars will grow outdoors in a sheltered position against a wall or among other shrubs. For preference a site should be selected which is not subjected to continuous full sunshine. They can also be grown in tubs.

Camellias dislike lime and should be planted in good ground containing plenty of peat or leaf mould and decayed manure. The

Kerria japonica flora pleno – The large bright yellow rosette flowers mak
this a cottage garden favourite. It does well planted against a wall

easiest camellias to grow outdoors are the japonica varieties with white, crimson or pink flowers some being prettily striped and either single or double. Apart from the flowers which appear from March onwards the foliage is valuable and individual leaves may be used for various decorative purposes, although it is the wax-like flowers for which this shrub is chiefly prized.

The named varieties will be readily available from specialist growers and include: White Swan and Jupiter, red, both singles. Elegans, salmon-rose, Lady Clare, soft pink; and Adolph Audusson, blood red, all doubles. There are several good multicolours including: Donckelarii, semi-double crimson and white; and Lady Vansittart, blush pink with rose pink stripes.

The *williamsii* hybrids are free flowering and semi double, especially good being Donation, clear pink and J. C. Williams, blush pink with prominent yellow stamens.

Caryopteris clandonensis will produce quantities of deep violet sprays during August and September. Kept lightly pruned each spring it makes a shapely bush and is ideal for growing against a wall. This shrub thrives in most soils and apart from the attractive flowers the glossy green foliage is useful for including among cut flowers.

Ceanothus. This does best in full sun and with the protection of a wall. From July until the frosts come they produce a wealth of flower spikes of elegant appearance. Among the best cultivars are: Gloire de Versailles, powder blue; Marie Simon, pink and Topaz, indigo blue. The evergreen ceanothus are particularly suitable for growing against a south or west wall and can be kept in good condition by pruning immediately after flowering, the main flush of which is during May and June.

Among the best known of these evergreens is *C. burkwoodii*, bright blue; dentatus, rich blue flowers in round clusters; and *C. thyrsiflorus Edinensis*, having long spikes of rich blue. A variety which is rapidly becoming popular is Cascade, forming powder-blue flowers on arching sprays.

Chaenomeles. This is the flowering Quince which we have for so long known as Cydonia japonica or ' Japonica '. It will grow against a wall or fence or in the open as a bush. Early in the year it will produce its showy, cup shaped flowers in great abundance and either good sized branches laden with flowers, or one or two blooms may be used indoors. Apart from the red flowers of *C. japonica* itself there are many cultivars including: cardinalis, salmon; and flore plena, double pink. *C. maulei* Knaphill Scarlet is superb, its

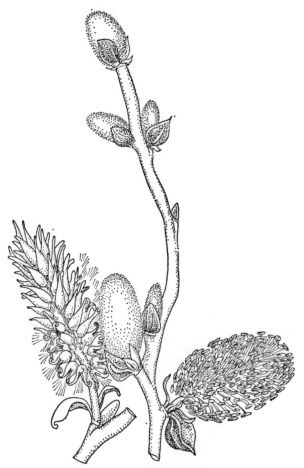

Salix daphnoides (Violet Willow) – Grows between ten and twenty feet high. Makes a nice specimen tree

bright orange scarlet blooms appearing during spring and early summer while *C. simonsii* is dark crimson. All make bushy growth and often bear edible quinces.

Cherry Flowering. See Prunus.

Chimonanthus fragrans or praecox is the Winter Sweet. The flowers are not brilliantly coloured but are interesting and pleasing both when growing and when brought indoors where they last well. The scented blooms are pale yellow with purplish centres and are borne on the bare twigs throughout the winter, however cold. The bushes dislike very heavy ground and a mulch of peat should be applied to the soil around the base of newly planted specimens. In the summer the bright green leaves give an air of dignity in the garden as well as when used with summer flowers. Pruning should be done as soon as the flowering period is over.

Choisya ternata is the Mexican Mock Orange which produces its handsome white sweetly scented star-like flowers during the late spring and summer. Its glossy cut foliage is aromatic when crushed.

Cistus. Often known as the Rock Rose this evergreen is very suitable for growing in dry positions and even on bare chalky soil. The showy blooms resemble the wild rose and appear from May to July. Individual stems often carrying several blooms being most useful for cutting purposes.

Among the cultivars which eventually grow more than 4 ft. are the following: *corbariensis*, producing large numbers of rosy-pink buds and slightly cup shaped flowers opening to white with a yellow flush; cyprius, has white flowers with a maroon blotch at the base of the petals; purpureus is purple-red, with red blotches in the centre; the foliage of all of these being pleasantly scented.

Smaller growing sorts include: crispus Sunset, deep rose; Silver Pink, delicate pink flowers with silver grey foliage; and *skanbergii* of spreading habit with delicate pink flowers and narrow pointed greyish foliage.

Cornus. All the species and cultivars in this most useful family are of easy culture. Of the flowering species, the Cornelian Cherry, *C. mas* is the most valuable for using indoors. During February and March its leafless stems are loaded with small yellow flowers. These are usually followed by red berries, not unlike the 'hips' of the wild rose. Cornus kousa is small growing with creamy white flowers surrounded by white bracts in June.

Forsythia is so well known and yet it might very well be used much more for indoor decoration than it is at present. It is extremely hardy and of easy cultivation, the yellow flowers being freely produced all along the branches which since they are so abundant may be cut without hesitation. F. intermedia and its varieties make vigorous shrubs of 8 ft. or more. F. suspensa is of rather rambling habit but suitable for growing against a wall. These flower from early February onwards but *F. viridissima* blooms in April. *F.*

spectabilis, Lynwood has bright well shaped yellow petals on erect branches.

Fuchsia magellanica riccartonii is one of the most reliable of the hardy fuchsias and has been used for hedge making with great success. Most of the previous season's growth dies back annually, but plenty of new shoots are made, the scarlet and purple flowers being most effective when cut and placed in vases. A smaller growing sort is *F. procumbens,* while the little *F. pumila* is charming indoors. Mrs. Popple is one of the hardiest, the carmine and violet flowers appearing on arching stems.

Garrya elliptica is a distinctive evergreen which in the colder Midland and Northern districts should have the protection of a wall. The grey-green leaves are attractive in themselves for indoor decoration, but coupled as they are during January and February, with long hanging, yellowish-green catkins they are really superb, especially as flowers are usually scarce at that time. It is generally possible to obtain both male and female plants, the former being much more effective with longer catkins.

Genista hispanica, the 'Spanish Gorse' thrives in a sunny, dry place. The low growing bushes produce wiry branches wreathed in myriads of yellow flowers from April onwards.

Halesia carolina produces miniature snowdrop-like, silvery-white flowers on leafless branches from the end of April. It thrives best on a chalk-free soil and eventually grows 6 to 8 ft. high.

Hamamelis. This is the Witch Hazel which flowers from December to March withstanding the severest weather. It likes a humus rich deep soil and will not do in shallow, chalky ground. The curious undulating petals are strap shaped and are followed by quite large leaves. *H. japonica* is of spreading habit with yellow flowers, and *H. zuccariniana* is lemon-yellow. *H. mollis* is probably the best species with fragrant golden yellow flowers. Sprays of these flowers used alone or with other subjects create a pleasing decoration.

Hebe. See Veronica.

Hydrangea. Apart from the indoor pot specimens there are some species which are quite hardy. All like well drained rich soil and they resent dryness at any time. *H. arborescens grandiflora* forms clusters of large, white flowers from July to September. In milder districts, the attractive varieties of *H. hortensis* can be grown. There are many colours available although hydrangeas do not blue naturally in all soils so that where really blue flowers are required it is necessary to add blueing powder to the soil. H.

macrophylla mariesii has flat rounded heads of rosy pink with large ray florets which in acid soil turn rich blue.

Hypericum. The St. John's Wort revels in almost any soil and position. Some species are excellent for ground covering. Others grow 3-5 ft. high, the flowering period extending from July to early October. *H. calycinum* is the Rose of Sharon and has cup-shaped flowers 3 ins. wide, the sub-evergreen leaves colouring to a purplish shade in autumn. *H. moserianum* is good and the varieties of *H. patulum* are first class, all have single rich golden-yellow flowers with prominent stamens which look grand when seen arranged in vases, particularly the form henryii which has crimson red foliage in autumn and rich bronze coloured seed pods.

Ilex. Much better known as Holly. This subject in addition to making decorative hedges and trees can become a useful means of providing berried and even unberried branches or sprays much in demand during the few weeks preceding Christmas.

While in some districts there may be some of the common dark green holly growing wild, such trees and bushes are rapidly disappearing and it is becoming increasingly difficult to secure a supply from established trees.

There is no need to stick to the plain green leaved common type which is *Ilex aquifolium,* for there is a real demand for the gold and silver leaved varieties.

Apart from its popularity at Christmas time there is a regular use for leaves and twigs of these silver and gold varieties for the making of wreaths.

Hollies are diocious, that is male and female flowers are borne on separate trees. The berries are produced on the female species and it is necessary to grow a few male species to effect pollination and a good set of fruit. These female berrying specimens must not be confused with what the market salesmen often call ' female holly '. By this, they mean the smooth leaved non-prickly type which often grows at the top of the ordinary trees.

Holly will grow on most types of land but seems to prefer one that is slightly acid and contains plenty of leaf mould. Trees can be raised from seed or cuttings, the former method is cheaper but far slower, for the ripe berries first have to be collected and laid in heaps until the flesh rots away. Then they are stratified by being buried in sand for some months. Afterwards seed is sown in drills $\frac{1}{2}$ in. deep and a foot apart in frames or in a sheltered place in the open ground.

Cuttings are taken from half ripe wood with a heel of the older wood attached. This should be done in late summer or early autumn, the cuttings being inserted in sandy compost in frames where they should be shaded in sunny weather and kept moist at the roots. Few holly varieties come true to type from seed and to ensure particular sorts, propagation must be from cuttings or grafting.

Variegated holly (Silver Queen)

Once established, holly grows fairly quickly, our native *I. aquifolium* species making up to 15 in. annually. The variegated kinds are rather slower, but all stand clipping.

Among the handsome coloured leaved sorts, is Silver Queen, with silver variegated foliage. In spite of its name, it produces male flowers. Golden King on the other hand, is a female holly and has broad almost spineless leaves enriched with a bright yellow margin.

Handsworth Silver and Silver Milkmaid, are both free berrying.

A compact growing green leaved holly is *Ilex crenata*, which rarely exceeds 5 ft. in height and which produces deep red berries. An interesting species is the one known as *Ilex aquifolium ferox* or the Hedgehog holly, because of its unusually sharp prickles, produced in rather clustered foliage.

Kalmia latifolia likes a lime-free, peaty soil and is a most beautiful flowering evergreen. There will probably never be a lot of bloom which can be cut without reducing the size of the shrubs, but where the clusters of pink flowers which appear in June can be brought indoors they always command attention. The glossy foliage increases the attraction of the subject.

Lavender is among the most highly prized of all fragrant shrubs and by reason of its grey-green foliage can be used in so many kinds of decoration. It will grow in almost any kind of soil and likes the sun. There are various species and varieties, varying in height from 9 in. to 4 ft. or so. The typical flower spikes are ready for cutting during July and August. L. spica is the old English lavender with long spikes of greyish-blue flowers. It has several varieties including Hidcote, deep purple-blue; Twickel Purple, with fan-like spikes of purple and Munstead Dwarf, deep lavender.

Leycesteria formosa, produces its white flowers surrounded by claret coloured bracts from July to September. In addition, the 3-4 ft. stems are a vivid sea-green colour during the winter, making them of value for indoor use.

Magnolia. This very large genus contains both deciduous and evergreen species and varieties, which provide a most magnificent display from March to June. Among their requirements are a good depth of soil, a sheltered position and shade from the early morning sun. Of the deciduous species *M. parviflora* has fragrant flowers with white petals and claret coloured stamens.

M. soulangiana is hardy, its white petals being stained purple. M. stellata has semi-double, pure white fragrant flowers appearing during March and April.

Magnolia grandiflora is a hardy evergreen usually grown against

Arbutus unedo (Strawberry Tree) – This lovely evergreen does well in a warm place. It can grow to 20 feet in ideal conditions

a wall. It has large, fragrant flowers and big, glossy leaves, both of which look grand when used indoors, either individually or together with other flowers.

Olearia haastii is the Daisy Bush which is hardy everywhere in Britain. Attractive and easily cultivated, this evergreen produces very many whitish daisy-like flowers throughout July and August, on good sized bushes anything from 4-6 ft. The foliage too, is excellent for mixing with flowers.

Phlomis fruticosa is the Jerusalem Sage which bears whorls of bright yellow, attractive flowers in the summer, and is very easy to grow in ordinary soil. The woolly leaves give this subject added value.

Phygelius capensis is a most handsome, pentstemon-like plant which must be grown in a warm, sheltered position in the full sun. The scarlet tubular flowers an inch or more in length, appear on 2-3 ft. stems in the late summer and autumn. The form *P. c. coccimea* has strong branching spikes of dangling flowers from August to October.

Prunus. This is the title of a very large family of flowering shrubs and trees. *P. amygdalus* is the flowering almond which in March produces a wealth of delightful pink flowers on leafless branches. Pollardii is a fine variety, so useful for its cut stems of single deep pink flowers.

P. persica is the flowering peach which is not quite so hardy as the almond, but equally as ornamental, although just a little later blooming. The variety Clara Meyer has double pink flowers. There is also a double white form.

Prunus cerasifera pissardii is the well-known purple leaf plum with very small pinkish-white flowers in March. *P. blireana* has coppery foliage and double pink rosettes.

P. cerasus is the beautiful flowering cherry of which there are literally dozens of species and varieties. One of the most popular is known as hisakura or kanzan with clusters of double rich pink flowers, the young growths being bronze coloured, making them of extra value for floral arrangements. There are other pink and white forms flowering in the spring, while *P. subhirtella autumnalis* produces its small pink flowers intermittently from the end of October until March. Branches of all of these flowering cherries can be cut when in full bud and taken into the greenhouse to open early.

Pyrus malus has long been recognised as the name of the flowering crabs, although it is now correct to refer to the genus as malus. Many varieties, apart from their showy flowers and coloured foliage, produce attractive fruits, some being of value for making jelly. Among the best for cutting are Cheal's crimson; John Downie; and sikkimensis.

Rhododendron. This well known shrub must have a peaty, lime-free soil. The range of varieties is extremely wide and very often a stem or two of flowers makes an ornamental vase without any addition. Some of the early flowering, small growing species are of particular value for bringing indoors. Individual leaves or clusters of foliage make a welcome addition to many colourful displays.

Ribes is the Flowering Currant and among the varieties of sanguineum which produce hanging bunches of showy flowers and of which long stems can be cut in March and April, are, carneum, flesh pink; and King Edward VII, intense crimson. All thrive in most soils and situations and will attain a height of 6 or 7 ft. So long as the young foliage is not handled too much the scent will not be unpleasant.

Philadelphus is often known as Mock Orange. This shrub is renowned for its scent. The flowers are mainly white adorning the long arching branches throughout June and July. They grow on ordinary good soil. If the old wood is kept cut out the shrubs will remain shapely. Among good cultivars are: Beauclerk, producing very large single white flowers flushed pink at base; Belle Etoile, beautifully scented single flowers flushed pink; coranarius has strongly scented flattish semi-double yellowish-white flowers. Virginal is the best double cultivar having enormous panicles of semi-double pure white scented flowers.

Romneya coulteri is the Tree Poppy thriving in warm, sunny places. The large, satiny-white flowers 4 in. or more in diameter have a showy centre of golden anthers, while the leaves are bluish-grey. Plunge the stems in water immediately they are cut.

Salvia grahamii is an attractive shrub which produces from July until October, quantities of showy scarlet flowers. It should be grown in a warm, sheltered border.

Senecio greyii is a handsome, compact shrub with bright yellow, daisy-like flowers throughout the summer. It is, however, for its silvery-grey foliage that this subject is of special value. It will succeed in all but the coldest districts and loves the sun and well drained soil.

Syringa. This is the correct name of Lilac (although it is often applied to philadelphus) which is not always satisfactory as a cut flower. Many flower decorators remove all the lower leaves from the stems and either hold the end of the stem over a light or plunge it into boiling water so as to seal the base. It is also satisfactory to crush the bottom of the stems immediately before plunging it into water. The lilac is a sun loving subject and although they will grow in any good soil, a fairly rich rooting medium will induce good results.

The colour range of the single and double varieties is very extensive. Among reliable varieties are: Michael Buchner, large heads of clear lilac, double flowers; Marechal Foch, pinkish-mauve, single flowers on upright stems; Massena, double purple; Charles

Statice sinuata hybrids

Clary, Art Shades

Perilla nankinensis

Calendula Radar

Papaver coonara mixed

Aster chinensis

Aster Giant Princess

Arctotis grandis

Joly, double, dark purplish-red; Souvenir de L. 'Spath, single wine red; Madame Lemoine, large panicles of double white flowers and Primrose, primrose coloured single flowers formed in graceful heads. Of particular value is the species S. persica, a graceful shrub with narrow leaves and small, fragrant, lavender coloured flowers.

Tamarix. This shrub succeeds in all but heaviest soils and is quick growing and attractive. The foliage is feathery and the flower spikes graceful. There are several species, particularly good being *T. pentandra*, pale pink with glaucous foliage; and *T. tetrandra* with rich pink flowers during May and June on arching stems.

Ulex is the proper name of Gorse which produces its bright, golden-yellow flowers from spring to autumn. It will grow well on poor, stony ground and may be used for covering banks. *U. europaeus* is at its best from February to May, while *U. gallii* will flower profusely from August onwards.

Veronica. A very large family of ornamental summer and autumn flowering plants which love the sun and grow well in any good soil. The spikes of blooms are available in very many shades of colour, some being on quite small plants, others developing to 5 or 6 ft. high. Reference to catalogues of shrub specialists will indicate the named varieties ranging in colour from white, lilac, pale blue, deep blue to pink and crimson.

Viburnum. In this extensive family there are both deciduous and evergreen species. The majority prefer a soil which does not dry out at any time and although liking the sun they will succeed in partial shade. *V. opulus sterile* is the Guelder Rose, a fine flowering shrub with white, ball-shaped flower heads. *V. opulus fructo-luteo* is of value because of the yellow fruits which form when the flowers have passed over. *V. tomentosum* has freely borne, white flowers and the form plicatum has ball-like, pure white blossoms.

Of the evergreen species *V. tinus* is outstanding. Often known as the Laurustinus it will, in time, form a dense shrub 8-10 ft. high, its particular value being that it produces clusters of purplish rose buds opening to white flower from November to March. It is first class when cut for winter decoration.

ROSES FOR CUTTING

Roses are among the most popular of all cut flowers. For this purpose they are treated in the same way as roses which are grown entirely for garden decoration. They flourish in deep well drained limy soil and it is helpful when preparing the site to work in

H

decayed manure, compost or similar bulky material, plus a good dressing of fish manure at about 3-4 oz. per square yard. This will provide feeding matter for a long period.

The pruning is an essential part in keeping roses free flowering and although there are differences as to whether this operation should be done in winter or spring, long practice shows that pruning of bush and standard roses at the end of March is satisfactory. Hard pruning results in stronger growth and better blooms although the floribundas should not be cut quite so severely as the hybrid teas.

For many years certain varieties have been grown by professional growers under glass, for length of stem as usually associated with cut roses is not readily obtained from outdoor bushes. Of recent years much more use has been made of many types of roses, and not just hybrid teas, as in the past.

Many of the really old fashioned groups, as well as rose species, are now included in floral arrangements. These often give a particular look to a design. Some of the species are not so long lasting as the hybrid teas or hybrid perpetuals, but the effect they produce is more than compensated for this drawback.

It is certainly possible to obtain long stemmed flowers from hybrid tea bushes grown outdoors. To achieve this a certain amount of disbudding is necessary. Selection of varieties is a matter of choice and with the additional introduction of new sorts the choice will vary. Among the best hybrid teas available now culture as buttonhole or indoor decoration flowers are the following: Alec's Red, apricot red, good foliage; Beaute, golden apricot; Blue Moon, lilac-mauve; Eiffel Tower, elegant soft pink with glossy foliage; Fragrant Cloud, bright coral red; Godfrey Winn, pinky-mauve, scented; Manuela, shapely buds opening to cherry pink; Pascali, cream in bud, opening to white, borne on long stems. Queen Elizabeth is a floribunda, but with hybrid tea shaped flowers of lovely pink. Sir Lancelot, an apricot floribunda, with semi-double flowers being freely produced in delicate trusses. There are many other floribundas which look well when cut including: Orange Sensation, golden; Treasure, Topsy and Masquerade, salmon orange.

All of the hybrid teas and floribundas are of more or less formal appearance, but there are many old fashioned species and so-called shrub roses which not only make informal growth, but produce flowers having individual shapes and not all in the same category as regards petal formation.

The group of Shrub roses known as *Rosa alba* contains a number of interesting varieties including Great Maiden's Blush, of which the scented flesh pink flowers gradually open to an almost white colour. The bluish green leaves set off these dainty flowers to perfection. Queen of Denmark is another Alba hybrid having scented rich pink flowers which are full of petals and are inclined to be crinkly in the centre.

The Bourbon Roses were originally the result of a cross between the China and Damask rose. Of these, specially good for cutting are: Boule de Neige, ivory white, rather like a camellia in appearance; and Mrs. Pierre Oger, of which the colour varies from white through pale pink to deep rose. The leaves have crinkled edges, the cup shaped blooms looking like old fashioned shell flowers.

Rosa centifolia is the Cabbage Rose which has been grown in Britain for almost 400 years, featuring in old flower paintings. Varieties still available include: De meaux, having scented rose pink flowers about an inch in diameter and Old Cabbage Rose is the name of a well known variety with deep glowing rose pink, cupped flowers, often on graceful recurving stems, so suitable for various arrangements.

Rosa muscosa, the Moss Rose, is most attractive with its bright green mossy growths. Of these, the old Pink Moss is the best known having pure rose pink cup shaped flowers, well mossed, with exquisite scent; Striped Moss is a fresh pink with carmine stripes framed in dark moss; while William Lobb is crimson in bud opening fuchsia purple at edges and shading lilac to almost grey giving a pleasing shot silk effect.

Rosa damascena, the Damask Rose is so called because of the tradition that they were brought to Europe from Damascus by the Crusaders because of their rich scent. These varieties have long been used for making attar of roses. The most famous variety is Omar Khayyam, which although not showy has scented light rose pink flowers with a tightly incurved centre. York and Lancaster is another old variety, the flowers being striped pale pink and white. The marking varies from bush to bush.

Rosa gallica is the French Rose. These were said to have been grown by the Persians about 1200 B.C. At times they have been used in France for medicinal purposes. The Red Gallica is brilliant light crimson with golden stamens, while Tuscany, the old velvet rose, is dark purple crimson again with golden stamens.

Rosa, Austrian Briars. These are small growers with yellowish green foliage and attractive copper brown wood. The main briar is known as Austrian Copper having brilliant orange flowers, while

Austrian Yellow is a beautiful single buttercup yellow, although a little shy flowering.

Rosa moschata is the Musk rose which have been favourites in English gardens from the time of the first Queen Elizabeth. The flowers vary in size but always appear in clusters. The variety Cornelia is one of the best, its salmon pink buds opening to shell pink flowers with a delightful scent. Pax is pure white with a lemon centre, Penelope is creamy-white suffused soft pink, and Prosperity is white tinged gold.

Rosa rubiginosa is the Sweet Briar of which there are several good named sorts including Amy Robsart with single deep rose flowers, and Lady Penzance rich orange single flowers.

Rosa rugosa is a very valuable group with attractive leaves and most of the varieties produce hips after the flowers have finished. Blanc Double de Coubert makes a good shrub with snowy white flowers showing a green boss in the centre. Frau Dagmar Hartopp has single flowers of flesh pink and Roseraie de L'Hay makes a big bush, the wine-purple flowers showing up against the rich coloured foliage. Rosa rugosa scabrosa has single flowers of fuchsia-pink followed by brilliant hips.

Rosa spinosissima. This is the Scots Briar which makes dense growth down to the ground and in May, becomes covered with buttercup yellow flowers. There is also a double flesh pink variety.

Apart from these separate sections there are a number of rose species. These are technically wild roses which have not been used by hybridists. Especially good for providing sprays for cutting are Rosa moyesii, having dainty foliage and dusky red flowers followed by bottle shaped hips, *R. m. var.* Geranium is a form having more brilliantly coloured flowers. *R. highdownensis* is a hybrid of *R. moyesii*, the flowers being carmine and the hips red.

Rosa multibracteata makes arching stems covered with the daintiest tiny foliage and brilliant pink single flowers. R. rubrifolia has glaucous foliage with a deep pinkish tinge, the stems are red and the flowers a rather inconspicuous pink.

R. xanthina Canary Bird makes a large bush with single yellow flowers as much as 2 in. in diameter; the young reddish shoots are practically thornless.

There are a number of so-called modern shrub roses, the result of cross breeding, which are perpetual flowering and of value for that reason as well as for their attractive foliage. These include: Constance Spry clear pink, scented flowers in mid-summer, the foliage being tinged red and yellow.

Fruhlingsgold makes a marvellous shrub with masses of large creamy flowers having prominent golden centres, the shining leaves being gold tinged.

Marguerite Hilling is very strong growing, the rose pink flowers which have prominent golden stamens hiding the foliage.

Will Scarlet has pure scarlet flowers produced in abundant clusters. All of these rose species and shrub roses can be grown as individual specimens and do not depend on their neighbours to enhance their show. In addition all are useful sources of supply of cutting material of both flowers and foliage, the stems of many are also of attractive value.

CHAPTER 9

BULBS TO GROW FOR CUT FLOWERS

THE discerning gardener endeavours to fill his home as well as his garden with flowers. So as not to sacrifice garden display a special cutting garden is the answer to a constant supply for the home.

Even a small patch in the garden will yield quantities of cut flowers and utilising part of the vegetable garden, or an odd sunny spot behind a garage or shed is often practical.

Bulbs are excellent subjects for cutting and their flowers follow one after another from late winter into spring and summer and well into the autumn.

The small early flowering bulbs, such as Snowdrops, Grape Hyacinths, Glory of the Snow and Siberian Squill, which are so delightful for intimate arrangements, can be gathered from bulbs planted in shrubberies or in grassy areas. When these bulbs are planted in their hundreds, handfuls for floral decoration will never be missed.

Of course, trumpet Daffodils and other narcissi can often be picked from naturalised plantings without noticeable loss of display, but if they are not liberally naturalised in your garden then include members of the impressive Daffodil family in your special cutting garden.

When planning a cutting garden allow sections for all types of bulbous subjects from miniatures to tall growers. Plant gladioli and dahlias, which are lifted at the end of the growing season and replanted again the following spring, in the first section. Plant tulips, daffodils, lilies, montbretias and other bulbs that remain in the ground year after year in the second section.

The availability of bulbs for flowering virtually the entire year round has made bulb cultivation a fascinating hobby. As more and more gardeners discover that a fantastic selection of bulbs are hardy in Britain they are experimenting with varieties and types that they have never grown before.

Bulbs are miracles of nature containing all the essentials to transform the bulbs into a beautiful flower. Because they are so easy to grow the beginner at bulb cultivation can, with a little common sense, match the results of the experts. As experience with application in the garden is gained, bulbs can literally transform the garden into a year-round pageant of colour and glory.

Bulbs, including true bulbs, corms, rhizomes and tubers, produce the best results for those who handle them with care and observe a few simple principles in cultivation.

It is essential to buy bulbs of good quality from reputable firms or nurserymen. Always buy the best. Don't fall for offers of parcels of bulbs at impossibly low prices.

Fine quality bulbs are good to look at. The tunic should be intact and the bulb firm to the touch when pressed with the thumb, its weight corresponding to its size. The tunic or coat of tulip bulbs sometimes splits and may fall but so long as the bulb is firm and unblemished it can be planted with confidence.

Order your bulbs early for better selection and prompt delivery. The best plan is to plant the bulbs immediately they arrive but should this be inconvenient open the bags for ventilation and keep the bulbs in a cool, dry place until you are ready to plant.

It is important not to put off planting for too long. The planting period for spring flowering bulbs in Britain extends from the beginning of September to mid December, but daffodils or narcissi should always be planted before the end of October. Autumn flowering bulbs should be planted in July-August, and summer flowering bulbs from April.

Bulbs will do well in almost any porous, well drained soil. They appreciate well dug ground and organic matter for a depth of about 8 ins. for their roots extend well down. Clays and compact soils often retain too much moisture.

Humus-forming organic matter is essential to plant life. The various species of bulbous plants prefer varying quantities of humus. Lilies and gladioli, for example, are greedy. Never use fresh manure with bulbs. Decomposed manure, composted for several months, can be dug in the soil ahead of planting. Peat and leaf mould are excellent sources of organic matter.

Planting is the most important operation in bulb growing. It is misleading to generalise on the precise depths at which bulbs should be planted for the depth varies according to the size of the bulb and the nature of the soil. Tall stemmed bulbs need deep firm rooting. The bigger the bulb, the lighter the soil, the longer the stem, the deeper the planting is a good guide.

As a general rule a depth of 2 to 3 times the bulb's largest diameter will prove satisfactory and the depth should be measured from the top and not the bottom of the bulb. In practice this means about 5-6 ins. deep for daffodils, tulips and hyacinths in average garden soil and 3-4 ins. deep for crocuses, muscari and most other small bulbs. Less harm is done by planting too deeply than too shallowly.

Spacing can vary considerably according to the effect one wants to create. Remember that bulbs like breathing space so that tulips daffodils and hyacinths should be planted 5-6 ins. apart at least and most small or miscellaneous bulbs 3-4 ins. apart.

Bulbs can be grown anywhere in the garden – in beds, borders, edges, shrubbery, rockeries, lawns, woodlands, below, in and on walls, between paving stones, in tubs, urns or window boxes – although various types and varieties are more suitable than others for particular sites.

Bulbs do well in sun or partial shade. Some bulbs prefer full sunshine but few require it. When planting in partial shade the blooms of bulbs will last longer.

Plant bulbs in groups or clusters of a dozen or more for the best and most colourful effects. Use extra bulbs for cut flowers in the vegetable garden or special area not required for display. Avoid spoiling your pleasure garden show by cutting flowers for indoor decoration.

Bulbs appreciate having the surface soil around them loosened in spring. By doing this and removing weeds the rain can do its proper job. All bulbs should have moisture when growing. Water in dry weather and avoid moisture touching the flowers as far as possible.

Few require staking but some taller types like lilies, dahlias and gladioli benefit from supports, particularly in gardens subjected to strong winds. Use stakes proportionate in size to the plant and conceal the support as much as possible.

Never leave faded or dead petals to drop as this is bad for the bulb and for the soil. When bulbs pass peak bloom remove the flower heads and allow foliage to die down naturally. This permits the bulb to replace energy and flower the next year instead of becoming weakened through seed production.

Most bulbs, except the tender species, can be left in the ground for flowering the next season but you should lift, clean and store them in a cool, well ventilated and frost free place for replanting the following autumn. Save only the largest bulbs for replanting for display. Medium sized bulbs can be relegated to the cut flower garden.

If space is needed for other flowers you can lift bulbs with green foliage provided you immediately heel them in carefully in a corner of the garden to allow the foliage to die down before cleaning and storing.

Handle bulbs carefully to avoid physical injury. It is easy to puncture, slice or scrape bulbs when lifting or cultivating. Use a fork for lifting rather than a spade. Appropriately mark the locations of bulbs planted in areas where soil operation are likely to be carried out during times when the bulbs have no top growth. If bulbs are unavoidably injured promptly smooth the edges of the wounds and dust with yellow sulphur.

Don't be afraid to experiment. It is only by planting different types and varieties of bulbs in different parts of your garden that you can enjoy an ever changing colourful panorama of bulbs in bloom.

Naturalisation not only adds a new dimension to flower gardening, it makes maximum use of space in the era of the smaller garden.

The philosophy behind this method of bulb gardening is that vigorous and hardy bulbs happily located will fend for themselves and multiply rapidly over the years, creating enchanting garden pictures with a minimum of maintenance and expenditure.

Naturalised bulbs are planted in selected landscapes to appear as if they had arisen from chance sown seeds and from natural offsets. The spacing rules are abandoned and you simply scatter the bulbs, planting them at the normal depths where they fall. To heighten the effect you select types of bulbs that fit into the landscape and that are not too developed horticulturally. Generally speaking single flowers are preferable to double flowers, but this is not an unchangeable rule.

If a special cutting garden is planned, even a small plot will yield quantities of cut flowers. Almost all bulbs lend themselves to floral arrangements. Their flowers are long lasting and with proper selection will follow one another from winter into spring and summer and into the autumn as well.

A cutting garden need not be devoted exclusively to bulbs. For continuous bloom for indoor decoration, plan one section for annuals and biennials and another section for perennials.

With annuals and biennials in the first section plant summer flowering gladiolus, montbretias, freesias, galtonias, dahlias and other bulbs, corms and tubers which are lifted at the end of the growing season and replanted again the following spring.

But it is with the second section for perennials that you should plant tulips, daffodils, lilies and other bulbs that remain in the ground year after year. Although bulbs look best grown in clumps or groups if space permits they can be planted in rows for easy cultivation. Weeding can be minimised by mulching. Lilies prefer shade on their roots and can be interplanted with low growing perennials like paeonies which retain their foliage during the summer. Daffodils and other early flowering bulbs which lose their foliage by early summer can be planted with perennials that do not make much foliage until late spring.

When choosing bulbs for the cutting garden, consider first the types of bulbs you want in terms of flowering time, form and colour. Cater for your own individual taste and what you know looks particularly effective in your home. The other factor is, of course, quantity and here you should be as generous as space allows.

For longer lasting beauty in the home cut all bulbs, except May-flowering tulips, when their buds first open and cut in the early morning or late evening, leaving as much foliage behind as possible. Your arrangements will last longer and you'll have all the pleasure of watching the blooms develop. Stand freshly cut blooms in 2 in. of water in a cool shaded place for 8 hours or more before arranging them.

Don't be misled into thinking that the tall-stemmed types and varieties are the only ones suitable for cutting. Many bulb flowers are useful in arrangements in shallow containers and stems can range from a few inches to several feet.

The small early flowering bulbs like snowdrops, Grape hyacinths, Glories of the Snow, and Siberian squill are delightful for small, intimate arrangements in bedrooms, living-room, dining-room or even the kitchen. If you plant enough of these in grassy areas or in shrubberies those you take for floral decoration will not spoil the garden display.

Try Iris histroides major, those lovely nemophila-blue flowers with a golden crest that bloom in January and February. The fragrant Iris reticulata in blue and Iris danfordiae in yellow, flower shortly afterwards. Spring Snowflake or Leucojum vernum, sends up lovely white green-tipped single flowers similar to the snowdrop but larger, from January onwards.

Crocus species and the handsome Chrysanthus varieties, are superb for indoor decoration. Flowering in February and March they provide a wide range of colour such as Blue Pearl, Cream Beauty, Snow Bunting and the golden yellow Zwanenberg, while Anemone blanda produces flowers in pastel shades during March and April.

Miniature narcissus are both elegant and dainty. Don't overlook *N. triandrus albus* (Angel's Tears) for despite their short stems they make lovely little arrangements. The multi-coloured ranunculus with large double flowers in charming pastel shades flower in June and are gorgeous for indoor decoration. And the dainty and sweet ixia flowering in June and July and obtainable in varieties ranging from blue through white, yellow, pink and orange to scarlet are also well worth growing for table decoration. These items and many others are detailed in the following list.

Acidantheras are closely related to the genus gladiolus having been known in this country since the latter end of the last century. *A. candida*, the pure white form; and bicolor, white with a purple blotch at the base of each petal, being the two chief varieties.

Over 40 years ago a striking form was sent from Abyssinia by Captain Erskine to Mr. James Kelway of Langport. It was recorded that when the first plants flowered he was enchanted not only by the grace and beauty of the blooms but by their strong, yet most attractive fragrance. It was suggested that the variety should be called *A. erskinei*, but the discoverer wished the plant to be named after his wife Muriel Erskine, which accounts for the corms being distributed for some years under the name of Gladiolus murielae.

The strong spikes reach a height of $2\frac{1}{2}$-$3\frac{1}{2}$ ft. the large flowers being of the purest silver-white, all excepting the top petal, being marked with a conspicuous deep maroon blotch near the centre, while the foliage is typically that of a gladious, although a little narrower. Not the least of the attributes of this delightful plant is the fact that it continues to bloom over a long period and it is not unusual to be able to cut blooms from the end of July until well into October.

It is a subject which does particularly well in pots or in the greenhouse and if planted late January or February it makes a good indoor plant which is most attractive on account of its beauty and scent, the flowers when cut, lasting well in water. Its culture is of the simplest and although at first acidantheras were regarded as tender and requiring indoor cultivation, A. bicolor Murielae can be treated in exactly the same way as an ordinary gladiolus and planted 3 or 4 ins. deep out of doors towards the end of March.

It is noticeable that they are very slow to start outside in a cold soil, so that a favourable spot should be selected. They like plenty of sun during the summer, in fact the more the better, but they must be copiously watered when in full growth. It has been found that a site on the heavy side but with a gravel sub soil, suits them best and a little silver sand at the base of the corms will be of further encouragement to produce the best results. As with gladiolus, acidantheras should be lifted in October and stored in a frost proof place during the winter.

Anemones. This is one of the most versatile of plant families the flowers being particularly suitable for all kinds of decorative arrangements. Coming from Southern Europe and Asia Minor, *Anemone coronaria* has given rise to many other excellent single and double varieties. One of the earliest records of this variety is in the latter part of the sixteenth century when some corms were sent from Constantinople to the then well known Dutch botanist Clusius, whose name has been commemorated by a number of bulbous subjects.

Over a century ago a special strain of Single Coronaria anemones was sent to France where a French grower in Caen, cultivated them with such success that they were soon listed as Anemone de Caen under which name they are still officially grown although they are also referred to as Giant French or Poppy Anemones. It is a most handsome strain growing 9-12 ins. high, the large saucer shaped blossoms being of most brilliant colours and so valuable for cut flowers.

Apart from the mixture of magnificent Single Poppy anemones they are now available in separately named sorts including the pretty Gertrude, rosy-salmon with black central boss; His Excellency, bearing very large blooms of vivid velvety vermilion, with a blue black centre, and often measuring 3 ins. in diameter; and The Bride, with spotless white flowers. The double Poppy Anemones are also greatly prized for cutting and many brilliant colours are to be found in the mixture. Among the separate colours are Cornflower, a frilly double dark amethyst blue; Queen of Brilliants, with particularly vivid cherry-scarlet flowers and Scarlet King having perfectly formed strikingly effective scarlet blooms.

St. Brigid anemones are of very graceful habit with large semi-double flowers all showing a dark black central boss. Greatly prized for cutting they grow 10 ins. high and the mixture contains very many hues. The Creagh Castle strain is especially good.

All anemones appreciate a rich deep sandy loam and this is essential if the tubers are to be left in the soil through the winter for they are not so likely to rot as would be the case in a wet cold soil. Many gardeners lift annually storing the tubers in a dry airy place until the next planting time. This method certainly prevents the untidy appearance of the plants as they are dying off.

Bone meal dug into the soil before planting the tubers will prove greatly beneficial and if a sprinkling of nitro chalk is worked around the plants when flowering begins it will encourage the continuous production of a plentiful supply of long stemmed blooms.

Corms planted in the autumn will produce flowers from early spring, while spring plantings will provide decoration from May onwards although in a well drained soil plantings may be made at very short intervals during the winter months thus ensuring a regular supply of blooms. Planted 2 ins. deep in clumps of 6 or more they are most effective.

Propagation. It is possible to increase stock from seed which should be sown under glass in the early spring or later out of doors.

Antholyzas are handsome and showy gladiolus-like plants from South Africa. While they will grow outdoors at the base of a south wall or other similar position, they also do well in pots in which they should always be grown in cold localities.

They flourish in well drained, loamy soil where there is leaf mould or peat, and if the soil is enriched with bone meal or old manure these will provide nourishment over a long period. Plant the corms in the early spring burying them about 3 ins. deep.

Antholyza aethiopica grows 3 ft. high and produces in the summer elegant spikes of scarlet and yellow tubular flowers, while *A. crocosmioides* has in September strong branching spikes of brilliant red and gold-yellow blooms. There are also several other species including *A. paniculata*, brownish red and yellow; and *A. fulgens*, rich coppery-rose, although these two are much less common.

They propagate themselves annually in the same way as gladiolus by producing new corms. It is also possible to increase stock by sowing seed in boxes of sandy loam in gentle heat in the spring.

Alliums. The ornamental garlics are part of a huge genus of some 300 species. The lovely flowers are massed together in a ball which is solid or tasselled and strike a note of distinction in any garden. These hardy bulbous plants will thrive almost anywhere.

Alliums flower freely from May into July, the smallest being only some few inches high while the tallest measure over 2 ft. The taller ones look very showy in borders and shrubberies and are most impressive when mixed with ornamental grasses. They can be used in long lasting arrangements if the stems are immersed in tepid water overnight and they do *not* give off a distinctive ' onion ' smell unless bruised.

Many shades can be obtained from the purest white to the deepest purple as well as cream, yellow, pink, red and blue.

Plant them in the autumn covering the bulbs 2 or 3 times their own depth. Smaller varieties can be planted 2 in. apart and taller ones about 6 in. apart. They need not be lifted and replanted until the bulbs become overcrowded and the flowers tend to become sparse.

The following species are worth growing for cutting purposes.

A. aflatunense carries dense rounded heads of lovely purple-lilac starry flowers in May and grows 2-3 ft. tall. A good border variety and excellent for vases.

A. albo-pilosum has in June on 2 ft. stems heads of starry lilac as much as 12 in. in diameter. It is one of the finest alliums for planting in groups and makes splendid cut flowers.

A. azureum (*caeruleum*) has handsome globular heads of deep cornflower-blue on 2 ft. stems in June and July. They are really charming in flower arrangements.

A. karataviense is most distinctive with broad, flat, mottled leaves. The scapes are about 8 ins. tall and bear dense umbels of pink flowers in May.

A. neapolitanum grandiflora grows 20 ins. tall with handsome heads of sweet scented white blossoms flowering in June and July. It can be forced under glass for early flowering.

A. sphaerocephalum has 2-3 ft. stems bearing striking heads of crimson-maroon in July making an attractive cut flower.

Brodiaea. This is a little known cormous plant with long leaves that trail on the ground and floral stems bearing clusters of umbels of bell-shaped flowers. This member of the lily family is also known as triteleia and all species come from North America. Two of the species available from larger bulb merchants can add beautiful colour to the summer garden.

Brodiaea laxa produces in June wide mouthed tubular flowers, sumptuous violet-purple in colour with blue anthers. The stems are very stiff and sturdy and some 18 in. tall, thus making an excellent cut flower in June.

Brodiaea ixioides sometimes called the Golden Star, produces umbels of several deep golden yellow flowers with a deep stripe on the outside of segments in June and July. Stems are from 1½ to

2 ft. in height and the magnificent flowers are excellent for cutting. Both like sunny warm positions like the foot of a south wall and sand should be added to the soil to make it a bit gritty. Plant the corms in March-April some 3 to 4 ins. deep and 2 to 3 ins. apart. They do not need much space as foliage is scant and usually dies before the flowers are over.

Brodiaeas need only be lifted and replanted every 4 years but in all but southern districts it is advisable to protect the corms with a mulch during the winter.

Calochortus are sometimes known as Mariposa or Butterfly tulips, whilst on other occasions certain varieties have been described as Star or Globe tulips. They come chiefly from California, and their light, graceful growth and charming brightly coloured flowers, make them altogether attractive and so valuable for cutting.

The flower consists of 6 petals, the 3 outer ones being shorter and narrower than the remainder, many varieties being of striking colours with vivid markings. They are especially valuable for cutting, having long stems and when established many blooms are produced over a long period. Calochortus are hardy, although they do best in a sunny position where the soil is light and sandy and drainage good. A bed raised above the surrounding soil is helpful preventing possibility of excessive moisture settling around the bulbs in the winter.

Mariposa tulips should be planted during October and November, covering them with 3 ins. of soil, and placing them 4 in. apart. It is a good plan in winter especially when there are heavy rains, to cover the beds with straw or similar material, which can be removed in the early part of the year. This gives protection and keeps the surface soil from caking.

The varieties known as Globe tulips are best planted in March. They like partial shade, with porous soil. They flower from June until August and during dry spells should have occasional soakings of water.

Some varieties are difficult to obtain but are well worth any effort needed to procure them. They include: Clavatus, very large golden-yellow expanding flowers. Kennedyi, dazzling orange-scarlet with black central blotches. Venusus Eldorado, a large strong growing sort of unusual colouring varying from creamy white to lilac, through to pink and rosy-purple, the centres of all being blotched brown.

The best of the Globe Tulips include: amabilis, with beautiful pendant, golden flowers and Amoenus, having drooping blooms of delightful rose, both growing about 8 ins. high. Of those described as Star tulips, Benthami, clear yellow with dark central blotch and Maweanus Major, a most delightful species with large cup-shaped white flowers and prominent blue central haris, are among the finest.

Although it is normal to increase stock by the young bulbs which form at the base, calochortus may also be propagated from seeds which should be sown as soon as they are ripe, either in pots, or in the cold frame and then planted out the following season.

Camassia. Easy to cultivate and so adaptable and useful, it is surprising that camassias are so little seen in our gardens. In North America the small bulbs are known as ' quamash ' to the Indians, who actually eat them.

Camassias have graceful linear-shaped leaves and the small flowers are borne in loose racemes. They grow 2 or 3ft. high and bloom in June and July before the herbaceous subjects are at the height of their glory. Camassias will thrive almost anywhere in sun or shade and in any well drained soil. They bear a profusion of starry flowers and a delightful effect can be achieved by planting them in quantity in herbaceous borders or in a special plot for cutting.

They do not require special treatment and grow vigorously, soon increasing if left undisturbed. They can be lifted and divided about every third year. Plant the bulbs about 3 ins. deep and 3-5 ins. apart.

A number of species are available including the following: C. cusickii, producing 2 ft. elegant spikes of pale lavender blue star-shaped flowers with pale golden anthers and having a rosette of glaucous green foliage.

C. esculenta has graceful tall 1½ ft. spikes of showy rich blue flowers, giving an illusion of a blue haze from the distance. This species is excellent for naturalising.

C. leichtlinii atrocoerulea produces very striking brilliant blue flowers on immense 2 ft. spikes.

C. leichtlinii alba, the white form, grows just 2 ft. tall, and although more expensive is well worth having in the garden.

Chionodoxa. This is known as Glory of the Snow and a hundred bulbs or so will produce a carpet of blue in your garden. Chionodoxa seed themselves rapidly and also increase by offsets when naturalised in sunny locations. Flowering in March and April

Anemone de Caen

Dahlias, different types

Zea Quadricolour

Zea multiflora

Ornamental gourds

they are most effective too at the base of spring flowering shrubs like yellow forsythia and creamy white magnolias.

Their lovely sky blue flowers are a most welcome sight in the garden, appearing soon after snowdrops fade, and along with the deeper blue scillas which they somewhat resemble. Once seen together, however, you cannot mistake them for the chionodoxa's cluster of blue flowers, each with its starry white centre always faces up to the sky, while the early scilla nod their heads and are deeper blue. Cut and used in miniature arrangements they never fail to attract attention, adding grace and beauty to all indoor displays.

The bulbs should be set about 2 or 3 in. deep and up to 2 in. apart. The lovely Cambridge-blue *C. luciliae* which has a clear snow white centre, is the best known. Six to 12 flowers develop on each 4 to 6 in. stem the broad linear leaves appearing at the same time. *C. luciliae* Pink Giant produces sturdy spikes with beautiful cattleya-violet blooms of fine shape. *C. gigantea* is a somewhat taller species with fewer flowers to each stem, but each flower is larger almost 2 in. across, in a lovely shade of gentian-blue with a lighter centre. There are white forms of both *C. luciliae* and *C. gigantea*. *Chionodoxa sardensis* is one of the earliest to bloom. The small flowers are a true gentian blue with a tiny white centre.

All chionodoxa last well in water, making delightful little arrangements in small bowls.

Colchicum. Spring is synonomous with bulbs but every gardener can beat the clock by planting these prolific and rewarding autumn flowering bulbs. To produce gay colour in your garden in September, October and November, plant the bulbs in July and August.

Colchicums are commonly known as Autumn Crocus but they are not crocuses at all. Catalogues often list colchicums as Meadow Saffrons and some gardeners refer to them as Naked Ladies.

This nickname stems from the fact that colchicums are naked of leaves at flowering time. The broad foliage does not emerge until spring and colchicums should therefore be sited so that their very effective long foliage will not interfere with spring flowering subjects.

Easy to grow in any well drained soil, they flourish best in rich, sandy loam. Despite the size of the corms they do not have to be planted deeply, a covering 2 in. of soil is sufficient. They thrive in full sun or in partial shade.

The flowers, many from each bulb, appear shortly after planting and the foliage which emerges in spring grows on until early

I

summer. When the foliage dies down you can if you wish lift the corms separate the clusters and replant them.

A wide choice of colchicums is available including Autumnale major (Byzantinum) 6 in. soft lilac-mauve, free flowering and one of the earliest. *C. autumnale minor*, with abundant rose-lilac starry shaped blooms on 6 in. stems is late flowering.

Colchicum speciosum boasts lovely deep purple flowers of erect habit on 8 in. stems and flowers late. *C. speciosum Illyricum* has blooms of soft rosy carmine with a white centre and yellow anthers.

Among the best of the large flowered hybrids are Lilac Wonder, pinkish-violet; The Giant, pinkish-mauve with white base; and Water Lily an enormous lilac-mauve double flowered hybrid. All range in height from 6-8 in. and are useful as cut flowers.

Commelina. A native of Mexico, this plant is sometimes known as the Blue Spiderwort. There are many species, but the best in general cultivation is C. tuberosa. This likes a warm sunny position and although in sheltered districts the little clusters of tubers can be left in the ground during the winter, they are best lifted and stored in sandy compost in a frost proof place until the following spring.

Commelinas are useful for the cool greenhouse where they flower from late June onwards. The clear gentian blue flowers are produced on 15-18 in. stems and are set amid long lance-shaped leaves. Not among the top flight of cut flowers, they certainly provide a touch of the unusual, particularly where a good blue flower is required.

Crocus species. Most of these are considerably smaller than the spring flowering varieties but they are superb for indoor decoration. Planted 2 in. deep in September they flower in February and March, and provide a wide range of colour.

Among the best for cutting are the Chrysanthus varieties: Snow Bunting, pure white with golden throat and purplish feathered exterior; Blue Pearl, soft pearly blue with orange stigmata; E.P. Bowles, heads of yellow with dark grey markings at the base of the petals; and Zwanenburg, bright golden yellow with brownish exterior.

Crocosmia. Somewhat like a large flowered montbretia this subject is showy in the border and are ideal cut flowers lasting 2 weeks or more in water. It also makes a fine pot plant. Place the corm 2 in. deep in rich sandy well drained soil.

Plant in early spring and give winter protection. C. masonorum $2\frac{1}{2}$-3 ft. produces long sprays of brilliant orange scarlet flowers from early autumn onwards.

Cyclamen. The dainty fluttering flowers of hardy cyclamen look so fragile that they suggest the plants are delicate when in fact, they are tough. They like to be planted where the soil is rich in humus matter, and also contains grit. If leaf mould or peat are present it will be helpful. Most species grow well where lime-stone chippings are added to the soil, although Cyclamen repandum is said to dislike lime.

Hardy cyclamen will often thrive where little else will grow and it is not unusual to find them flowering freely at the base of hedges or under trees. In woodland gardens where the grass is not long they look superb. While it is usual for suppliers to offer corms as ' dry bulbs ' this is not always the most satisfactory method from the buyers points of view.

If the corms are kept out of the ground for a prolonged period they develop a dry, rather corky skin or bark. When this becomes really hard the corms may remain dormant for a long period, after planting. During this time the corms are alive but sulking and take some time to recover.

In spite of the custom of selling dormant corms, cyclamen can be moved as growing plants over a period of many months and this certainly avoids any stagnation of growth. When the corms are dormant it is easy to plant them upside down. The rounded side should go underneath.

There are many species and it is possible to have colour from July until April. Flowering in the autumn *C. neapolitanum*, white; is easy and very popular. The heavily marbled leaves develop as the flowers begin to fade and have an attractiveness of their own.

C. europaeum has scented flowers from the middle of July. These are of bright crimson paling slightly, towards the tips. The flowers and leaves usually appear together. *C. graecum* has slightly twisted pink flowers.

C. cilicium has the smallest and daintiest flowers of all, the narrow slightly twisted petals being pale pink, and showing in September and October. Cyclamen coum is a distinct winter flowering species having several forms. All have round dark green leaves without marbling, the flowers showing from early January onwards. Among the forms are *C. album*, blush-white, crimson, and *C. roseum*. When established they flower over a long period.

C. ibericum and *C. atkinsii* are early spring flowering, their pretty blossoms of white or rosy-pink with their beautifully marked foliage making them attractive in every way.

Cyclamen repandum has marbled well cut leaves which appear before the show of pink to carmine-red flowers in March and April.

Propagation. Many of the species seed themselves freely and left undisturbed they will in time, form a real carpet of colour. Seedlings raised under glass are best grown on in small pots for a year or two until they become well established, then they can be transferred to the open garden. Another method is to cut the old healthy tubers into pieces. Each piece should have one or two eyes or buds in it.

Dahlias. Named after Dr. Dahl a Swedish botanist this plant has become a great favourite for garden and indoor decoration. The plants are not hardy and top growth will be cut down by the first severe autumn frost.

The normal practice is to start the tubers in warmth in February and to take cuttings of the new shoots when they are about 3 in. long. Both the tubers and rooted cuttings can be planted out of doors from the end of May onwards in deeply moved well prepared soil which does not dry out during the summer. Taller varieties will need staking and excessive side shoots must be removed, particularly as the season advances. To increase the size of the flowers where necessary some disbudding may be necessary.

Cut the flowers when they are two-thirds open, preferably early in the day and place them immediately in water. To prevent the water becoming stagnant a few pieces of charcoal should be placed in the vase. Other ingredients used to prolong the life of the flowers includes aspirins, glucose and glycerine. The latter is a favourite with many gardeners the rate of application being one ounce of glycerine to a gallon of water.

Dahlias produce many varied petal formations in all hues and colours fortunately they are divided into sections making it easy to identify them. Among the sections are the following:

Single flowered. These have blooms with a single outer ring of florets, which may overlap the centre forming a disc. Formerly called mignon dahlias most are 1-1½ ft. in height and produce an abundance of brightly coloured flowers through the summer and autumn. Most catalogues list them as single dwarf bedding varieties. Within this group come the beautiful new strain of Topmix dahlias, ideal for massing or edging in the border because of the free flowering and dwarf habit. Stems are only about 10 in. tall.

Anemone flowered dahlias have blooms with one or more outer rings of generally flattened ray petals surrounding a dense group of tubular florets. These are longer than the disc florets in single flowered dahlias and show no disc. Most are dwarfs like the single flowered dahlias. Only a few named varieties are available but a mixed collection is just the thing for a small bed.

Collerette dahlias boast single flowers with an outer ring of generally flat ray florets and a ring or collar of small florets in the centre forming a disc. No flower arranger should be without them. They flower on erect slender stems 2½-4 ft. tall, their long lasting qualities making them superb cut flowers. They are easiest to obtain as mixed collections but a few named varieties are available.

Paeony flowered dahlias have flowers with 2 or more rings of generally flattened ray florets, the centre forming a disc. Useful for bedding most are dwarf in stature although a few varieties grow up to 3½ ft. high. They flower prolifically and last well when cut.

Decorative dahlias make up one of the biggest and most popular groups and have fully double blooms with broad, flat petals usually bluntly pointed. This group along with the cactus and semi-cactus groups have been graded into five classes according to the size of their flowers. These classes are giant flowered (over 10 in. in diameter), large flowered (8-10 in.), medium flowered (6-8 in.), small flowered (4-6 in.) and miniature flowered (under 4 in. in diameter).

Decorative dahlias make most effective border plants because of their strong habit and long lasting qualities and range in height from 3-6 ft. For giant flowered varieties try the chinese coral Holland's Festival, and the delicate lavender pink Lavender Perfection both 4 ft. tall. Among large flowered decoratives available are the purple-violet Ludwig's Score and the dark red and white Mrs. McDonald Quill, both 4-4½ ft. tall. For medium flowered gems choose the purple and white tipped Deuil du roi Albert, the coppery orange 4 ft. tall House of Orange, the rose and salmon-pink 6 ft. tall Jersey Beauty, the pure white Snow Country, the purple-red and white tipped Tartan and the blood red Terpo on 6 ft. stems.

Among the lovely small flowered varieties are the deep blood red 2½ ft. tall Arabian Night, the orange red on yellow 4 ft. tall Chinese Lantern, the saffron-yellow and tangerine 3 ft. tall Front Row, the deep pink 4 ft. tall Gerrie Hoek, the lemon yellow 4½ ft. high, Glory of Heemstede, the dark lilac 4 ft. tall Requiem and the orange-red Magnificat both on 3 ft. stems.

Miniature flowered decoratives are enchanting and none more so than the bronze Lilianne Ballego and the clear red and white tipped Musette both $3\frac{1}{2}$ ft. high and the bright red Kochelsee or orange-red Magnificent both on 3 ft. stems.

Ball dahlias make up another group and come with flowers 4 to 6 ins. in diameter or as miniature ball dahlias with blooms less than 4 ins. across. These were formally classified as large and medium pompom dahlias. These have globular flowers with petals which have blunt or rounded tips and are quilled inwards for most or all of their length. Both the ball and miniature ball dahlias have fully double blooms. Ball dahlias can be purchased in mixed selections or by named varieties.

Pompom dahlias under the new classification are those with blooms similar to the ball dahlias but with flowers not exceeding 2 in. in diameter. Varieties available with real charm include the pure white Albina, the orange-bronze Master Michael, the gothic purple Moor Place and the bright purple Purple Gem, all on stems 2-3 ft. tall.

Cactus dahlias with their fully double blooms and narrow quilled or rolled petals sometimes twisting and incurving comprise a huge group. They vary in height from 3-5 ft. and have cane hard stems. They come in a wide range of colours and flower well in beds and borders. They make striking cut flowers.

Few giant and large flowered cactus dahlias are catalogued, but an outstanding available variety is the bright cyclamen pink large flowered Pride of Holland. Among the medium flowered cactus varieties select the cattleya-pink Apple Blossom, the red and yellow De Ruyter's Sensation, the deep mauve-rose Good Earth, the deep purple Orfeo and the light pink and bronze Orly.

Small flowered cactus dahlias worth room in any garden include the cardinal red Doris Day, the dark pink and purple Pontiac and the light pink Silvretta.

Semi-cactus dahlias have broader petals than cactus dahlias and they are quilled for less than half their length. They are classed in five divisons according to size of flower. Frontispiece is a giant flowered example in ivory-white and a host of large flowered, varieties are obtainable. These include: Belledame, orange and deep pink; Gina Lombaert, deep pink and yellow; Independence, bronzy orange; Miss Universe, flame; and Royal Sceptre, orange and yellow.

Medium flowered semi-cactus varieties are also worth having including the deep pink Beauty of Aalsmeer, the red and yellow Carnaval, the dark red Eclipse and the dark pink Fortune.

Small flowered semi-cactus varieties of real merit include the lovely yellow Hoek's Yellow, the neat lilac Nocturne, the lavender-pink Pink Profusion, the salmon-pink Preference and the glorious white Purity.

The last group consists of those cultivars which do not fall into the other groups, including the rarer species dahlias. Within the cactus and semi-cactus groups, however, are some unusual fimbriated varieties whose flowers are fringed or frilled or feature laciniated petals. Among these is the medium cactus Dentelle de Venise in pure white with split petals. Fimbriated medium semi-cactus varieties on the market include the soft pink Popular Guest and the clear sulphur-yellow Promise.

There are demonstrably dahlias to every taste and they bloom freely throughout the summer and autumn and frost permitting even into November. No other plants have such a variety of colour or wealth of bloom.

Dahlias should always be planted in sunny positions for they flower less well in shade. All dahlias are excellent for beds and borders and for cutting. The dwarf bedding varieties can also be used most effectively in window boxes or in tubs or urns on the terrace or roof garden.

Do grow some dahlias just for cutting and do remember when cutting these long lasting blooms to use a sharp knife. Always collect your dahlias for floral arrangements in the morning or evening and never in the heat of the day.

Eranthis. Best known as Winter Aconites, the little flowers when cut are invaluable for giving the finishing touch to the smaller flower arrangements.

The golden yellow buds set in a rosette of frilly, finely cut leaves are among the first to flower, often emerging through snow or hard frost as early as January in southern areas but a little later further north.

The flowers open up like buttercups and look charming in their green ruff which consists of bracts and not true leaves. The foliage, develops beside the flower stalk, appearing as the flowers open forming a delicate carpet of green.

Plant the little rhizomes immediately they are received for they do not like being out of the ground for any length of time. Choose positions near deciduous bushes or trees where they will get the maximum amount of winter sunshine and shade during the summer. Plant an inch deep in colonies setting the tubers about 2 to 3 in. apart.

Eranthis hymalis, with golden-yellow blooms on 3 in. stems, is the earliest to flower. *E. cilicica* has pinkish 4 in. stems and larger deeper yellow flowers which bloom a little later.

Eremurus. Often known as Foxtail lilies, these are good plants for the back of the border where they can be sheltered from high winds. The common name is given in reference to the tail-like flower spikes. Whilst they look remarkably good when planted alone, best effects are produced when they are grown among plants and shrubs. Their elongated spikes make them ideal for cutting where a particular tall decoration is being planned. They form a spreading horizontal rooting system so that care is needed not to damage the fleshy roots when cultivating the soil nearby. Young plants can be left in their flowering quarters for 3 or 4 years before they need be lifted and divided.

Planting time extends from October to November, covering the tubers with 4 in. of soil. An annual top dressing of loam and decayed manure will keep the plants in free flowering conditions.

There are several good species, all with strap-like leaves and tapering spikes of saucer-shaped flowers. Among these are *E. bungei*, with golden-yellow flowers appearing in June and July, *E. himalaicus* has spikes of white flowers with orange anthers from mid-May onwards, while *E. robustus elwesianus* has delicate pink flowers.

Unless specific colours are needed, the Shelford hybrids should be grown. These take in a wide range of beautiful colours produced on sturdy spikes.

Propagation is by carefully dividing the crowns in the autumn, although such divisions do not flower for a further 2 or 3 years. Seed can be sown in late summer or early spring. Keep the seedlings in the frame during the first winter.

Erythronium, otherwise known as the Dog's Tooth Violets give constant delight through March, April and May. The most familiar are the cyclamen-like flowers of E. dens-canis or Dog's Tooth Violet, for the mixtures of shades of clear pink, red, deep violet and white, all produce in March graceful and dainty reflexed petal blooms on 4 to 6 in. stems. They have the added attraction of lovely marbled leaves making attractive groups of foliage when flowering time is over.

Another species, native to California, is *E. tuolumnense* which produces 2 or 3 orchid-like flowers of rich buttercup-yellow on each 8-10 in. slender stem in April. The foliage is uniform green, glossy and unmottled and this species in particular makes a lovely cut flower.

Erythroniums are not difficult to grow although these woodland plants have small whitish bulbs which tend to dry up easily. They should, therefore, be planted upon receipt in the autumn, choosing slightly shady positions in rich soil, burying the bulbs 4-6 in. deep and always planting in groups. Do not disturb them, but leave them to bring you fresh delight year after year when they will provide interesting and unusual cut flowers.

Freesias. The delicate pastel freesias of remarkable fragrance you buy in florists shops can now be grown in your own garden. Specially prepared corms for outdoor cultivation are available in a glorious rainbow mixture.

Named after one F. H. Freese, these members of the iris family are natives of South Africa but no single pure species is cultivated these days. Since the beginning of this century, the Dutch have undertaken the selection and systematic hybridisation of freesias and the hybrids now available are really super flowers.

This is good news for every flower arranger for the blooms are every bit as colourful and sweetly scented as those commercially forced under glass for the florists. Outdoor freesias have sturdy stems 10-12 ins. high, making them suitable both for garden display and cutting.

By planting corms from mid-April you can have an abundance of elegant flowers in your garden from late July to October. They thrive in average garden loam which is well worked over and like sunny, sheltered positions. Plant the corms about 2 ins. deep and 2-3 ins. apart, remembering to water them regularly in dry weather, particularly during the early growing stages.

There is a whole range of lovely colours – white, pink, yellow, orange, red, mauve, purple and blue. Each stem bears about half a dozen erect trumpet-shaped flowers.

Fritillaria. Although not long lasting when cut, where something out of the ordinary and exotic-looking is required, these are strikingly attractive. Ideal grouped in sunny or shady borders or in rockeries, all varieties must be planted no later than October, in humus filled soil some 6 to 8 in. deep and about 12 in. apart, for April-May blooming. Plant the small bulbs in colonies in autumn on receipt, in cool spots in the garden. They can also be naturalised in grass where they seed themselves freely and can easily be grown in pots.

Fritillaria meleagris are delightful April flowering plants only 10 to 12 in. tall and known as ' Checkered Lilies ' or ' Snakeshead Fritillary '. They have six-pointed, squared-off, drooping bells, 2 or 3 of which appear on each leafy stem. They are available in mixtures of chartreusy tones, in reddish-browns and purples with deeper markings or in named varieties. A white form, alba, has creamy-white bells on slender stems. F. meleagris Aphrodite has almost pure white flowers, Artemis is a prettily chequered grey-purple, Charon is a very deep purple.

F. citrina is a dainty little gem from Asia Minor, flowering in late April on 9 in. stems. Its bell shaped blooms of pale yellow flushed green, are glossy inside. Available only from a very few suppliers is the more expensive, but very hardy, *F. pallidiflora*, a superb species from Siberia growing 8 to 12 in. tall with 3 to 12 bell-shaped flowers of pale greenish-yellow flecked brown showing in April.

For an inexpensive odd-fritillary plant *F. pinardii*, a small-flowered species with drooping campanulate flowers of dusty purplish-brown, flushed green. It does particularly well in the alpine house and when grown outdoors it welcomes a little winter protection. Flowering time is April.

Galanthus. Although almost everyone calls them Snowdrops botanically they are classified as galanthus which means 'Milk Flower'.

As early as January, the bulbs send up pearl-like buds protected by two green leaves. If it is cold, the buds will remain closed waiting for the warmth of the sun.

Snowdrops should be out of the ground as short a time as possible. The bulbs should be planted as available in September or October up to 4 ins. deep in light soils and about 6 ins. in heavy soils. They actually flourish in fairly solid, damp, heavy soil.

Snowdrops spread rapidly by bulb division and self seeding. If the clumps become too thick, they should be divided after flowering but before the foliage changes colour. They do well in sun or semi-shade and they can be planted with winter aconites and other small bulbs. Never cut the foliage, even if you use snowdrops as dainty cut flowers, but allow to ripen naturally.

Galanthus nivalis is the common or classic snowdrop species of European origin. Naturalised they form vast white carpets as early as January.

G. nivalis flore-pleno is an exquisite double form with large globular blooms. Both have 6 in. tall stems.

Specialist nurserymen have other forms such as *G. nivalis maximus*, a very large flowering variety of vigorous habit on 8 in. stems; and *G. nivalis* S. Arnott, the giant single snowdrop with sweetly scented large snow-white flowers on taller 10 in. stems. *G. nivalis viridiapice* is a handsome and robust cultivar producing green-tipped white globular flowers on 7 in. stems. *G. elwesii* has on 8 in. stems distinct and beautiful single flowers of globular shape, the inner segments of the white blooms marked a rich emerald-green.

Galtonia candicans is the botanical name of the Summer Hyacinth, that tall, conspicuous, sweetly-scented pure white flower that apart from size so resembles the familiar hyacinths of spring.

It is closely related to the hyacinths of the Middle East although this particular member of the lily family comes from South Africa. The large bulbs produce a tuft of large strap-shaped leaves and strong, erect flower spikes, on which in July and August appear loose racemes of 15 to 20 delicately scented and large drooping pure milky white bells. Stems, in contrast to the spring flowering hyacinths soar $2\frac{1}{2}$ to 4 ft. high.

Galtonia candicans likes sunny, well drained positions in the garden and appreciates a winter mulch of peat or leaf mould if not lifted. It is a marvellous subject for the back of the border, for planting among shrubs, for siting in clusters. Bulbs can be planted from late February into April 5 and 6 ins. deep and between 6 and 8 ins. apart. If you do not plan to lift them after the foliage has died down do double the space between bulbs.

Summer Hyacinths make excellent cut flowers and many gardeners grow them in the cutting garden or raise them in pots in the warm greenhouse. If potted in early spring, they will flower in the late summer.

Gladiolus. For a riot of colour in the garden and a succession of spikes for cutting few flowers compare with gladiolus universal leader of the summer flowering bulbs.

What's more you need not spend much, because many varieties are inexpensive for producing excellent flowers for the home and garden from July to September.

Today there are available types of gladioli for all purposes ranging from special beds and mixed border clumps to cut flowers, flower arrangements and exhibitions. Many types will be satisfactory for a combination of purposes.

The successful cultivation of all types of gladiolus is the same. Almost any soil will do, but to produce the best spikes and flowers, soil should be well enriched and also contain plenty of humus, supplied by compost, organic matter or peat. Always prepare the ground well in advance, digging at least 8 in. deep and working in

3 ozs. of a complete garden fertiliser per square yard. Do remember that gladiolus do not like freshly manured ground but soil manured for a previous crop is ideal.

When choosing planting sites select sunny situations and avoid wind swept positions. Gladioli make excellent decorative plants in beds or borders but don't plant them among tall plants in the herbaceous border or among shrubs. Those you want for cutting purposes can be planted in separate beds or in rows in the vegetable garden.

Planting can begin any time after frost is out of the ground and it is dry enough to work readily, usually from mid March. Succession planting may continue, at intervals of 2 to 4 weeks, as late as mid May for fine spikes in the autumn.

Place the corms 5 or 6 in. deep and about 8 in. apart in groups or clusters of a dozen or more. If your soil is heavy some sand placed underneath the corms will assist their drainage, but on lighter soils this should not be necessary. Shallow planting will lead to a lot of staking and many good spikes may be lost in heavy winds.

By mid-May the young shoots of the early plantings will begin to show above the soil. From then on the soil around the plants should be hoed frequently taking care not to snick the young shoots. Cultivation should be shallow to prevent damage to the new corms developing underground. If there is a dry spell in June or July, you should water the gladiolus regularly. One good soaking is much more effective than a number of sprinklings and gladiolus like an abundance of moisture. Mulching with compost or moist peat is helpful and also keeps down weeds.

Always leave at least 3 leaves when you cut gladiolus so that the developing young corms for the following season obtain sufficient nourishment. To produce healthy corms gladiolus like a spell of dry weather for about 6 weeks after they have finished flowering, by which time the foliage will have turned brown and they will be ready for lifting.

When lifting corms save all the small corms and cormlets. Label each sort carefully, and then cut off tops, an inch or so above the corms. Dry off for a few weeks then discard the husks and old remains and place the new corms in paper bags or ventilated boxes for winter. The very small cormlets can be planted in the spring close together in rows about 2 in. deep to produce larger specimens for the following year.

The large-flowered section provides the widest choice, it is the most adaptable and generally the most satisfying. They are easy to grow, the plants reaching 3½-5 ft. in height and ranging in colour from white to almost black. They are equally suited to garden decoration and cutting being particularly valuable where large arrangements are needed.

Large Flowered gladiolus can be timed to flower since the early flowering sorts bloom 90 days after planting, the mid season 100 days, and for the late flowering allow 120 days from time of planting.

For those who want to have a few smaller varieties with lighter, daintier and hooded flowers on 2-3 ft. stems in front of the taller large flowered varieties a good idea is to buy a mixture of Primulinus hybrids.

A newer race of small flowered known as Butterfly gladioli are becoming increasingly popular. They grow 3 ft. or so tall and each spike has 6 to 8 florets open at a time and the flowers are beautifully ruffled with vivid throat markings. Again collections can be bought relatively cheaply consisting of about ten very charming and blotched colours varieties, most useful for cutting.

Rather smaller growing than the Butterfly type is the group known as Miniature gladioli. This is a somewhat misleading name since they are not dwarf, but are about the same height as the Primulinus hybrids, the size of the flowers being a little smaller than the Butterflies. They are distinct in having heavily frilled and ruffled petals.

Much more recently introduced are the new Early Peacock Hybrids which are earlier flowering than the other types. The size of bloom, stem and height resembles that of the Primulinus but the petals are more pointed and reflexed. They are dainty and graceful being excellent for cutting.

The value of gladiolus as cut flowers cannot be over emphasised. They should be cut with a minimum of foliage when the bottom flowers are just opening and plunged into deep water in a cool place. The florets will gradually open all the way up the spike. As the blooms die they should be removed and the stem shortened. The last few flowers can always be used in small, shallow bowls very effectively.

The so-called Hardy gladiolus are altogether smaller than the other sections. They are often planted in sheltered positions out of doors in November or may be grown in pots in the frame or greenhouse.

Gladiolus nanus and its varieties have long been grown. *Colvillei*

The Bride is pure white; Peach Blossom, rosy pink; and Spitfire is a scarlet-red with a crimson blotch. Hardier than all of these is *Gladiolus byzantinus* which can be left in the ground undisturbed for years. The flowers are a crimson-wine colour. All of these hardy gladiolus flower from May onwards.

New varieties of gladiolus are introduced each year, but the following Large Flowered varieties are reliable, although they have been in cultivation for quite a long time.

Early: *Acca Laurentia*, orange; Flower Song, yellow; Memorial Day, purple; and Snow Princess, white. Mid season: Atlantic, garnet red; General Eisenhowever, pink; Sans Souci, red; and Morning Kiss, white. Late: Aristocrat, scarlet; Flower Dream, pink; Picardy, salmon pink and Johan van Konyenburg, bright red.

The Primulinus gladiolus are available in a very wide range of art shades and a mixture of these usually provides a grand display.

Hyacinths make superb, long lasting cut flowers. Although daffodils, tulips, irises and freesias top the list of spring flowers for home floral arrangements, sweetly scented hyacinths with their gorgeous long heads of dainty florets are becoming increasingly popular as more and more amateur flower arrangers discover their advantages.

No flower can equal the perfume of the hyacinth and whether the floral heads are completely or only partially filled with florets they are delightful from all angles. The stems are surprisingly sturdy, the blooms lasting well in water.

Hyacinths are attractive in floral arrangements whether used alone or in mixed arrangements with other spring flowers. A few will go a long way in any floral display.

The red, blue or mauve hyacinths will contrast well with yellow or cream coloured daffodils, while white and blue hyacinths will give a balance to the brilliance of many spring flowering subjects used for indoor decoration. Hyacinths also look well in a spring display of other bulbs particularly the gay tulipa hybrids. Even simple material such as yellow forsythia, primroses and wallflowers can be made into a striking display by the judicious use of hyacinths.

To keep the bulbs in good condition so that they produce flowers for several years running, they should be lifted as soon as the leaves have died down. Store them in a cool place during the summer for replanting in September, which should be in well drained ground that has been thoroughly dug over.

Few gardeners seem to appreciate what superb long lasting cut flowers hyacinths make. Thus second year bulbs are best allocated to a portion of the garden where their blooms can be used for cutting. Hyacinths are reasonably priced enough to enable gardeners to afford renewing the bulbs every year for garden display. This also provides an opportunity to try different varieties and create different colour schemes in the garden or window box or in terrace tubs or containers.

There is no need to purchase the largest sizes of hyacinths for the garden. For outdoors use, second, third and bedding grades which give excellent results and are cheaper than the exhibition or first size bulbs used for indoor forcing. They will produce flower spikes almost as large as the larger bulbs because they grow more slowly outdoors and have a longer time to develop strong roots.

Among good named varieties are: white – L'Innocence, Carnegei, Arentine Arendsen; creamy-white – Edelweiss; yellow – City of Haarlem, Yellow Hammer; orange – Orange Boven, Salmonetta; pink – Lady Derby, La Victoire, Pink Pearl, Princess Margaret; red – Cyclops, Jan Bos, Tubergen's Scarlet, Amsterdam. Mauve and purple – Amethyst, Distinction, Lord Balfour, Purple King; blue – Delft's Blue, Queen of the Blues, Marie, Myosotis, Bismarck, Grand Maitre.

Once you have started to grow hyacinths for cut flowers you will never want to be without these lovely blooms in the house.

Hippeastrum. One of the most satisfying of bulbs any amateur can grow is the Hippeastrum often known as Amaryllis.

The bulbs of the Giant Amaryllis, correctly classified as *hippeastrum* but rising to spectacular popularity as amaryllis, are enormous, often 4 or 5 ins. in diameter. They are brown, tunicated, with flattened leaf scars at the top and semi-dry roots at the bottom and more often than not you can see the green tips of the leaves or even the flattened flower buds just emerging.

Amaryllis bulbs have become popular since recent extensive hybridisation in Holland has increased the number of giant varieties on the market. These hybrids show refinement in texture and substance of the petals, richness and subtlety of colour, and the coarseness of the earlier hybrids has disappeared. Excellent as pot plants the spikes can, of course, be cut and used in floral arrangements.

The massive lily-like flowers – often bigger than a man's outstretched hand – are superb. Each fat stalk, tall and light green, bears up to 4 to 6 of these giant flowers and the larger bulbs can have 2 or 3 stalks and up to a dozen flowers or more. And they come in the most beautiful of colours: pure white, all shades of red, vermilion, orange-red, scarlet, deep red, bright red with a pure white star in the centre, rose, salmon, orange, pink, salmon-pink, violet-pink, cherry and even striped.

The flower stalks usually appear before the bright green strap-shaped leaves, but the latter develop quickly as the flowers open. Occasionally leaves will appear simultaneously with the flowers or even precede them. The flowers last 3 or 4 weeks if kept under cool conditions.

Hymenocallis narcissiflora sometimes known as the Peruvian Daffodil or the Summer Daffodil is often catalogued as Ismene calathina, having glorious umbels of 2 to 5 large, pure white trumpet-shaped blooms of great fragrance.

This species is almost hardy and an improved hybrid called ' Advance ' has been developed and is available to British garden-ers. They look rather like large fantastic daffodils in full bloom, for each flower so white and fragrant, is trumpet-shaped with long narrow reflexed segments. They bloom in July and August on stems 18 in. or more tall, with decorative long leaves.

The bulbs of both must be kept dry and warm in winter, and not planted in the garden until late May. Choose sunny sheltered positions and bury the bulbs 5 to 6 in. deep in well drained soil, rich in humus, consisting of a mixture of peat, leaf mould and sand. They will, of course, thrive in pots in a cool greenhouse.

Peruvian Daffodils grow very quickly, the first flowers appearing as early as a month after planting. The plants must be lifted before the first frosts and the bulbs stored in boxes filled with dry peat or sand and kept in a dry, warm store until planting time comes round again.

Spectacular in the summer garden, Peruvian Daffodils also make long lasting cut flowers.

Irises Tall and Dwarf. Dutch iris are probably the largest cul-tivated group of the huge iris genus, popular not only with gardeners who like them best in clumps in the rockery, in borders or to set off evergreen shrubs, but with housewives who find them invaluable for floral decoration in the home.

Dutch iris are widely grown commercially as cut flowers, being forced under glass and are available in the shops from before Christmas to well into May.

Aptly enough, the word ' iris ' means ' rainbow ' and Dutch iris in no way detract from this definition, for they are more colourful than any other types of iris. They come in white, yellow, blue,

Scabious caucasica

Thalictrum dipterocarpum

Begonia Rex

Tithonia Torch

Cosmea Fiesta

mauve and purple varieties with contrasting standards and falls, many varieties beautifully blotched.

They are particularly fine plants with larger flowers than the somewhat similar Spanish iris, and sturdier and stronger in growth. Compared with English iris, the Dutch iris are not only more colourful (there are no yellows among English iris) but boast more exotic and delicate blooms with more graceful stems and foliage.

Dutch iris produce large flowers of great substance on tall stems ranging from 20 to 24 ins. in height. They are long lasting and the first of the cultivated iris to bloom. When planted outdoors in September and October some 3 to 4 ins. deep and about 5 to 8 ins. apart, they flower as early as mid-May, depending upon the season, or in June. Spanish iris bloom at least a fortnight later and English iris do not flower until late June or July.

Dutch iris are hardy and accommodating plants which will flourish everywhere in a well drained soil and under almost any conditions. For best results plant them in sunny positions in soil with plenty of humus. They need little care and attention, and need not be lifted, for the little bulbils that develop around the mother bulb will flower too after 2 or 3 years. If taken up when the foliage dies down the bulbs should be kept dry until it is time to replant them in September. Normally lifting is unnecessary until such time as a site becomes overcrowded and division of the bulbs and replanting is advisable.

Nothing can beat Dutch iris for late May or June cutting or colour in the garden. Gardeners will find the varieties Wedgwood and Imperator particularly easy to force in the cool greenhouse. When using iris from your garden or greenhouse for floral arrangements cut them in bud, just as they are showing colour, and they will last in vases for an extraordinary long time.

Iris hispanica, better known as Spanish iris can be treated similarly to the Dutch varieties. They are a little later in flowering but the mixture of varieties will prove first class for cutting.

English irises are also valuable in mixture flowering finishing later than the Spanish and most useful for cutting, retaining their beauty in water for a long time.

Dwarf Iris. These flower months before their bigger sisters and are inclined to be often overlooked. Yet they are as enchanting as butterflies and provide an incredible range of colour early in the year.

For best results they should be planted in autumn about 4 in. deep and 4 ins. apart in semi-shaded positions where their rich

K

colourings are more pronounced and their flowering period is lengthened than when grown in full sun. The secret of cultivating them is to keep them moist while they are growing and dry and warm during their summer resting period.

There is a marvellous choice of species iris now available including the sweetly scented *I. bakeriana* which has slender lavender-blue standards and unusually marked falls of ivory heavily dotted deep purple. They grow 4 in. tall, and flower early in February. Their stiff leaves are well ribbed.

I. danfordiae has slightly scented lemon-yellow blooms spotted dark green-grey down the throat. The dainty flowers on 3 in. stems last well when cut. The bulb sometimes splits up into many off-shoots which themselves flower in 3 to 4 years. This means the same bulbs cannot be depended on to flower in succession again.

Ixia, the African Corn Lily is very free flowering producing on strong, wiry 16-18 in. stems, graceful heads of delightfully coloured blooms in a wide range of brilliant colours. Flowering outdoors in June and July, each stem boasts 6 or more flowers of striking beauty, most having a prominent dark centre. The narrow grassy foliage is an added attraction.

You can buy ixias in beautiful mixtures of yellow, orange, pink, red and purple. Plant them outdoors about the end of October or November, about 3 ins. deep and 3 ins. apart in a sandy loam and in a sunny position where they can be left undisturbed. In cold winters provide a cover of straw or bracken to protect the top growth.

For late spring or early summer flowering, plant ixias between September and November, 5 or 7 corms in a 6 in. pot containing a mixture of sand, leaf mould and good garden soil. The pots should then be buried to their rims in peat or ashes in a frame or in the shelter of a wall and protected from frost by glass or straw. In February, when the shoots appear they can be brought into a cool greenhouse and placed on a sunny shelf. They like a fresh, cool atmosphere and should be kept moist by regular watering.

Ixiolirion. Frequently referred to as 'Ixia lilies' these two subjects are very different from each other. Ixias are members of the Iridaceae family while Ixiolirions are members of the Amaryllidaceae family and come from the steppes of Central Asia.

Both deserve to be more widely grown, and they bring a new dimension in grace and beauty to the garden after the tulips cease flowering. They are a welcome asset to the rockery or border and both are ideal as cut flowers and they can be cultivated in the cool greenhouse for earlier flowering. Ixiolirions flower in the garden towards the end of May and throughout June, producing on thin, stiff stems 12-16 ins. tall, a number of handsome, rich, violet-blue tubular flowers in form much like hyacinth florets. The long narrow greenish-grey leaves are also very attractive.

Ixiolirions like warm, sheltered positions and rich well drained sandy soil. Plant them 3 ins. deep and about 3-4 ins. apart in October where they can be left undisturbed. Like ixias, they appreciate protective covering in the winter. You'll find they make the most elegant of cut flowers, showy and long lasting.

Of the few species available, I. pallasii is the most outstandingly suited to British gardens. They produce lovely large flowers of violet blue tinged with rose, and with a darker coloured band down the centre of each segment.

For cultivation in the cool greenhouse, grow them just as you would ixias or freesias.

Leucojum, better known as Snowflakes, their cultivation presents no problem, because they adapt themselves to almost any soil and every kind of aspect although the Summer Snowflakes welcome rich, moist soil. The bulbs should be planted in the autumn 3 to 4 in. deep, with 3-4 in. between the bulbs.

The Spring Snowflake is *Leucojum vernum*, flowering in March and April, and is about 6 in. tall, the tunicated bulbs producing lovely little white bells tipped with pale green, somewhat larger than the blooms of the Snowdrop. They are particularly valuable for massing and naturalising in almost any situation although they like somewhat shady positions.

The Summer Snowflake, *Leucojum aestivum*, flowers in April and May, and like the Spring Snowflake produces umbels of 4 to 8 white flowers, a bit larger and of nodding habit, but on stems 15-18 in. tall. They flourish best in a cool place.

L. aestivum Gravetye, an improved form, flowers simultaneously, its elegant drooping white bells tipped green, making it a lovely cut flower.

Lilies. Developments in the breeding of lilies in recent years have brought this magnificent genus of beautiful and graceful plants into the realm of the average amateur gardener.

Many lilies are as easy to grow as hyacinths or daffodils, largely due to the work of hybridisers who have bred new strains by inter-crossing many different types of wild lilies, then carefully selecting the best and re-hybridising and selecting again until new varieties were achieved which are more vigorous and adaptable than ever before both for garden decoration and for cutting.

These new hybrids are strong, sturdy, tolerant, adaptable and resistant to disease, while they introduce beautiful new colours and shapes so that together with the many species available, most of which are very easy to grow, the gardener now has a tremendous choice.

Lilies vary in height from $1\frac{1}{2}$ ft. to 10 ft. Some flowers are cup-shaped, others being bowl-shaped. Many are fragrant and the colour range is wide, though there is no blue. The flowering season extends from the end of May to October.

There are now so many types and varieties of lilies that attractive places can be found for them almost anywhere in the garden. Far from being delicate and fragile many lilies are the hardiest of all summer flowering bulbs. They are surprisingly inexpensive and there is no reason why every garden should not have a selection. They can be left undisturbed to bring beauty to the garden each year.

In size, colour, form of flower, fragrance and flowering time, lilies offer great scope to the gardener. The secret of success involves good drainage, a cool rooting medium in open porous soil, protection from cold winds and for most lilies, shade from hot sun near the roots. These conditions are easiest to provide by planting bulbs in herbaceous borders or among rhododendrons, azaleas or other shrubs.

Lilies can be planted in November and December, but it is best to wait for early spring before planting stem rooting types. Lilies prefer neutral or slightly acid soils which most gardens have in this country but a few like *L. candidum, henryi* and *martagon* not only like but need lime.

Prepare the ground for lilies in advance by turning it over to a depth of 12-18 in. and incorporating plenty of humus and organic matter. Remove broken or bruised scales and when planting put plenty of sand round the bulbs to help drainage and discourage slugs. Base rooting lilies like *candidum, martagon* and *pardalinum* should be planted 4-6 in. deep and about 10-12 in. apart.

Stem rooting lilies can be planted 7 or 8 in. deep in light soil but in most gardens 4-6 in. deep is enough. It is better to make little mounds of earth above the bulbs rather than plant them too deep. As soon as the stem rooting lilies begin to grow put a 4 in. layer of leaf mould on top and keep mulching during the growing period which will keep the stem roots active.

Lily stems are usually sturdy enough without staking. In the autumn all lilies welcome a mulch of peat or leaf mould and a fresh top dressing will be appreciated each spring.

While lily lovers may not be keen to spoil their garden display it is easily possible to devote a small area for growing lilies for cut flower purposes. Florists are still rather conservative and tend to concentrate on *Lilium longiflorum* and its hybrids.

Lilium auratum the Golden-rayed lily of Japan, is stem-rooting and produces highly scented pure white flowers with brown and crimson spots, each petal marked with a golden ray. The flowers on stems 4-5 ft. high often measure 10-12 in. across and bloom August to October. There are several beautifully marked varieties.

Lilium candidum is a base rooting lily and the oldest lily culti- vated in Europe. Known as the Madonna lily this snow white beauty flowers in June and July on 4-5 ft. stems and likes full sun. Plant only an inch or so deep in early autumn.

Lilium hansonii, the yellow martagon lily, thrives in any position in well drained soil. The pendant flowers are bright golden-yellow with crimson-maroon spots and reflexing petals. It flowers in June on robust 3-4 ft. stems.

Lilium henryi is a graceful tall, stem rooting lily growing 6 to 8 ft. tall and flowering profusely in August and September. The spikes carry up to 18 large orange-yellow flowers with reflexed petals and prominent stamens. They like lime and appreciate deep planting.

Lilium longiflorum is stem rooting producing lovely trumpet- shaped flowers of pure waxy white on 3 ft. stems in June and July. It does best in sheltered positions.

Lilium martagon, the Turk's Cap lily, has handsome purple flowers spotted with various shades of purple-red on 3-4 ft. stems in June and July. It does best in sheltered positions. It likes partially shaded positions in the border. These flowers are effective in providing a softening touch to an otherwise gaudy display.

Lilium maxwell is a beautiful hybrid of the *willmottiae* type, the orange-red flowers with brownish-red spots, appearing in July. Stem rooting, it likes partially shaded positions. Plant up to 7 or 8 in. deep for it grows 6-7 ft. tall.

Mid-Century hybrids. This is a fabulous group of lilies. Flowering in June and July, the stems do not require staking unless exposed. Plant the bulbs 4 or 5 in. deep or 6 in. deep in light soil in either sunny or partially shaded positions. Named varieties include: Enchantment, cherry red, 2-3 ft.; Harmony, rich bright orange, 2-3 ft.; and Tangelo, orange, 2½ ft.

Lilium pardalinum, the Californian lily, bears 12 to 20 recurving orange-red flowers with maroon spots on 5 ft. stems in July. Of pardalinum type are the Bellingham hybrids, a strain containing a wide colour range from clear yellow through orange-yellow to bright orange-red mostly spotted rusty brown. The 6-7 ft. stems carry as many as 20 flowers on a pyramidal head. These long-lasting beauties are ideal both for cutting and for informal woodland planting.

Lilium regale, one of the most popular. Easy to grow. It has strong 3-5 ft. stems crowned with large trumpet-shaped flowers, externally streaked soft brown, pure white interior with golden-yellow shading and golden anthers. This sweetly-scented lily blooms in July and prefers sunny positions.

Lilium speciosum is a glorious Japanese species with pure white, crimson and pink spotted flowers of exquisite fragrance. Thriving in sun or partial shade they flower in August and September on 3-5 ft. stems. Stem rooting, they deserve to be grown more extensively. L. speciosum album is glistening pure white with golden anthers; roseum is heavily spotted pink; and rubrum, well spotted carmine-red.

Lilium tenuifolium is regarded as the daintiest of all lilies. In June it bears up to 10 glossy and brilliant Turk's Cap flowers on slender $1\frac{1}{2}$ ft. stems with narrow grassy foliage.

Lilium tigrinum, the lime hating Tiger lily is invaluable as a border plant. Its imposing spikes of richly coloured Turk's Cap flowers, red with purple spots, bloom in August and September on 2-4 ft. stems. L. tigrinum fortunei giganteum has a large head of orange flowers spotted glossy black on sturdy 4-5 ft. stems.

Lilium umbellatum is the group name of a showy section of easily grown lilies of rare beauty for the garden or cold greenhouse. They flower in late June. Many varieties of this stem rooting species are available ranging in height from $1\frac{1}{2}$ to 3 ft.

To be really effective lilies should be cut with a long stem which means removing most of the leaves. If too many stems are taken from any plant it makes it difficult for the bulb to build up nourishment for the following season.

Particularly in the case of pure white lilies, it is advisable to remove the stamens since these are so rich in yellow pollen which is apt to spread all over the petals causing discoloration as well as marking the surroundings where the lilies are placed.

Lily of the Valley. The Latin name of this well-known plant is convallaria but the common name gives a good indication of its preference for moisture and partial shade, although of course, it will not succeed under water-logged conditions. The old type Lily of the Valley, *C. majalis*, is reckoned to be a native of Britain, although now rare in the wild state. There are also a number of other species and forms which, however, are much less well-known.

Although the pure white Lily of the Valley is the only well-known variety nowadays there is reason to believe that in the forests there were, early in the 19th century, pink and red sorts, as well as an unusual double red form which appears practically unknown today.

In addition to *C. majalis*, with its several forms, *C. globosa* and its two varieties *japonica* and *latifolia* are sometimes to be obtained as well as *C. alba marginata striata* with its attractive variegated foliage, all flowering outdoors during May and June.

As to general culture, Lily of the Valley require partial shade to be entirely successful, and new beds should be deeply dug, with old manure, peat and leaf mould added, while weathered soot is a useful addition. Generously prepared sites enable the plants to continue to flower well over many years and they need only be disturbed and thinned when they become really over-crowded. If the crowns are spaced 3 or 4 in. apart, they will have ample room to develop.

It is most helpful to apply an annual top dressing of really decayed manure and compost material when the foliage has died down in September. This treatment will ensure the continued production of large bells instead of the small ones gathered from neglected plants. When picking the flowers, always leave at least one leaf, since the foliage acts as lungs for the plants, and it is partially through the work of the leaves that the following year's flowers develop.

Lily of the Valley respond to forcing treatment. The pips are packed closely in 6 in. deep pots or boxes of sandy compost or peat with just the points left exposed. Plunged in leaf mould, sandy soil or fine weathered ashes, speedy rooting will occur. If the pots are then brought into a moist atmosphere, where the temperature remains about 75 deg. F. and kept from the light, they will soon push out their flower spikes, being then brought into full light and given plenty of water. From that time the temperature should be gradually lowered so as to give the plants more strength.

Many specialist growers first place the retarded pips in a hot bath with a temperature about 80 deg. F. Left there for twelve hours or more, they are then planted immediately on being brought out of the water.

When Lily of the Valley are left in position for some years to provide a regular cutting bed, two important points to remember are the annual top dressing of old manure or leaf mould and the refraining from cutting too much foliage. In this connection, it is well worth while bedding out a patch of crowns solely for their foliage; then it will not matter if these particular plants fail to flower.

Montbretias. These decorative plants of elegant growth have long been grown in this country and continue to be deservedly popular. South African in origin and sometimes offered in catalogues under the name of tritonias, the fibrous rooted corms produce narrow leaves and graceful arching flowering spikes.

In some old cottage gardens will be found clumps of the older hardy montbretias and of these *M. pottsii* is a particularly reliable sort. Growing about 2½ ft. high, it produces dainty spikes of glowing vermilion shaded golden yellow. The much branched spikes of *M. crocosmaeflora* are well furnished with orange-red flowers. Etoile de Feu is a charming red cultivar, with a bright yellow centre, the spikes often attaining to 3½ ft. Prometheus is a vigorous grower with large open flowers of golden orange.

All of these have been rather put in the shade by the Earlham Hybrids which originated at Earlham Hall, Norwich. A great advance on the older types, being taller and stronger in growth, the individual flowers often measure 3 or 4 in. in diameter.

Always decorative in the border it is hardly surprising that the Earlhams have become very popular for cutting. Among the largest of these hybrids are Comet, a beautiful rich golden yellow, each petal being banded crimson; Fiery Cross, has stems of 3 ft. bearing flowers of brilliant orange with large primrose centre. Hades, vermilion-scarlet with gold throat and small crimson blotch; Henry VIII is particularly handsome and strong growing often reaching 3½ ft. The broad petalled flowers are an attractive velvety scarlet colour, shading down to gold, thus making it a choice sort. Lady Wilson is bright yellow overlaid with an orange sheen. Mephistopheles, the brightest of all, has showy petals of vivid scarlet marked crimson-maroon, the reverse side being a flaming red. A mixture of Earlham Hybrids produces a delightful display the colours blending in a remarkable way.

The older types of montbretias are normally planted in the autumn. The best way with the Earlhams is to plant in February or early March when the corms should be given a deep, well drained loamy soil to which leaf mould has been added. A surface covering of peat or litter gives light protection and provides a summer mulch which is of great value later in the year.

Plant the corms 3 ins. deep in a sunny situation.

Muscari or Grape Hyacinths are among the most adaptable of bulbs. With flowering time stretching from March to May according to variety, they are ideal for the rock garden and the sunny border. They can be naturalised in wild gardens or woodlands, particularly M. armeniacum and the little clusters of close-set bells atop sturdy stems looking like an up-ended bunch of grapes, are superb when cut and grouped with the early daffodils, both white and yellow varieties.

Although of dwarf habit, ranging from 5-8 ins. in height, muscari make delightful and long lasting cut flowers. Among the earliest to flower in March are the 5 in. tall *M. azureum*, with dainty spikes of soft azure blue and its white variety album. They contrast pleasantly with snowdrops.

The best known Grape Hyacinth is probably *M. armeniacum* with its clusters of deep cobalt blue to blue-violet rounded bells, tightly packed on 8 in. stems, 4 or 5 flower stalks coming from each bulb. This strongly scented variety begins to produce its large flowers in April.

M. botryoides has neat erect foliage appearing with the flowers. It is often listed as a bright blue variety, *M. botryoides coeruleum*. *M. botryoides album* produces in April, a neatly compact cone of fragrant white flowers, looking like an elongated bunch of miniature pearls, appearing on 6-8 in. spikes. It is lovely planted on its own at the base of a clump of grey birch trees or grouped with blue muscari in other choice open spots in the garden.

M. tubergenianum sends up a tightly compact, somewhat oval cluster of flowers from mid-April, with the bells almost completely closed, and in two colours. This variety has been nicknamed the Oxford and Cambridge muscari, for when in full flower, the top half is bright clear blue and the lower part deep blue. The buds are a distinct turquoise blue. It flowers on strong 8 in. spikes.

M. plumosum which makes such an unusual and excellent cut flower, should be planted rather closer together than most varieties so that the feathery amethyst plumes on 8 in. stems support each other. This variety is often known as the 'feather hyacinth'.

Narcissus. This genus is generally reckoned to be named after the youth in Greek legend who changed into this flower. This subject has been the theme of writers and poets for many years and it is really poetic licence which has made the name daffodil synonymous with narcissus.

Today we usually think of the daffodil as being the flower with a trumpet, although this is of course one of the sections of the large narcissus family. This family has now been divided into a number of groups so that the varieties in each group can easily be identified. Generally speaking narcissus are recognised as the varieties having a cup or corona as distinct from a trumpet, although the size of the cup varies considerably.

Narcissus can be left in the ground for several years and to ensure a good display each year, it is a good plan to enrich the soil with humus and incorporate bone meal at the rate of 1 oz. per square ft. before planting. In subsequent years bone meal can be used at the same rate on any areas planted with narcissi by merely scattering it on the ground in late winter, allowing the rain to wash it down to the roots of the bulbs.

Narcissus flower prolifically. A cluster of a dozen will increase in 2 or 3 years to produce as many as 50 to 100 blooms. Thus when planting it is advisable to allow 6 to 9 in. between the bulbs. As to depth of planting, 5 to 6 in. of soil on top of the bulbs is required for their proper development. Plant an inch deeper in lighter soil than in heavy soil.

Narcissus should be kept growing after flowering. Pick off old blossoms before they start to make seed pods. It is a mistake to cut off leaves before they die down. It takes a good month or more for the leaves of narcissus to complete their vegetative cycle after the flower has faded. The leaves should be allowed to wither naturally before being removed after they have turned yellow.

Grass where narcissus bulbs are naturalised should not be cut until the leaves are mature. In borders, annual flowers and nearby perennials will fill the space in the summer when the daffodils die down. You can, of course, turn the leaves over and fasten them with a rubber band or soft twine if the dying leaves interfere with other plants. This action however often gives an artificial look to the garden.

The small or miniature daffodils are cultivated in exactly the same way, and should be planted so that they are covered with 3-4 in. of soil and they should be spaced 3-5 in. apart depending upon height of stem and size of flower. When planting bigger narcissus in a cutting bed, cover them with at least 4 in. of soil and space them 6 in. apart in even rows about 8-10 in. apart across the bed. Plant different types and varieties and label each variety as it is planted.

Narcissus, like tulips, have the flower already formed inside the bulb that is planted in the autumn. But it is possible for more than one flower to be inside a daffodil bulb. With narcissus bulbs there is no size but there are those which are called double-nosed. These bulbs have 2 distinct points on the top, which indicates that 2 flowers will develop in the spring. Such a bulb is in effect 2 bulbs fused together.

Narcissus are amazingly adaptable. They are easy to grow, require very little care and will flourish in just about any soil in any garden. Put them in sun or shade, near water or rock ledge, clustered in rough grass under trees, they thrive everywhere. The beauty of the narcissus is unquestioned and they look at home wherever they are sited on their own or with other flowers. The bulbs should be planted in clusters or groups of no less than 5 of the same variety.

Narcissus will make a carpet of bloom under choice flowering trees and shrubs in focal spots in the shrub and flower borders. Since varieties flower at different times, many colourful combinations with other garden flowers can be planned.

There are many problem spots around the garden where conventional garden flowers cannot be grown. Most common of these is in the shade of deciduous trees where the ground is not cultivated. This is an ideal place to naturalise narcissus – in other words, plant them in large informal groups as if they were growing wild. Trumpet and large and small-cup varieties are particularly suited to naturalising as are the sweetly scented Poet's narcissus.

Narcissus have the stamina to compete with rough grass growing in an unmown area beyond the lawn. Here the narcissus foliage can ripen, as it should, before the tall grass is cut like hay.

When naturalising narcissus avoid planting bulbs in rows or in clumps having an even outline. Scatter the bulbs on the ground at random planting them where they fall, always ensuring that they are spaced about 8 to 10 in. apart. Holes are made with the sharp blade of pick or similar tool. Naturalising hundreds of bulbs in the lawn or rough grass can be done quickly in this way. They can be fed by spreading the bone meal directly on the grass. This should be done in winter before new growth is up, so as to avoid damage to tender shoots.

Narcissus make excellent long lasting cut flowers and every

gardener should have a cutting bed in some out of the way part of the garden.

Start planting narcissus early in September and ensure that all kinds are planted by the end of October at the very latest. They will thrive in any well cultivated and well drained garden soil. Stagnant water is injurious to them but they don't mind moist soil. Where there is room a cutting bed can be made in the vegetable garden which overcomes the objection sometimes raised that cutting the blooms spoils garden display.

Narcissus will flower better if their bulbs are left peacefully in the ground from year to year. The clumps may be divided once the leaves have died down after 3 or 4 years. When doing this, it is best to replant bulbs immediately or in any case, no later than August.

Although new varieties of narcissus, including trumpet daffodils are regularly introduced, some of the older sorts remain unbeatable for cutting purposes. Among these are the following.

Daffodils. Yellow Trumpets: Golden Harvest, King Alfred, Kingscourt.
Bicolour Trumpets: Queen of Bicolours, Spring Glory, Patria.
White Trumpets: Beersheba, Mount Hood.

Narcissus. Yellow petals, coloured cup: Carbineer, Carlton, Fortune, Flower Records.
Pink varieties: Mrs. R. O. Backhouse, Rose of Tralee.
All white narcissus: Follies, Castella.
Double narcissus: Irene Copeland, Texas, Van Sion.
Jonquils: *Odorus rugulosus*, Trevithian.
Narcissus poetaz: having several flowers on strong stems, Geranium, Primrose Beauty.
Poeticus: Actaea, Old Pheasant's Eye.

Apart from these larger flowering varieties there are a number of small growing species which are first class for cutting, growing only 3-5 in. high. These include: *N. bulbocdium conspicuus, canaliculatus, cyclamineus, lobularis, juncifolius* and the *triandrus* varieties. *Narcissus minimus* is a miniature yellow trumpet daffodil only 3 in. high. Flowering in February and March, it is superb for miniature arrangements.

Ornithogalum thyrsoides. This lovely plant which carries great clusters of white star-shaped flowers from July to September, was dubbed the Chincherinchee by the local inhabitants of its native land, South Africa, because of the sound made when the dry stems rubbed together in the wind.

Nearly everyone calls it the chincherinchee with only professional horticulturists and botanists referring to it by its official name of Ornithogalum thyrsoides. This is understandable and in any case, Chincherinchee is a rather nice sounding name.

The most remarkable attribute of the Chincherinchee is that it probably lives longer in water than any other flower. If the flowers are picked in bud and water is changed regularly, a bunch of Chincherinchees may last up to 6 weeks with every bud opening.

Each bulb throws up 2 or 3 sturdy stems 1½-2 ft. tall bearing triangular-shaped clusters of 30 to 35 beautiful white star-shaped flowers with long yellow stamens. Gather the stems as soon as the buds show colour and so enjoy a long lasting display indoors. Flower spikes are normally available in succession from July until September.

The leaves do not develop fully when grown out of doors and therefore the bulbs starved of nutrition, will not flower a second year. Since the bulbs are inexpensive it is worth buying a fresh supply each spring. If you grow them in a cold frame or greenhouse the bulbs will flower regularly every year.

Chincherinchees should be planted from March to May in well drained soil in warm sunny spots in the garden placing them 2-3 in. deep and about 4-6 ins. apart.

Oxalis. This name is derived from the Greek ' oxys ' meaning ' sharp ' or ' sour ' because of the bitter taste of some of the leaves of this tuberous and rhizomous genus, but they are among the sweetest little gems you can have in your summer garden and give an exotic look to any flower arrangement.

Oxalis deppei, commonly known as the ' Good Luck plant ' or the ' Four-leaved Clover ', is the species all gardeners can grow to bring radiant colour to the rockery or front of the border and for indoor displays.

It has 6-12 in. stems bearing dainty clusters of copper-red flowers appearing from July to September, and contrasting well with the attractive foliage. The broad leaves have four red-spotted leaflets each, like those of red clover which accounts for the common names of this species.

Plant them in March-April in warm garden borders or semi-shaded positions, setting the tubers 4-6 ins. deep and the same distance apart in well drained soil. The plant grows prolifically and you can obtain an ever increasing show of colour by dividing them in October.

Puschkinia. This pretty scilla-like plant of the lily family is native to the Caucusus and Asia Minor and was named puschkinia after the Russian botanist, Count Puschkin.

Drifts of these in partially shaded positions create a pleasing effect in the spring garden. The fluffy striped bells resemble scillas each small 4 to 6 in. stem bearing a cluster of a dozen or more pale silver-blue blooms, each segment lightly marked with a slightly darker blue line. There is only one known species in cultivation, *P. scilloides*, which is listed in bulb catalogues as *P. libanotica*, the Lebanon or Striped Squill. The white form, *P. libanotica alba*, is pure white, flowering at the same time. The small tunicated bulbs should be planted in autumn about 3 in. deep and 3 in. apart, where they can be left undisturbed. They also like sunny spots in the front of the border or rockery. The flowers are excellent for including in small arrangements and posies.

Puschkinia can be grown indoors like crocus. Plant them in rich, light soil in October, about 1 to 2 in. deep and a $\frac{1}{2}$ to 1 in. apart, in 5 in. pots. Plunge the pots outdoors in the garden or place in a cool cellar for 6 or 7 weeks before bringing them indoors to a cool living room.

Ranunculus. Few plants produce a more gorgeous effect in the border in May, June and July than the multi-coloured ranunculus with their large double flowers in magnificent pastel shades.

This large genus of fibrous and tuberous rooted plants derives its name from the Latin ' rana ', which means ' frog ', apparently because so many species grew in damp places similar to those inhabited by frogs.

The tuberous rooted ranunculuses are the most beautiful and are highly valued by knowledgeable gardeners as well as professional florists. They are useful for beds, borders, cut flowers and greenhouses.

All thrive in ordinary soil but they like moisture as well as shelter from the north. Plant them in sunny positions about $1\frac{1}{2}$ ins. deep and 6-8 ins. apart claws downward, but not before the end of February. They grow from 18-24 ins. tall, producing many double globe-like yellow, orange, scarlet, crimson, pink or white blooms. Combined with anemones, or planted alone, ranunculus are splendidly colourful and particularly effective as cut flowers.

Once you've got ranunculuses in your garden you'll never want to be without them. They need not be lifted after the foliage has died down but for season after season of gorgeous flowers, give them a dressing of organic fertiliser each autumn and protect them carefully from frosts and winter cold by placing bracken, straw or similar material over the site during very severe weather.

While soil preferably gritty and peaty, should be saturated with water before planting ranunculus, claws down, about 2 ins. deep and 6-8 ins. apart, all sites must be well drained. Do not water too much after planting until the plants are full grown. They make very effective cut flowers and can also be grown in a cool greenhouse if planted in pots and plunged outdoors until well rooted. Flowers range in colour from white to deepest purple and running through the whole spectrum of yellow, pink, red, scarlet and orange. The plants have deeply scalloped leaves and each stem is crowned with a magnificent flower 1-4 ins. in diameter, according to type and variety.

There are four main types of ranunculuses:

French ranunculus. This type was evolved in France about 1875 and later the semi-double flowers were improved by the Dutch. A vigorous strain with large blooms in many delightful shades, all have a central black blotch.

Paeony-flowered ranunculus. The large double or semi-double flowers of this strain were first developed in the early 1900's by an Italian horticulturist, blooming from May into July on 10-14 in. stems they thrive in a sunny, well-drained border. While they can be planted in sheltered positions in December and given winter protection, it is usually best to wait until February before planting.

Persian Ranunculus. This type has medium or small flowers either single or double with stems 10-16 ins. high. Buy them in mixed or named varieties and plant from the end of February in sunny positions.

Turban ranunculus. Hardiest of the four types and available for planting from December to April. They have large, globular or rose-shaped double or semi-double flowers on 9-12 in. tall stems. Extremely showy when planted in mixture in sunny sheltered positions.

Scillas or 'squills' are particularly lovely seen in masses and drifts and are effective when planted in the border in clusters near early flowering bright species tulips or miniature narcissi. They are also ideal for including in spring floral arrangements.

Scilla bifolia is the earliest to flower, sometimes in February sending its small nodding star-like bells of deep blue on 4 to 6 in.

wiry stems right through any snow. *S. bifolia rosea*, about the same height, has pale pink star-shaped flowers studded with golden stamens. Both like a protection in cold winters.

S. siberica is the best known species, its prussian-blue bells intensified by grey blue anthers on 3 to 4 in. stems. *S. siberica alba* is the very fine pure white form, a little less robust than the blue species. *S. siberica* Spring Beauty is a remarkable improvement on the common form with flowers twice the size on 6 in. stems. The bells are bright china blue with a touch of ultramarine. The flowers are sterile and thus last a long time in bloom. They are produced in succession over a long period.

Latest of the species to flower is *S. campanulata* (*hispanica*) otherwise known as the Spanish bluebell. It produces on stems 10-12 in. tall, spikes of bell-shaped violet-blue flowers which bloom in May.

S. campanulata Azalea is deep pink; Blue Giant deep blue; Mount Everest is white; and Queen of the Pinks is deep rose. Collections of mixed hybrids are also offered by the larger nurserymen and garden centres.

Scilla like well-moved soil and should be planted in October or November 3 to 4 ins. deep. All species multiplying freely.

Sisyrinchiums are usually classed with bulbous subjects, although they do not really produce bulbs or tubers, but form a thickish base. Most of the species flower from April onwards. The petals of some glisten when seen in the sun, and this has given them the common name of Satin flowers. They deserve wider cultivation for although their slender appearance suggests that they are fragile, this is not so and they are not difficult to grow. All flourish in light sandy soil, and seem to like to get their roots into peat or leaf mould, while they prefer a sunny situation, which however, should be sheltered.

Taking some of the species alphabetically, *S. augustifolia*, also known as *S. gramineum* is a native of Mexico and parts of the United States. Slender growing, with 6-8 in. stems it carries lavender-blue flowers, each with a yellow centre. *S. burmudiana* grows 6 to 10 in. high, and although it will sometimes flourish outdoors in favourable places, it is safest given glass covering. The narrow flat leaves remind one of a miniature iris, and from the end of April onwards, the mid-blue flowers appear, being brightened with a yellow eye.

S. striatum is another Chilean species, grow 1-2 ft. high, and looking very much like a small iris, until the rather sad appearance

Spring flowers

Gladiolus three types

of the flowers shows what they are, the colour being yellow striped brown. This too is inclined to spread.

S. tenuifolium of Mexican origin has narrow foliage and rather pale yellow stems. *S. junceum* or *roseum*, is another dainty species with nodding pink flowers, and as its specific name suggests, the foliage is rush-like. First introduced to Britain about 1832, the tubers of this species have claws, rather like those of ranunculus. Other less hardy species include *S. californicum* and *S. graminifolium* both of which are yellow.

Sparaxis. The blooms of sparaxis provide such brilliant colour combinations that this small genus of bulbs native to South Africa has won the common name of Harlequin flower. Sparaxis are members of the Iridaceae family and are closely related to both freesias and ixias, although they have larger flowers – averaging 2 ins. across – and shorter stems – 6-9 ins. in height. The narrow foliage is both colourful and graceful. The colour combinations of these soft delicate flowers defy description and are a tremendous asset in the garden from late June into August.

Plant the small globular corms from the beginning of April onwards in light, well-drained soil in sheltered and sunny positions. Plant about 3 in. deep and 3 in. apart and do remember they like a bit of protection in frosty weather.

There are now many beautiful varieties and the most economical and colourful purchase is a mixture. If you want to try a named hybrid, you can't do better than Sparaxis Scarlet Gem which boasts a flaming red flower with conspicuous yellow pencilling and black at the base. They look particularly lovely in the rockery. Like freesias and ixias, sparaxis can be easily grown in pots in the cool greenhouse and cultivation is precisely the same.

Sprekelia. This striking and decorative Mexican flower, known as the St. James' Lily because the segments of the perianth look rather like the red cross embroidered on the cloaks of the Knights of St. James, used to be strictly a greenhouse plant. But classified officially as Sprekelia formossisima it adapts itself perfectly and easily to garden cultivation in Britain provided it is not planted outdoors until the end of April.

Sprekelia, and there is only one species in the genus, is related to the popular hippeastrum, the main difference being that it always produces a solitary flower. But this flower is truly magnificent, a six petalled flower in gorgeous red, curiously orchid-like in appearance with slim and erect upper petals partially enclosing the stems. The large oval-shaped, long necked bulbs with black

L

tunics produce several long stems, each crowned with an imposing vivid crimson-scarlet flower. They are in full bloom in the garden in June-July, and the flowers are extremely long lasting.

Sprekelia formossisima bulbs should be planted shallowly in well-drained soil about 12-18 ins. apart in sunny positions. It is best to lift the bulbs in autumn before the first frosts, and to keep them in a dry, temperate storage place during the winter. You'll note that the bulbs increase by division, the offshoots usually taking two years to flower.

Sprekelias can be grown in pots in the greenhouse or house, planting them just like hippeastrums in John Innes No. 3 compost, leaving the top half to third of the bulb exposed. When planted in pots sprekelia should be allowed a prolonged period of dryness after flowering when the leaves begin to turn yellow, to ensure flowering again the following year.

Whether grown outdoors or indoors the leaves usually appear at the same time as the flower, but don't be alarmed if the flower sometimes blooms before the foliage appears or vice versa.

Tulips. These are available in all colours of the rainbow from white to almost black, from softest pink to deepest purple. They come in broken colours, self colours, striped, streaked, shaded and tinged. They even come with touches of green in the blooms. And they come at different times with a flowering season ranging from February through May. These facts alone make them indispensable for cutting and the creation of both simple and the more elaborate indoor floral displays.

They flower in a host of forms and shapes. Some have oval flowers, some are shaped like turbans, and others are square at the base. Some tulips resemble double paeonies, others are elegantly reflexed to resemble a lily. Petal formation greatly varies too with laciniated petals, fringed petals, curled petals and pointed petals. Most have one flower on a stem, a few produce several flowers on a single stem. In some cases the flowers are tiny while others produce blooms as large as the span of a man's hand. Some have stems of a few inches, others soar to almost 3 ft.

With such a wide choice of tulips all kinds of different planting schemes can be devised and tulips do equally well in tubs and windowboxes. They prefer being planted late in the season, from November to mid-December. Place the species or botanical tulips about 4 in. deep and about 4 to 5 in. apart, except *T. fosteriana* hybrids, which should be planted 5 to 6 in. deep and some 6 in. apart, except for the taller-stemmed rarer species, the taller stemmed

T. greigiis and all the garden tulips. Tulips are easy to cultivate thriving in any well-drained soil. Species tulips do best in sunny positions but garden tulips can be planted in sun or partial shade.

A small group of flamboyant *T. fosterianas* will dominate a rock wall or shine across a front lawn if clustered in front of evergreen shrubs. They are also excellent for planting at the base of light trees, like cherries or crab apples.

Garden tulips from Single Earlies to Parrots show up well in either formal or informal plantings. Placed in groups of a single colour, tulips lend sparkle and drama to the garden. By planting in plenty there will be good supplies of cut flowers available over a long period.

The tulip species are the earliest to flower and they vary greatly in size and colour. Their brightness and oriental appearance make them worthy of notice. Ideal for cutting when used in spring floral arrangements they impart a tone not given by any other flowers. Plant the bulbs in autumn about 4 in. deep, or where the soil is lighter, 5 or 6 in. is not too much. Among the finest of the species are the following.

T. acuminata having long narrow pointed segments of red and yellow. *T. australis* of dwarf habit, the star-shaped yellow flowers being flushed red. *T. biflora* has clusters of 2 to 5 creamy-white flowers tinged green. *T. chrysantha* has small yellow flowers and wavy leaves. *T. clusiana* the Lady tulip, has rose and white flowers, while *T. eichleri* is scarlet with a black centre.

T. fosteriana is brilliant crimson, but it is the hybrids of this species which are notable, especially Red Emperor, vermilion-scarlet. *T. greigii* is usually recognised by its grey-green leaves which are blotched purple-brown, the flowers being fiery red. This species, too, has given rise to many marvellous hybrids.

T. praestans is scarlet-vermilion with a yellow base, the flowers sometimes being borne in clusters. *T. kaufmanniana* produces carmine flowers, edged white. Here again, it is the hybrids which are so remarkable, taking in shades of salmon, apricot, orange and pink.

The earliest of the garden tulips to flower are the Single Early varieties. Derived from crosses between *T. gesneriana* and *T. suaveolens*, they form sturdy stems 10-15 ins. tall. They are available in striking shades of almost every known colour and are very popular.

They normally flower in mid-April being invaluable for massing in beds and borders to produce the earliest dramatic splashes of colour in the garden. Varieties available for both indoor and out-door culture include: Bellona, golden-yellow, scented; Couleur Cardinal, purplish-crimson; De Wet, fiery orange, stippled orange-scarlet, scented; Dr. Plesman, orange-red, scented; Prince of Austria, orange-scarlet and Keizerskroon, crimson with broad yellow edge.

Double Early tulips bloom somewhat later than Single Early tulips, about the end of April. While about the same height as the Single Early varieties, they have large widely open double flowers which on the whole last longer.

In 1665 this attractive race of tulips first appeared. There are both self-coloured and variegated sorts. Unrivalled for mass plant-ings in beds and borders they do particularly well in sunny, partially sheltered positions. Their neat even growth makes them ideal for bedding. The following are good Double Early varieties; Electra, deep cherry-red; Marechal Niel, yellow and orange; Mr. van der Hoef, golden yellow; Orange Nassau, orange-scarlet; Peach Blossom, rosy pink and Scarlet Cardinal, bright scarlet.

Darwin tulips are important, for not only have they proved themselves to be fine tulips but have shown an exceptional capacity for being hybridised with other classes. From Darwins have come the Mendel, Rembrandt, Darwin Hybrid and Lily-flowered tulips.

Darwin tulips are superb in beds and borders as they have long sturdy stems 25 to 32 in. in height, which also make them superior cut flowers. The large cupped flowers are squared off at the base and tops of petals, come virtually in all colours, and have a dis-tinctive satiny texture. All varieties are resistant to wind and rain, and can be grouped effectively among shrubs or evergreens or interplanted with roses and other subjects.

Darwin Hybrid tulips represent a fine achievement in the tulip's history. Obtained recently from crosses between Darwin varieties and *T. fosteriana* Red Emperor, these hybrids are the newest of the garden tulip classes, boasting the biggest flowers yet produced. They are also notable for their brilliance of colour. Of superb stature with stems ranging from 22 to 28 in. in height, the giant flowers are huge, single cups, particularly noted for satiny shades of red.

Although modern varieties, they are surprisingly inexpensive and quite a choice is available. These include: Apeldoorn, orange-scarlet; Dover, poppy-red; General Eisenhower, orange-red; Gudoshnik, sulphur-yellow and Holland's Glory, orange-scarlet.

Cottage tulips have more variation in form than any other

class. They are so named because they were originally found in old cottage gardens. Many have slender buds with long pointed petals. Distinct of habit, these single-flowered gems are strikingly effective when planted in bold masses. Always plant in groups of 3 or more, remembering that these elegant tulips have long stems ranging from 20-32 in. making them superb for cutting.

The large egg-shaped flowers come in pastels and pastel blends and in light hues of many colours and bloom early in May. In this class come the viridiflora or green tulips as well as some multi-flowering varieties, each carrying 3 to 6 flower heads per stem.

Outstanding Cottage varieties include: Artist, 9 ins. salmon-rose and green; Dillenburg, 26 ins. salmon-orange; Golden Artist, 9 ins. golden-orange, striped green; Golden Harvest, 26 ins. lemon-yellow; Mother's Day, 24 ins. lemon-yellow; Monsieur Mottet, 22 ins. ivory-white, multi-flowering; Mrs. John T. Scheepers, 26 ins. clear yellow; Princess Margaret Rose, 21 ins. yellow edged orange-red; and Smiling Queen, 30 ins. rosy-red edged silvery-pink.

Lily-flowered tulips are among the most graceful and elegant of all. They create most beautiful pictures when planted in groups in beds, borders or in terrace tubs or window boxes. Beautifully reflexed and pointed petals form flowers of handsome beauty on tall, wiry stems some 20 to 24 in. tall. All Lily-flowered varieties make excellent cut flowers.

The distinct shape of the blooms somewhat resembling lilies is responsible for their having been placed in a separate division. The colours are deep, rich and glowing and groups of different varieties grown for cutting invariably make a splendid display. Among good varieties which bloom in May are: Aladdin, 20 ins. scarlet edged yellow; China Pink, 22 ins. satin-pink; and Mrs. Moon, 24 ins. pure yellow.

Mendel Tulips. These help fill the flowering gap between the early and late or May-flowering tulips. They are the result of a cross between Duc van Thol and Darwin tulips, but they produce large, handsome single flowers in a wide colour range on stems 16 to 24 in. high.

They like somewhat sheltered positions, and flower from the last week in April and at least a fortnight before the Darwin tulips appear in a normal season.

They are self-coloured or edged with deeper or contrasting hues and look most elegant in clumps in beds and borders or beneath light trees.

Among the varieties available are: Apricot Beauty, 16 ins.

salmon-rose tinged red; Athleet, 18 ins. pure white; Sulphur Triumph, 22 ins. primrose yellow.

Triumph tulips come in a wide range of colours on stiff stems 16-24 in. tall and are weather resistant to all but the extremes of our late April climate. They have large single cup flowers striped and margined, not to be found in other divisions of tulips. They are particularly valuable for exposed positions in beds, borders and other garden sites. They usually bloom immediately after the Mendel tulips. Whether grown indoors or in the garden they make graceful and useful cut flowers.

Choice varieties include: Bandoeng, 20 ins. mahogany-red flushed orange; Bruno Walter, 19 ins. deep orange yellow; Emmy Peeck, 22 ins. deep lilac-rose; Kees Nelis, 20 ins. red, edged yellow; Paul Richter, 25 ins. geranium-red; and Telescopium, 24 ins. violet-rose.

Parrot tulips. These are beautiful flowers with strikingly fringed, scalloped or wavy segments, sometimes narrow and elongated. Detailed selection has led to stronger, sturdier stems and breeders have introduced many charming varieties.

Flowering in May on strong 20 to 26 in. stems, the flowers in a wide colour range are often tinged with green. The foliage is light green and provides a lovely contrast for the brilliancy of the blooms. Excellent for cutting and indoor arrangement, Parrot tulips like sheltered positions and make a gorgeous splash at focal points in the garden.

All the varieties are sports of tulips from various classes and with the exception of their larger flowers and laciniated segments, have all the qualities as the varieties from which they originate.

Varieties include: Black Parrot, 24 in. purplish-black; Blue Parrot, 26 in. bright violet; Fantasy, 24 in. soft rose streaked green; Orange Favourite, 22 in. orange with green blotching; and Texas Flame, 26 in. yellow, flamed red.

Rembrandt Tulips began with ' broken coloured ' tulips and date back to 1554. These magnificent tulips were once all the rage and fabulous prices were paid for a single bulb. They can still be admired in old paintings and Rembrandt himself loved them as subjects.

For many years ' broken coloured tulips ' were classified as Bizarres, Bijbloemen and Rembrandt tulips according to parentage and colour, but now all have been incorporated into a single Rembrandt class.

All varieties have large single cups with stems ranging from 20 to 30 in. and come in the most artistic colours with feathered or flamed blooms. Although lovely in clumps in the garden, they are mostly grown for cutting for indoor flower arrangements. Varieties which flower in early May include: Absalon, 25 in. coffee-brown on yellow ground; Dainty Maid, 18 in. magenta-purple on white ground; Insulinde, 23 in. violet on yellow ground; and Victor Hugo, 18 in. cherry-rose on white ground.

PART II

CHAPTER 1

FOLIAGE FROM SHRUBS AND TREES

THERE are many easy to grow plants, shrubs, trees and pot plants from which it is possible to obtain individual leaves or leafy twigs and branches. These can be used with great effectiveness when properly selected and placed among any arrangement of cut flowers. Used alone many make a pleasing decoration.

While it is true that flowers often look best when displayed with their own foliage, this is by no means always the case. There are leaves in many shades of green, others are tinted yellow or bronze-red, some are variegated and others assume remarkable autumn tints.

The greatest quantity of such foliage can be gathered from shrubs and it is well worth planting some of these, especially for cutting. There are quite a number which have the simplest of cultural requirements.

Among the many suitable berberises are *B. darwinii*, of which the green foliage is attractive throughout the year, apart from its orange flowers and autumn berries. *B. juliae* is compact growing with rather larger leaves, while B. verruculosa has dark green, glossy leaves (which are white on the undersides) which colour up well in the autumn. *B. stenophylla* has graceful, arching branches of small leaves which become tinted red in October. Valuable for cutting during the winter is *Cotoneaster salicifolia* with long, dark green, rather drooping leaves which are white underneath with red veins.

Copper beech can be used in many colour schemes, while the very young green foliage is also decorative. Particularly on chalky soils, *Corylus avellana atropurpurea* or the Purple Nut should be grown. The deeply veined leaves colour up well and it is suitable for cultivating where space is limited.

Almus. This is the alder, which should not be confused with the elder, of which the proper name is sambucus. *A. glutinosa* is the common alder, of which the shoots and leaves are sticky when

Skimmia japonica – Beautiful dwarf evergreen shrubs that do as well in
strong clay as in sandy soil and peat

young. The form known as *A.g. imperialis* makes a tree of more than 20 feet the foliage being finely cut.

It is *Almus incana aurea* which is the most attractive, the young shoots and leaves being yellow. Red tinged catkins develop as the wood assumes an orange colour in winter. A. laciniata is the cut-leaved grey alder. Odd leaves, stems and catkins taken from these shrubs or trees provide valuable material for including in mixed arrangements.

Amelanchier canadensis is noted for its drooping racemes of white flowers in April. What is so often overlooked is the fact that the half grown leaves are tinged with pink and in autumn, the foliage assumes rich colourings. There is the bonus of berries in July, while in winter the twiggy habit of the shrubs gives a purple effect.

This subject can be grown as a bush or tree and here again, a few leaves or a little cluster of dormant stems give added value to floral designs.

Crataegus. While one does not usually think of the hawthorns as being foliage plants there are several worth considering for this purpose.

The three-lobed leaves of *Crataegus pinnatifida* are often as much as 6 in. across. As autumn approaches they take on many pleasing coloured tints making them first class where a leaf or two are needed to complete an arrangement. The large red haws add to the showy display.

Crataegus tanacefolia has very divided foliage which at first is covered with a whitish down. Here again the subsequent display of yellow haws increase the value of this subject.

C. tomentosa also has foliage which when young is covered with grey down, but it is the autumn colouring of orange and scarlet that make the leaves so desirable.

Eleagnus. This is an outstanding evergreen of dense rounded habit. The leaves being enhanced by neat brown stalks and twigs. It does produce small silvery white scented flowers in autumn, but it is for its foliage this shrub is valued. *E. pungens maculata* is deservedly the most popular of golden variegated evergreens growing 5 or 6 ft. high.

Enkianthus campanulatus. It is the way in which the leaves develop which makes this subject useful. They grow in whorls and change in autumn from green to beautiful shades of rich yellow and red.

Attractive cream bell-shaped flowers are produced in spring.

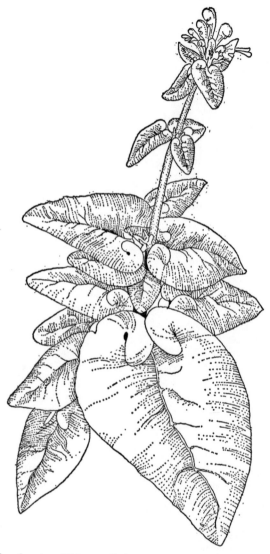

Stachys lanata – This woolly-leaved plant thrives in any soil!

Plant in a sheltered place and where early morning sun does not reach the foliage otherwise the leaves may be discoloured.

Eucalyptus. Most of the species in cultivation are not fully hardy but *E. gunnii*, the Cedar Gum, which is sometimes catalogued as *E. whittinghamensis* can be grown in the open perfectly safely so long as the position is not exposed or badly drained. A little protection given the first winter after transplanting will be of great help.

E. dalrympleana is another good species but not better than E. gunnii for the average sheltered garden. Of special interest is the fact that the juvenile leaves of *E. gunnii* are round and glaucous-blue while when they mature, they are grey-green and sickle shaped. A fast grower, this species needs supporting from its earliest stages while the stems are slender.

In course of time the trees make quite large specimens but they will stand a certain amount of cutting.

The bark of the trunk and older branches is renewed annually, the old bark peeling off to reveal the pleasing greenish-white trunk and boughs. Small white flowers are often produced but these are not significant.

All eucalyptus transplant best when young, in fact they resent root disturbance once established, often taking some time to recover after a move.

Eucalyptus can be raised from seed without difficulty, in fact, where the foliage is needed for cutting it is a good plan to raise a few seedlings annually in order to have both round and sickle shaped leaves available.

Fagus. This is the botanical name for the lovely beeches. The so-called Common beech is *F. sylvatica*, of which the green foliage is particularly lovely in spring and autumn and does much to enhance the appearance of an arrangement of cut flowers. The form *F.s. heterophylla* is particularly fine, the graceful well dissected leaves turning a delightful golden tone in September. Another form, purpurea, is particularly attractive in spring since the young purplish foliage is tinged with red.

Fagus sylvatica cuprea is the Copper beech the coppery red foliage being indispensable for many floral designs especially if the arrangements are placed so that the sun can be seen shining through the leaves.

All the beeches will in time make large specimens although regular cutting will retard the size.

Ginkgo biloba is the Maidenhair tree. A hardy subject, it still

Forms of ivy foliage

Cornflower Carnival Mixed

Sweet Sultan Mixed

Dianthus Sweet Wivelsfield

Coreopsis, Mayfield Giant

Sweet William Mixed

Pansy Superb Mixed

Cineraria maritima

appreciates a good deep, well-drained soil, sun and congenial conditions. The pale green fan-shaped leaves vary from 2-3 in. long, and half the width, the edges being crenulated. They turn to a beautiful golden tone before falling in autumn. In its native China it sometimes produces fruit but rarely if ever does so in Britain.

Koelreuteria paniculata is usually grown for its pannicles of yellow flowers, but it is worthy of cultivation for its attractive leaves which are useful for cutting. When young, the colour is a pleasing peach pink, but by the autumn when the foliage is much larger, sometimes a foot or more long, the colour will change to golden yellow.

Perfectly hardy, this subject likes good soil where the roots can penetrate deeply.

Hedera. This plant, better known as ivy, is very versatile being suitable for many purposes. The so-called English ivy is useful for covering walls, tree trunks, and as an edging to window boxes and terrace pots where their tracery shows up like lace.

Many ivies are now grown as pot plants in the living-room and greenhouse, while trailings of the coloured forms are excellent for including in bouquets or for house decoration.

The large glossy leaves of Hedera colchica dentata have beautiful creamy markings, while another form is gold. *H.h. cristata* has smaller shiny leaves crimpled at the edges. *H. canariensis* Gloire de Marengo has shadings of grey, pale green, silver and pink against a darker green background.

Hedera h. Glacier has small leaves suffused silver grey edged white.

All hederas are easy to grow flourishing in ordinary soil, with the minimum of attention.

Liquidambar styraciflua is another tree which likes a position where the roots can go down easily and does not object to fairly moist conditions, so long as it is not in the shade. This tree will, in the course of time, grow quite large. The leaves are often 5 or 6 in. wide and as much long, and are somewhat like those of the maple. It is in the autumn that they are so lovely, for then they usually take on most beautiful hues from showy orange to brilliant crimson red.

Magnolia leaves are quite frequently used by flower arrangers. Very often one or two leaves are sufficient to finish off an arrangement. All magnolias are slow growing and like a rich neutral soil although they sometimes flourish in slightly acid ground.

Magnolia campbellii although noted for its crimson-pink flowers

M

Liquidambar Styraiciflua foliage

which however do not usually develop until the plant is up to 30 years old, is notable for its very large oval green leaves one of which is usually sufficient for adding to quite a good sized floral display.

Magnolia grandiflora Exmouth has handsome glossy green leaves with a brown felty down covering the undersides.

Metasequoia glyptostroboides is known as the Dawn Redwood. Of ancient origin it was rediscovered in China in 1940 and plants are now available from specialist growers. Quite hardy and a fast grower, it prefers a situation where the soil never dries out. It has vivid green feathery young foliage, which by the autumn turns to many beautiful shades of bronze. This is an indispensable subject conifers in cultivation.

Mahonia japonica sometimes known as *Berberis aquifolium* is where graceful foliage is needed and it is one of the few deciduous

often cut because its glossy, dark green leaves may be used throughout the spring and summer and again later when they assume
beautiful autumn colours. It will grow almost anywhere. The large
pinnate foliage consists of a number of leaflets each of which may
be as much as 4 in. long, while often reaching a length of 10-12 in.
The leaflets have serrated edges often armed with spines.

Apart from their pleasing foliage these shrubs produce heads of
attractive lemon-coloured pendulous flowers in March. These are
much used for indoor decoration, not least because of their strong
Lily-of-the-Valley scent.

Mahonia bealii

M. bealei is similar, but the flowers are produced in erect
racemes and are somewhat shorter. *M. lomariifolia* has long slender
leaves. This shrub is inclined to make leggy growth being shy at
producing side growths. Give it a sheltered place and it will produce
its erect heads of flowers from December onwards.

Perovskia atriplicifolia is a lovely shrub having grey aromatic
foliage and stems which may be used to advantage with lavender
blue flowers. It likes light and sun and should be pruned annually
in the spring.

Pittosporum is a fine evergreen, but unfortunately not hardy in all districts. It can be raised from seed or cuttings, the most suitable species being P. tenuifolium with bright, pale green leaves and almost black twigs. Of special value at Christmas time it may be used in the summer months too when the stems should be plunged in water as soon as they are cut.

Several of the prunus are of value for their foliage. *P. pissardii* has rich ruby-bronze foliage in spring darkening to purple. *P. nigra* is darker still and seems to like a chalky soil. *P. blireiana* has rich bronze leaves throughout the summer, while *P. spinosa rosea* is invaluable as a foliage tree. The dainty purple tinted leaves turn matt purple with age.

There are a number of oaks or quercus having tinted leaves, and Q. coccinea being especially good, the form Knaphill Scarlet is really handsome until the end of November. These have the virtue of producing many basal growths, if and when stems have been cut.

Nandina domestica is related to the berberises. It is reliably hardy only in sheltered situations. Sometimes known as the Chinese Sacred Bamboo, the long pinnate green foliage emerges a delicate pink shade and in autumn turns to purplish crimson. It likes deep rich soil. The white flowers in June are occasionally followed by red berries.

Olearia, the Daisy Bush, is often grown because of its large heads of flowers during the summer. Several evergreen species are notable for the value of their foliage both when growing and cut. *O. haastii* is the best known and reliable species. The small oval leaves are green on the upper surface and silvery grey beneath. *O. mucrodonta* has grey downy, holly-like foliage without spines. *O. illicifolia* has larger leaves and is less hardy than the others. All like well-drained lightish soil.

Photinia serrulata both flowers and produces berries. In addition, its evergreen foliage has much merit. Individual leaves are 6 to 7 in. long and 2 or 3 in. wide and slightly toothed. When young they are a coppery red colour, turning to deep green in maturity. Since new leaves develop very frequently, their coppery shade makes the bushes noticeable. In addition, the young leaves or shoots provide just the right touch of colour for certain arrangements.

Rhododendron. Although no one would think of denuding individual specimens, a leaf or two included in an arrangement of flowers can greatly enhance the display. Such action will not normally hinder the flowering strength of the bushes.

R. luteum, sometimes known as Azalea pontica with yellow

honeysuckle-like scented flowers, has foliage which in autumn assumes rich hues of red and crimson.

R. ponticum, an evergreen, with purplish-pink flowers, has dark, glossy leaves attractive in any season.

Lime free soil, enriched with peat and leafmould is needed for good growth and an annual mulching of peat, bracken and decayed leaves will prove beneficial.

Rosmarinus. The well-known Rosemary is valued for its aromatic grey-green linear leaves, felted on the undersides. To keep the bushes shapely, trim them annually after flowering.

R. officinalis is the best known, but Miss Jessop's variety is useful when a stiff, regular branch is needed in a floral creation.

Rubus cockburnianus. This is a Bramble and therefore needs handling respectfully. It grows well in almost any soil. For the flower arranger the value of this subject is in its strong stems looking as if they are white-washed, the pinnate leaves being white beneath. Small purple single flowers appear in June followed by black fruit.

Ruta graveolens, Jackman's Blue. This shrubby plant has striking opalescent blue semi-evergreen leaves, which can become a focal point in a display of foliage and berries as well as adding beauty to a mixed arrangement of flowers.

Salvia officinalis. There are several coloured forms of the bushy Sage. They must be grown in sheltered positions, but if damaged by severe frosts soon recovers, particularly if grown in light soil. S.o. icterina has grey-green leaves variegated yellow, while S.o. purpurascens has soft purple foliage.

Santolina. These are low growing aromatic evergreens especially attractive seen growing near the coloured leaved berberis, and producing a striking effect when used with berberis foliage indoors. This subject likes light soil and sun.

S. chamaecyparissis or *S. incana* is the Cotton Lavender 2½ ft. with narrow closely set, saw edged silvery leaves. The dwarf form nana grows about a foot high.

S. neapolitana has looser more feathery foliage.

Senecio. These are quite important grey foliaged shrubs. The persistent foliage makes it a useful subject at all times, especially when used as a contrast to other foliage subjects. It produces yellow daisy-like flowers in summer and grows about 3 ft. high. The oval to lanceolate grey leaves are 1½-2 ins. long and spring from white felted young shoots.

Spiraea bumalda, Anthony Waterer, forms flat clusters of pinkish red flowers in May and June but its delightful spring foliage which sometimes shows yellow variegations makes it doubly worth growing, especially as often traces of pink, red and cream are to be seen in the young leaves.

S. prunifolia plena produces little double white flowers on arching stems in May but it is the lustrous green leaves which turn red in autumn that are so useful for cutting.

Leaves of various trees and shrubs can be preserved in good condition by the glycerine process. This changes their colour to varying shades of brown. The stems should be bruised at the base in order that they absorb the liquid into which they are placed. This liquid consists of one part glycerine and two parts water. The stems are placed in this and it is usually about 3 weeks before they have absorbed sufficient liquid to lead to the full coloration of the leaves.

Leaves may also be skeletonised. Although the process needs care and patience, it is not difficult. Results are really exquisite for only the midrib and vein structure remains when the job is completed. It is a very old-fashioned practice, the principle being the softening of the leaf substance so that it can be removed from the skeleton.

Various methods are employed, one of the simplest being to immerse the leaves in a pan or tub of water for several weeks. Keep them in the same water for decomposition takes places more easily when it has been standing for some time. If the leaves are examined from time to time, they can be lightly rubbed, which makes it easier to remove the leaf tissues. Another method of skeletonising leaves is to simmer them in a solution made of 3 oz. washing soda and $1\frac{1}{2}$ oz. quick-lime, mixed into 2 pints of boiling water. When the skin has loosened, take out the leaves and lightly scrub them to remove all pulp so that only the skeleton remains. These skeletons can be bleached by using the ordinary household bleach. When they are white, gradually dry and either press them flat or leave them to curl. Good leaves for this treatment include magnolia, laurel, beech, rhododendron and holly. Seed pods can be treated similarly.

CHAPTER 2

HARDY PLANTS WITH GOOD FOLIAGE

ALTHOUGH it may seem odd to some people to grow plants for their foliage it is a fact that there are many subjects which have leaves of outstanding colour and shape, and which may be gathered individually both for their own beauty and as a background to flower arrangements. Foliage plants are in a class by themselves and very often the leaves are of great value for indoor decoration in the spring before the main display of blooms develops.

Among these are bergenias which have the common name of Elephants Ears, the large rounded greyish, virtually evergreen leaves being beautifully shaded purple in their young stages, *B. cordifolia* being particularly fine. *Clematis recta purpurea* has plum-coloured leaves, while Dicentra eximia has green filigree, ferny leaves. *Foeniculum vulgar* has a blackish-red tinge, to its leaves.

Hostas are among the most widely used of foliage plants and a single leaf or a group of this foliage will make all the difference to a floral display. *H. lancifolia fortunei* has blue-grey leaf blades, while the form known as Thomas Hogg has leaves which unfold a bright butter yellow edged green, later turning to soft green. *H. lancifolia albo-marginata*, has sage green foliage beautifully edged white.

Lamium macaulatum has white stripes down the centre of its rich green foliage. This plant should be cut back after flowering in order to increase the effectiveness of the later foliage. *Ligularia clivorum* has bold green heart-shaped leaves which are rusty brown underneath.

Mellissa variegata is the Golden Balm. Several of the paeonies particularly *P. lactiflora* have shoots and leaves which are a beautiful reddish tone while young.

Polypodium emodi has brightly mottled leaves, while Pulmonaria officinalis has leaves marked and blotched white.

Where a large leaf or two is required Rogersia aesculifolia is a handsome metallic bronze. Ruta graveolens has striking opalescent blue foliage, and the shrubby Salvia purpurescens has soft purple leaves, other varieties being grey-green and variegated with yellow. *Sedum spectabile* forms mounds of fleshy grey-green.

Plants with golden leaves which may be gathered individually if required include: *Valeriana aurea, Veronica teucrium Trehane*, and *Origanum aureum. Acanthus mollis latifolius* which has leaves of architectural merit. They are a shining green 18 to 20 in. long and handsomely arching and undulated with deeply lobed edges.

The thistle-like foliage of both *eryngium* and *echinops* are invaluable as are the greyish well cut leaves of the Globe Artichoke. There are several irises with variegated leaves, particularly good

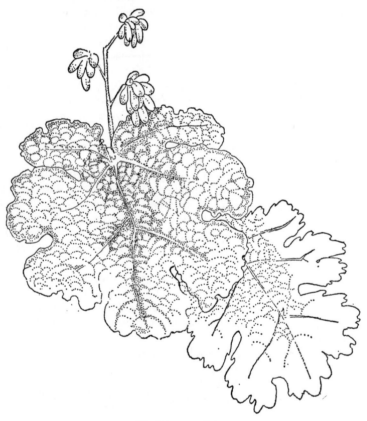

Macleaya cordata

being Iris japonica and Iris foetidissima variegata. In addition the heads of scarlet seeds which succeed the rather dingy-looking flowers are invaluable for cutting.

Reference to the catalogues of specialist plant growers will reveal many other subjects with attractive foliage which one should not overlook.

Apart from all of these it is sometimes quite easy to gather the leaves from both cultivated and wild plants which are not usually used indoor and which if placed in water immediately, will remain decorative for a long time.

Several irises have variegated foliage including *I. foetidissima variegata*, a form of the old Roast Beef plant. The greyish leaves of *Nepeta faassenii* are attractive, while *Nepeta hederacea* the rather invasive Ground Ivy, has leaves with a white centre.

Pachysandra terminalis variegata is another ground covering plant which spreads rather rapidly, the leaves produced in whorls, being variegated white.

Macleaya cordata make a lot of growth and should be given plenty of room in the garden. The foliage is bronzy green and silvery grey on the undersides.

Onopordon arabicum is the Scotch thistle. It does have deep purple flowers but its chief value is its silvery leaves and stems. It is best to cut off the seed heads before the seed falls. This prevents the appearance of unwanted, inferior seedlings.

Hostas are invaluable to the flower arranger, not only on account of their flowers but because of their attractive foliage. *H. elata* has dark green leaves, glaucous on the undersides, while H. fortunei and its forms usually have bluish-tinted foliage. Several other species have handsomely variegated leaves.

Paeonies are usually grown for their impressive flowers but as the new shoots unfurl they are usually a pleasing reddish tone and they frequently turn crimson in autumn.

The elegant arching stems of Solomon's Seal are most useful in certain arrangements, particularly when the hanging white bells are opening. They grow well in partial shade.

Thalictrum has most dainty foliage fit to grace the choicest of floral schemes.

With all of these perennials it is sometimes only necessary to use one or two leaves and their removal will not harm the plants in any way.

CHAPTER 3

ORNAMENTAL GRASSES AND FERNS

ORNAMENTAL grasses are of value for including in flower displays since they give a light airy effect. There are both annual and perennial species and although the colour and variety of flowers now available has tended to eclipse the flowering grasses, many of them are now coming into favour again. The fact that they are attractive both during the growing season and when dried for winter use makes them doubly useful.

The annual grasses can be bought in small packets and can be treated in exactly the same way as seed of annual flowering subjects. They can be sown out of doors where they are to flower when danger of frost is past or in boxes or pots under glass for planting out when conditions are right.

Agrostis nebulus. Cloud Grass, has dainty spikes of cloud-like formation 1-1½ ft.

Aira cappillaris, splendid flower spikes with many branchlets, 1-1½ ft.

Avena sterilis is the Animated Oat often grown as a curiosity, for when mature the seeds, when placed on the ground, move about like insects, 2 ft.

Briza maxima. Quaking Grass, a handsome species with well-branched spikes. 1½ ft. B. minor is similar but smaller, 9-12 in.

Bromus brizaeformis is the Quake Grass with large drooping spikelets, 1-2 ft.

Coix lachryma jobi. Job's Tears. Grown for its attractive ornamental seeds which resemble pearly-grey beads, 2-2½ ft.

Eragrostis elegans. Love Grass, having feathery panicles of small spikelets, 2 ft.

Hordeum jubatum. Squirrel's Tail. Nodding feathery spikes of silvery green passing to light brown, 1½ ft.

Lagurus ovatus, Hare's Tail. Neat fluffy heads, 1 ft.

Panicum capillare. Graceful arching heads of greyish-purple, 1½ ft.

Briza maxima

Pennisetum villosum attractive long-stemmed flower heads, 2 ft.

Tricholaena. Although perennial, is usually treated as an annual. Known as Wine Grass it produces pretty rosy spikes, 1½ ft.

Cut the spikes before they are fully open and hang in bunches in an airy place, preferably in dull light. By autumn, the stems will have hardened and they can be arranged in vases or used in posies or miniature arrangements with, or without, other dried flowers when they make splendid winter decorations.

Perennial grasses are also most useful and can be planted in the autumn or spring, the latter time being best where the soil is on the heavy side. Among the best of these ornamental species are the following:

Alopecurus pratensis variegata, having narrow green arching foliage, striped old gold.

Avena candida. This is a perennial Oat, its foliage being an intense steel-blue. The plant makes quite a large clump and will not suffer in any way by some of the stems being picked. In the summer, the 2 ft. arching stems are crowned with oat-like flowers.

Carex morrowii. This is another plant which forms a clump and from which individual stems can be taken. The foliage is dark green, edged gold, the little flower heads appearing in the spring. It grows well in shady positions.

Elymus canadensis. A miniature grass which does particularly well in sandy soil.

Festuca glauca forms neat grey hummocks with short flower plumes on 8 or 9 in. stems. It thrives in the sun.

Holcus mollis variegatus. This is a brilliant silver and pale green grass growing only 7 or 8 in. high.

Luzula maxima. This has grass-like leaves, usually margined white.

Milium effusum aureum. Often known as Bowles' Golden Grass, it is most effective arranged with bright coloured blooms.

Miscanthus sinensis zebrinus. This has broad golden bands across the leaves which arch gently.

Molinia caerulea, leaves striped green and cream.

Pennisetum alopecuroides. This forms a compact plant of rounded outline, the flowers looking like grey-pink bottle brushes, carried on short stalks.

Phalaris arundinacea picta is known as Ribbon Grass, or Gardener's Garters. White striped leaves form in dense clumps, and look superb when mixed with cut flowers, particularly if blue and purple are included.

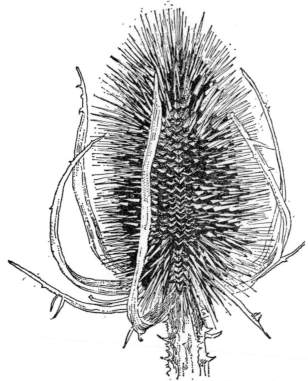

Dipsacus sylvestris (the Common Teasel) – Provides good material for a dried flower arrangement

Stipa pennata, the Feather Grass, has bright green foliage, in addition to which the creamy buff flowers on 2 ft. stems are useful for including in the larger decorations.

Uniola latifolia. This forms tight, strong flowering spikes so useful for floral decoration.

The Pampas grass is undoubtedly the best known of the perennial ornamental species. These plants make magnificent specimens often being used as a centre piece for large sized lawns or ornamental gardens.

Cortaderia argentea is the most widely grown species making spikes of feathery plumes as large as 10 ft. high. There are several lesser known forms including *C.a.* Sunningdale Silver; *C.a. pumila*, which rarely grows more than 4 ft. and *C.a. rendatleri* of which the plumes have a pinkish shade.

All Pampas grasses require careful siting, for although they may look good among shrubs, the latter must not grow in such a way that they hide the beauty of the cortaderias.

Both the leaves and inflorescence of these grasses can be used for many weeks during the winter since they dry well.

Apart from being so useful in the garden the great contrast in the leaf variations of ferns makes them almost indispensable for including in decorative displays. Sometimes a single leaf is sufficient to complete an arrangement. In addition many of them are useful for drying for using with seed heads.

Ferns prefer cool conditions usually in partial or complete shade, although some will grow in full light. The best fronds are, however, produced under cool conditions.

Adiantum pedatum is hardy so long as it is given a sheltered position. The leaf stems are wiry and black, the foliage being delightfully tinged with bronze when young.

A. venustum is a replica of the well-known Maidenhair fern, but much smaller, the leaves being tinted when young.

Athyrim felix-femina – the Lady Fern is a moisture lover which will also thrive in drier soil. The fresh green well-divided leaves create a lacy effect.

Blechnum tabulare is a really handsome fern which, however, does need some slight protection in the winter. The leaves are broadly divided.

Cystoperis bulbifera is a small growing plant with green leaves having chestnut brown streaks.

Dryopteris flex-mas is the Male Fern. A shade loving plant of graceful appearance and very hardy.

Matteuccia struthiopteris, a moisture loving fern with large divided leaves.

Osmunda regalis is the Royal Fern, of most handsome appearance, thriving on moist soil. When young the foliage is tinted a coppery brown.

Phyllitis siolopendium the Hart's Tongue fern has broad strap-shaped fronds in rosette formation.

Polystichum setigerium, hardy, dainty lacy foliage.

Woodwardia radicans, a graceful species for sheltered positions or the conservatory, having long large divided arching fronds.

CHAPTER 4

EVERLASTING AND DRIED FLOWERS

WITH the increase in floral decoration, there has come a great demand for everlasting and dried flowers. For long, many of these have had a bad name when used indoors, since they were often regarded as dust traps, and to be a variation of the artificial flowers sometimes seen decorating hotel tables and other public rooms.

Fortunately, many of the true everlastings are easy to grow and the annuals can be sown in March and April in boxes or pans in the warm greenhouse. After the seedlings have been pricked out and hardened off they can be planted in their flowering positions in late May. Alternatively, seed can be sown directly out of doors in May, although this will mean later flowering.

The following species are among the best for general decorative purposes:

Acroclinium, see helipterum.

Ammobium elatum. Growing about 18 in. high, this has silvery white flowers or bracts, with a yellow centre, making them particularly useful in large arrangements of colourful flowers, while they are a useful addition to silver and grey compositions.

Emmenanthe penduliflora. This little known subject requires a warm sunny situation, where the soil is light. Growing 9 to 12 in. high, it is when dry that the nodding bell-shaped flowers become useful as everlastings. The noise of the dry flowers moving in the wind has given them the common name of Whispering Bells.

Gomphrena. This is the Globe Amaranthe, of which the clover-like flower heads on 12-18 in. stems, are made up of bracts, between which are hidden the true flowers, the colours including white, yellow, pink and purple.

Helichrysum bracteatum, sometimes known as the Straw Flower, is probably the most widely used annual everlasting. Growing up to 3 ft. high it produces colourful bracts often referred to as petals, and these have a silvery sheen. Seed can be obtained in mixture, or in separate colours such as crimson, pink, rose, salmon, terra-cotta and white. In the garden where they can be planted in early June after hardening off, they look best growing in irregular groups.

Lonas. This rather uncommon annual is a branching plant rarely more than a foot high. From July to October it produces thickly clustered heads of yellow, ageratum-like flowers. These dry well under the same conditions as suggested for helichrysums and other everlasting subjects. Seed can be sown in late April and during May in an open, sunny situation, and usually the plants grow and flower well without any special attention.

Statice. Although the botanical name of this subject is limonium, it is widely known as statice. These annuals are useful both as fresh flowers and as everlastings. Seed should be sown in a temperature of 60 deg. F. from early March onwards, the seedlings being pricked out in the usual way and hardened off for planting out of doors from late May onwards. For drying, the flowers should be cut just as they reach full colour. If left too long they become somewhat faded looking. Once cut, the stems should be bunched and hung up to dry gradually in a cool, airy place.

S. sinuata is the species from which many large flowered varieties have been developed. Of these a number of individual colours are offered by seedsmen in separately named varieties. They include: True Blue, Lavender Queen, *S. rosea superba* and *S. alba*, white. The mixture offered as Art Shades takes in many shades not available separately. All grow from 1½ to 2 ft. high.

S. bonduellii is a fine yellow flowered species, of which there is a deeper coloured form. Yellow is a colour which is not freely found in the *S. sinuata* mixed.

Xeranthemum. This is a very useful everlasting, producing flowers in shades of purple, pink and white. These papery everlasting blooms, which vary from 1-2 in. in diameter, look well both when growing, and when used for winter decoration. The plants like an open, sunny situation where the soil is on the rich side.

X. annuum is widely used as an immortelle. There are several varieties producing double flowers, but the seed is usually offered in mixture.

There are many flowers which while not true everlastings will dry well and remain decorative for a long time. They may lose some of their brightness and the final result may to a large extent depend upon how well they are treated after being cut, but undoubtedly they bring greater variety. Especially in these cases, the drying off process demands extra care. It must be done very slowly, if otherwise, the stems become brittle and the flower heads will shatter. All of the following are worth trying and with perseverance they will prove rewarding.

Achillea filipendulina produces flat heads of golden yellow on sturdy 4½-5 ft. stems. This has the advantage of not needing special drying off, in fact it can be used as soon as cut, for mixing with fresh flowers and still be of service when the other subjects have finished. In such arrangements do not crowd the achillea but allow air to circulate so that the flowers dry gradually.

Achillea millefolium in its pink and white forms produces clusters of flowers which need to be dried properly. The flowers can be coloured with a floral dye.

Amaranthus caudatus or Love-lies-Bleeding has pendulous blooms which dry well and are specially useful in arrangements placed above eye level.

Echinops, the Globe Thistle, has silver backed foliage and lilac globe-shaped, thistle-like heads. They can be used as soon as cut if required.

The spikes of buddleia will keep well if gathered while the florets are still firm and well coloured.

Eryngium or Sea Holly is similar to echinops but less prickly. The bright coloured long stemmed large flowers are a deep violet colour. Cut the stems before they become old but not before they are really firm. If desired some of the many short branches may be removed.

Heathers. Most people have gathered heathers from moors and woodlands and have found them to be long lasting. So that the colour is retained, the sprays should be gathered while fairly young. Some of the golden leaved sorts should be included. All stems should be cut as long as possible. This gives more opportunity to use them in arrangements where they can be fitted in to provide curves and drapings.

Hydrangea heads have long been used for drying, sometimes more successfully than others. The flowers need watching as they develop so that the stems can be cut at the right stage. The heads are made up of bracts the flowers being very tiny and often unnoticed. Cutting should not be done until the bracts become thin and papery. If they are cut while still fleshy disappointment occurs in the drying process.

It is not uncommon, in some seasons, to be able to gather hydrangea heads in mid winter, the bracts having dried thoroughly while still on the plants.

Lavender is most useful both fresh and dried, for the spikes

N

bring a certain grace to other shaped flowers as well as being fragrant. It is important to cut the spikes before they are really ' ripe ' otherwise the flowers will drop and cause disappointment.

Salvias are not only showy summer bedding plants but if the flower spikes of the scarlet and salmon pink varieties are cut and put in water either as an arrangement with other subjects or alone, they will gradually dry. When this happens they can be kept for some weeks since although they may not keep their shape, the colour is retained.

Salvia farinacea, S. sclarea and the annual *S. horminium,* are most useful for their long lasting pink, blue or white bracts. These make them invaluable for using with many types of flowers over a long period.

Solidago or Golden Rod dries well too. The flower spikes should be gathered before they are fully developed but not while immature, otherwise the flower heads become discoloured, fluffy and fall.

When the colourful flowers are no longer available from the garden and when you would like a change from the everlastings, there are the seed heads of many subjects which will provide form or pattern, used alone or in conjunction with other material.

The range of seed heads suitable for using indoors is much wider than is often realised. When the petals have fallen and given way to the seed vessels the stems become more woody. They must be handled with care for they are then brittle and may easily break.

Poppy heads have long been favourites with flower arrangers, not only because they have such sturdy stems but in the case of large heads they can be used as containers for miniature displays.

Antirrhinum, aquilegia and delphinium seed heads are also invaluable while echinops and eryngium bring ' quality ' to a display. The stems of the wild thistle are useful too, if you have the courage to gather them, for their spines are formidable.

The seed pods of various lilies are most useful as are those of the flag irises and some of the other taller species. *Iris foetedissima* in particular is good, for as the pods split, shining red berries are displayed. Once the colour is seen the stem should be cut, otherwise the berries or seed will fall. If the splitting pods are given a coating of copal varnish it will prevent such a happening.

Honesty, Molucella or Bells of Ireland, should not be over-looked. *Physalis franchettii* although an invasive plant, usually atones for its aggressiveness by yielding a display of brightly coloured calyces which easily give the clue to why they are known as Chinese Lanterns.

Preserved globe artichoke flowers, pine cones, laurel and magnolia leaves, sprigs of ivy, and some ' switches ' from brook shrubs, can all be used for creating a display when fresh flowers are scarce.

Apart from the real everlasting flowers, a number of plants and shrubs have flowers which can be dried so that they remain ornamental for several months. Helichrysums and Statice sinuata varieties and *Limonium latifolia* come to mind immediately. The range is considerably wider than this as the following list will show.

Catananche blue, and blue and white. Often known as Cupids Dart, this plant grows in ordinary garden soil. Delphinium spikes should be cut before the top floret opens. Dry off gradually preferably in dull light.

Gypsophila paniculata. This hardy perennial is widely used, for its light feathery flower spikes introduces daintiness to what would otherwise be heavy looking displays.

Anaphalis triplenervis is another well-known reliable flower for drying. The white blooms on 10 in. stems keep well.

Trollius, the Globe Flower and the double varieties of helianthus or the perennial Sunflower, can be dried slowly. The same applies to double zinnias and the American spray chrysanthemums, while rosemary and lavender are also useful for the winter.

In all cases the aim should be to cut with a long stem, remove the lower leaves and dry very, very gradually.

Ornamental gourds are useful for winter decoration. Many of them have names descriptive of their appearance being known as crook-neck, pear, ostrich, egg and such like, some being smooth others warted. Most of these are varieties or types of vegetable marrows, and can be grown in the same way. Others which are varieties of lagenaria, are known as bottle, spoon, siphon, or dipper gourds.

Apart from their decorative value when heaped in bowls for a table decoration, they look superb against a background of foliage or when flowers are placed among them.

The fruits should remain on the plants as long as there is no danger of frost by which time the skin should be hard. They do not need storing but can be displayed as soon as gathered.

It is not essential to take out the inside of the gourds since if left, the inner tissues will shrivel. There are records of gourds being retained in good condition for upwards of 50 years. Long life can be encouraged by painting the fruits, when quite dry, with fine copal varnish. This makes it easier to keep them free from dust. Any one with an artistic turn of hand can paint attractive designs on fruits of good size.

CHAPTER 5

DISORDERS, DISEASES AND PESTS

ORNAMENTAL foliage and flowering plants, shrubs and trees are generally free from the ravages of diseases and pests where a healthy stock is planted and where they are grown in well-cultivated and thoroughly drained ground. Even so, it is possible for disorders of various kinds to arise. To prevent their gaining a hold it is essential for the trouble to be detected and dealt with at the earliest possible moment. It is easy to exaggerate such possibilities but even when pests or diseases are present in nearby gardens, keeping the plants under clean hygienic conditions not only lessens the likelihood of attack, but healthy plants are much more able to withstand and overcome attacks of all kinds.

In the case of annuals, diseases are less likely to appear, but if they do, quick identification and treatment will prevent the spread of the infection.

ANTS can be a nuisance. They are most likely to appear where greenfly are working, since the latter produce a sweet secretion known as honeydew. This attracts ants, which sometimes carry greenfly from one plant to another, and this is one way in which various diseases are spread. The aim should be to trace the ants' nests and destroy them by using one of the proprietary ant killers, or pouring liquid derris into the entrance to the nests.

APHIDS or GREENFLY. There are several forms of these sucking insects, the green and black forms being the most common. They often settle on the growing point of plants, piercing the shoots, leaves and stems, resulting in distortion and discoloration. In the case of sweet peas, they may cause the light coloured flowers to present a mottled appearance. The travelling of aphids from unhealthy to healthy plants is a means by which disease is frequently transmitted.

Liquid derris applied early and forcibly is an excellent check and there are many greenfly killers on the market. For preference, all should be applied in the evening or in dull weather to lessen the possibility of sun scorch. Ladybirds are a natural enemy of greenfly and should never be destroyed.

CAPSID BUGS of various kinds sometimes damage leaves and shoots or eat the buds, leading to malformed flowers. Here again, derris is useful. Keep weeds cleared from hedge bottoms or waste places which can become breeding places.

CATERPILLARS may attack the foliage of plants, leaving only a skeleton of veins. Keep a look out for clusters of eggs, which sometimes appear on the undersides of leaves and hand pick the caterpillars if seen. Dust or spray with derris or use a nicotine insecticide.

CUTWORMS will attack the stems of plants at or just above soil level, so that the plants snap off as if cut by a knife, or they may just wilt if the stems have not been quite severed. The surest method of catching these pests is to half bury pieces of cut vegetable to which the pests are attracted. Frequent examination of the traps will make it possible to destroy the culprits.

EARWIGS are a nuisance on all types of plants, causing malformed growth. They usually hide during day time under the cover of any rubbish which may be lying about. They can be trapped in inverted pots stuffed with hay or straw.

SLUGS and SNAILS are enemies of most plants, particularly in their young stages, where growth is soft and succulent, and during damp weather. Regular applications of one of the proprietary slug baits is usually effective, while the pests can be trapped by putting down pieces of orange peel or leaves of cabbage or lettuce under which the slugs will gather.

WOODLICE too, damage the stems of plants since they hide under rubbish and where there is rotting wood. The remedy is obvious.

MILDEW is another plant enemy. Of fungus origin, it often covers the leaves with a white powder-like growth. Dusting with yellow sulphur powder or spraying with liver of sulphur are good ways of controlling this disorder.

DAMPING OFF is caused by various fungi. It is a disease which frequently affects seedlings, particularly those under glass. Over-watering, a too humid atmosphere, and overcrowding pre-disposes the plants to this disorder. The regular use of Cheshunt Compound prevents this trouble from spreading, although it will not cure affected plants.

There are few pests likely to be troublesome on trees and shrubs. Ants and aphids are always liable to appear. Where large specimens are concerned it may be necessary to spray the entire shrub or tree. For this purpose, apart from the usual washes, a simple insecticide can be made by steeping 1 lb. Quassia chips in 1 gallon of water for $1\frac{1}{2}$ hours. Then add $\frac{1}{2}$ lb. soft soap and boil for 10 mins. Dilute this liquid to make 8 gallons of wash. This will deal with green and black fly, red spider, and woolly aphis, although the latter may have to be finished off by painting the lower infestations with methylated spirits.

BIRDS sometimes peck at the flower buds of crataegus, cotoneasters, and pyracantha, but they do so much good in other ways that nothing drastic should be used. Seed beds and polyanthus beds can be protected by means of black cotton stretched on short sticks over the beds.

BLACK SPOT is usually restricted to a few varieties of roses. Collect and burn all diseased leaves and shoots. Remove the top inch or two of top soil in winter and replace with fresh compost. Spray the bushes with Bordeaux Mixture or Liver of Sulphur. Alternatively use one of the modern Black Spot remedies.

CUCKOO SPIT or FROG HOPPER. The female lays her eggs on the plant and the grubs suck the sap from the flowers and leaves, covering themselves with froth. Spray with paraffin emulsion or better still, wipe off the spittle and insects with a rag or soft paper.

There are various moths which lay eggs of all kinds on ornamental plants, which they eat into and spoil. If the eggs, which are often covered with a web-like substance, and which catch up the leaves, are destroyed before they hatch into caterpillars, the life cycle of the moths will be averted.

There are some diseases associated with certain plants. Antirrhinum rust is one of these and it covers the plants with a mass of brownish coloured ' spores ' which increase rapidly. Where the trouble has occurred in the past it is best to grow the rust resistant varieties. The use of a copper based spray is a help but not a cure.

Aster stem rot, blackleg, or ' wilt ', is another killer that can ruin plants at all stages. The fungus works from the root upwards causing stunted growth. Burn all affected plants watering the healthy specimens with Cheshunt Compound and choosing a new site for asters the following year. There are now some wilt resistant varieties on the market. .

Sweet Peas are sometimes affected by botrytis which attacks at ground level causing the plants to die quickly or sometimes they produce a few flowers and then die. Burn affected specimens and use Cheshunt Compound on the soil around the remaining plants. Virus diseases sometimes strike but the mottling of the light coloured flowers is often due to greenfly sucking the sap.

Some of the troubles already referred to affect biennials and perennials. Eelworm can cause damage to many plants and bulbs. These microscopic creatures lay their eggs in the tissues of the plants often in the stem or bulb. If it is suspected that the pests are present plants such as phlox, oenothera and bulbs should not be planted on the same site for at least three years. This starves out eelworm.

Hollyhock rust is a fungus which can greatly disfigure hollyhock, mallow or lavetera. Weeds sometimes act as hosts to the spores which is one reason why they should not be tolerated. Affected plants should be sprayed several times with Bordeaux Mixture.

Bulbs are not particularly susceptible to disease and pests, but occasionally they are attacked. There are several forms of botrytis which can cause damage. Often they are encouraged by wet, badly-drained, soil. It is then that they can gain a firm hold. Any bulbs or corms found to be soft when lifted should be burned, as should those seen to have decaying black markings between the scales.

Leaf spotting on irises seems most likely to occur in a lime deficient soil.

Lily disease is fairly common in some seasons and is technically known as Botrytis elliptica. If it gets a hold the entire plant is disfigured. Lilium candidum seems the most susceptible. This is the species which produces a rosette of leaves near ground level in the autumn which possibly makes it easier for the spores to gain a hold. There are now several strains less liable to the disease.

Narcissus may become affected with basal rot, although this usually begins while the bulbs are in store.

Tulip fire is a fungus which, particularly in wet seasons, causes a greyish brown mould to appear on the foliage and can lead to the plants being entirely spoiled. Bordeaux mixture and Tulisan are good preventatives.

Narcissus are the most likely bulbs to be attacked by pests and in the case of eelworm and narcissus fly the most effective remedy is to subject the bulbs to the hot water treatment.

Thrips may appear and these suck the sap from the foliage leaving tell-tale silvery markings. They are most likely to appear on gladiolus, and the foliage of affected plants should be burned.

Grown under ordinary good conditions there is no need to fear disorders, diseases or pests, which usually flourish when growing conditions are poor.

CHAPTER 6

SELECTIONS FOR VARIOUS PURPOSES

SHAPES AND COLOUR OF FOLIAGE

The shape and colour of leaves varies considerably and the following are some of the variations to be found in herbaceous plants. In many cases there are differences within the same family. It will be helpful to know these distinctions when individual leaves or sprays are needed to complete a floral design.

Lobed	*Fern-like*	*Grassy*
Artemesia	Sansguisorba	Armeria
Dicentra	Senecio	Iris
Helleborus	Thalictrum	Kniphofia
Rogersia	Filipendulina	

Heart-shaped	*Woolly*	*Cut Edged*
Bergenia	Lychnis	Artemesia
Crambe	Phlomis	Cimicifuga
Doronicum	Stachys	Helleborus
Ligularia	Verbascum	Rudbeckia
Macleaya		
Omphalodes		

Blotched	*Rush-like*	*Shiny*
Erythronium	Crinum	Aconitum
Lamium	Galtonia	Hosta
Polypodium	Iris	Nerine
Pulmonaria	Tradescantia	Penstemon
		Rudbeckia
		Trollius

SHRUBS PROVIDING AUTUMN FOLIAGE

3 to 8 ft. high

Subject	Colour	Subject	Colour
Berberis thunbergii	red	Euonymus alatus	red
Callicarpa	purple	Spiraea prunifolia	orange
Clethra	purple	Stephanandra	yellow red
Cotoneaster divaricata	red	Viburnum dentatum	red

8 to 12 ft. high

Subject	Colour	Subject	Colour
Acer ginnala	orange red	Enkianthus	orange and red
Acer Osaka Zuki	red	Parrotia persica	golden and crimson
Amelanchier	orange red	Photinia villosa	scarlet, gold
Abronia arbutifolia	red	Rhus cotinus	red
Azalea pontica	red	Stranvaesia	red, orange
Contoneaster bullata	red	Viburnum opulus	red

A MONTHLY SELECTION OF CUT FLOWER SUBJECTS

January

Iris unguicularis	lavender
Chimonanthus	pale yellow
Winter Aconite	yellow
Mahonia bealei	yellow

February

Chionodoxas	blue
Cornus mas	yellow
Viburnum tinus	pink
Narcissus, February Gold	yellow

Subject	Colour
Galanthus, snowdrop	white
Jasminum nudiflorum	yellow
Helleborus niger	white
March	
Chaenomeles	pink, red
Daphne mezereum	purple
Helleborus orientalis	mixed
Pansies	various
Spiraea thunbergii	white
Tulip species	orange, red, pink
Viburnum fragrans	pinky-white
May	
Aquilegia	pink, blue, white
Lilac	many colours
Lily of the Valley	white
Anemones	mixed
Paeonies	pink, red
Trollius	yellow
Wallflowers	mixed
July	
Achillea	yellow
Alstromeria	orange, pink
Gaillardia	orange and red
Gypsophila	white and pink
Helenium	bronze, yellow

Subject	Colour
Pulmonaria	blue and pink
Garrya elliptica	green catkins
Cyclamen hardy	red, pink, white
April	
Doronicum	yellow
Daffodils	white, yellow
Muscari	blue
Myosotis	blue
Polyanthus	mixed
Prunus, peach	pink
Tulips, E.F.	mixed
June	
Anchusa	blue
Canterbury Bells	blue, pink, white
Carnations	various
Iris germanica	mixed
Heuchera	pink, red
Pyrethrum	mixed
Larkspur	pink, blue
August	
Coreopsis	golden yellow
Dahlia	various
Gladiolus	mixed
Echinops	grey-blue
Liatris	rosy-purple

Iceland Poppy	various
Nigella	blue, white
September	
Catananche	lavender
Chrysanthemum	various
Michaelmas Daisy	blue, pink, white
Montbretia	orange-red
Physostegia	pink
Rudbeckia	orange-yellow
Thalictrum	lavender-pink
November	
Ericas (heathers)	pink, purple
Lonicera fragrantissima	cream
Prunus subhirtella	pinkish-white
Symphoricarpus	white berries
Viburnum fragrans	white
Phlox	various
Scabious	blue, pink
October	
Nerine	steel-blue
Eryngium	pink, red, white
Cyclamen, hardy	pink, red
Schizostylis	pink
Physalis	orange seed pods
Solidago	yellow
Statice	various
December	
Helleborus niger	white
Erica darleyensis	pinky-purple
Hyacinths	various
Pernettya berries	various
Viburnum tinus	white and pink

HERBACEOUS PLANTS IN SEPARATE COLOURS

Blue Flowers

Aconitum, monkshood, various
Aconitum napellus
Agapanthus umbellatus
Anchusa, various
Aster, Michaelmas Daisy, various
Campanula, various
Catananche coerulea

Delphinium, various
Echinops, Globe Thistle
Iris, various
Linum perenne, Blue Flax
Lupinus (lupin), various
Meconopsis baileyi, blue poppy
Myosotis, Forget-me-Not

Platycodon mariesi
Polemonium, Jacob's Ladder
Pulmonaria azurea
Scabiosa caucasica, scabious
Veronica, various

Mauve and Purple Flowers

Acanthus mollis
Anemone pulsatilla
Aster, Michaelmas Daisy
Campanula, various
Delphinium, various
Erigeron, various

Eryngium, various
Galega, goat's rue
Geranium grandiflorum
Lupinus, lupin, various
Nepeta, catmint

Primula denticulata
Phlox, various
Statice latifolia
Tradescantia Leonora
Veronica, Speedwell, various

Red Flowers

Achillea Cerise Queen
Aquilegia Crimson Star
Armeria, Sea Pink, various
Aster, Michaelmas Daisy
Astilbe, spiraea, various
Bellis perennis
Chrysanthemum, various

Geum Mrs. Bradshaw
Helenium, various
Kniphofia, Red-Hot-Poker
Heuchera, Alum root
Lupinus, lupin, various
Monarda Cambridge scarlet
Paeonia, various

Papaver, poppy, various
Phlox, various
Potentilla, various
Primula japonica
Pyrethrum, various
Sidalcea, various
Wallflower, various

HERBACEOUS PLANTS IN SEPARATE COLOURS

Pink Flowers

Anemone, various
Armeria, Sea Pink, various
Aster, Michaelmas Daisy
Astilbe, spiraea, various
Centaurea dealbata
Centranthus, valerian
Chrysanthemum, various
Dielytra, dicentra, various

Erigeron, various
Gypsophila rosenchleier
Heuchera, Alum root, various
Incarvillea Bees' Pink
Lavatera cashmeriana
Lupinus, lupin, various
Lythrum, loosestrife, various
Paeonia, various

Phlox, various
Poterium obtusum
Polygonum bistorta superbum
Pyrethrum, various
Saxifraga cordifolia
Sidalcea, Greek mallow
Veronica, speedwell
Papaver, poppy, various

Achillea, yarrow or milfoil
Anemone, various
Armeria, sea pink
Aster, Michaelmas Daisy
Bellis perennis
Campanula persicifolia alba
Chrysanthemum, various

White Flowers

Galega niobe, goat's rue
Gypsophila Bristol Fairy
Helleborus, Christmas Rose
Lupinus, lupin, various
Paeonia, various
Papaver, Oriental Poppy
Primula various

Pyrethrum, various
Ranunculus aconitifolius
Scabiosa Miss Willmott
Sidalcea candida
Spiraea various
Tiarella cordifolia, foam flower

Achillea, yarrow or milfoil.
Alstroemeria, various
Anthemis, various
Aster, Michaelmas Daisy
Cephalaria tartarica
Yellow scabious
Cheiranthus allioni
Siberian Wallflower

Yellow and Orange Flowers

Gaillardia, various
Geum various
Helenium, various
Helianthus, sunflower, various
Heliopsis Orange Queen

Hemerocallis, Day lily
Iris, various

Oenothera youngi
Evening primrose
Primula, various
Rudbeckia, cone flower
Senecio, various
Solidago, Golden rod, various
Trollius, globe flower
Verbascum, various

PLANTS HAVING GREEN FLOWERS

Amaranthus caudatus
Euphorbia wulfeni
Gladiolus Green Goddess
Helleborus orientalis
Ixia viridiflora

Mignonette
Molucella
Nicotiana Lime Green
Tulipa viridiflora
Zinnia Envy

SILVER OR GREY LEAVED PLANTS

Achillea	Hybrid Pinks
Anaphalis	Onopordon
Artemesia	Santolina
Centaurea	Senecio
Cynara	Stachys
Lavender	Verbascum

SHRUBS AND PLANTS HAVING SCENTED FOLIAGE OR FLOWERS

Shrubs

Buxus	Lilac
Calycanthus	Lippia
Ceanothus	Myrtle
Cistus	Perowskia
Clethra	Phlomis
Daphne mezereum	Rosemary
Eucalyptus	Sweet Bay
Gardenia	Sweet Briar
Laurus	Viburnum fragrans
Lavender	

Plants

Artemesia	Lilium auratum	Pink
Freesia	Lily of the Valley	Roses
Heliotrope	Mignonette	Sweet Peas
Hesperis	Monarda	Sweet William
Jasmine	Oenothera	Violets
		Wallflower

INDEX

PART 1 – FLOWERS

Hardy Annuals

INDEX

Biennial Plants

Hardy Perennial Plants

Flowers Under Glass

Flowering Shrubs, Trees and Roses

Roses for Cutting

Bulbs

PART 2 – FOLIAGE

Foliage Shrubs and Trees

Hardy Foliage Plants

Ornamental Grasses

Everlasting and Dried Flowers and Seed Pods